Logic in Earliest Classical India

PAPERS OF THE 12TH WORLD SANSKRIT CONFERENCE
Vol. 10.2

Logic in Earliest Classical India

Edited by
BRENDAN S. GILLON

MOTILAL BANARSIDASS PUBLISHERS
PRIVATE LIMITED • DELHI

PAPERS OF THE 12TH WORLD SANSKRIT CONFERENCE HELD IN HELSINKI, FINLAND, 13-18 JULY 2003
VOL. 10.2

General Editors:
PETTERI KOSKIKALLIO & ASKO PARPOLA

First Edition : Delhi, ***2010***

ISBN: 978-81-208-3449-1

MOTILAL BANARSIDASS
41 U.A. Bungalow Road, Jawahar Nagar, Delhi 110 007
8 Mahalaxmi Chamber, 22 Bhulabhai Desai Road, Mumbai 400 026
203 Royapettah High Road, Mylapore, Chennai 600 004
236, 9th Main III Block, Jayanagar, Bangalore 560 011
Sanas Plaza, 1302 Baji Rao Road, Pune 411 002
8 Camac Street, Kolkata 700 017
Ashok Rajpath, Patna 800 004
Chowk, Varanasi 221 001

PRINTED IN INDIA
BY JAINENDRA PRAKASH JAIN AT SHRI JAINENDRA PRESS,
A-45 NARAINA, PHASE-I, NEW DELHI 110 028
AND PUBLISHED BY NARENDRA PRAKASH JAIN FOR
MOTILAL BANARSIDASS PUBLISHERS PRIVATE LIMITED,
BUNGALOW ROAD, DELHI 110 007

CONTENTS

CONTRIBUTORS

AKIHIKO AKAMATSU
Graduate School of Letters
Kyoto University
Yoshida-Honmachi
Sakyo-ku
Kyoto 606-8501
JAPAN
e-mail: aakamat@bun.kyoto-u.ac.jp

ELI FRANCO
Institut für Indologie und Zentralasienwissenschaften
Universität Leipzig
Schillerstraße 6
04109 Leipzig
GERMANY
e-mail: franco@rz.uni-leipzig.de

BRENDAN S. GILLON
Department of Linguistics
McGill University
1085, Avenue Docteur-Penfield
Montreal, Quebec
H3A 1A7
CANADA
e-mail: brendan.gillon@mcgill.ca

BIRGIT KELLNER
Institut für Südasien-, Tibet- und Buddhismuskunde
Universität Wien
Uni-Campus AAKH
Spitalgasse 2, Hof 2.7
A-1090 Wien
AUSTRIA
e-mail: birgit.kellner@univie.ac.at

KARIN PREISENDANZ
Institut für Südasien-, Tibet- und Buddhismuskunde
Universität Wien
Uni-Campus AAKH
Spitalgasse 2, Hof 2.1
A-1090 Wien
AUSTRIA
e-mail: karin.preisendanz@univie.ac.at

ERNST PRETS
Institut für Kultur- und Geistesgeschichte Asiens
Österreichische Akademie der Wissenschaften
Prinz Eugen Strasse 8-10
A-1040 Wien
AUSTRIA
e-mail: prets@oeaw.ac.at

CHIZUKO YOSHIMIZU
Section of Philosophy
Graduate School of Humanities and Social Sciences
Tsukuba University
Tsukuba-shi Tennodai 1-1-1
305-8571
JAPAN
e-mail: chizukoy@logos.tsukuba.ac.jp

Logic in Early Classical India: An Overview

BRENDAN S. GILLON

This book comprises seven papers delivered at a session of the World Sanskrit Conference, held in 2003 in Helsinki, Finland, entitled Logic in Early Classical India. Karin Preisendanz discusses reasoning in the early Dharma literature and traces out the various senses of the term *nyāya* in that literature in relation to the term's well-known sense in the logical literature. Ernst Prets presents the results of his investigations into the various editions, manuscripts and commentaries of the early medical text *Carakasaṃhitā*, which contains important passages pertaining to logic. The *Vaiśeṣikasūtra*, another early text, also contains discussions relevant to the history of logic in early classical India and Birgit Kellner addresses one form of inference mentioned in it, namely the inference from exclusion, or *virodhin*. Not all the relevant texts from this time have come to us in one piece. Eli Franco, in his contribution, reports on the discussion of the *pramāṇa*s, or means of epistemic cognition (that is, knowledge), in a Buddhist text which survives, alas, only in fragments. These fragments are known collectively as the Spitzer Manuscript, in honor of Moritz Spitzer, who initiated the work on them. Chizuko Yoshimizu treats a brief but perplexing passage on logic from the Buddhist text *Sandhinirmocanasūtra*. Next, Brendan Gillon reports on a confusion of obversion and contraposition in Vātsyāyana's commentary on the *Nyāyasūtra*. Finally, Akihiko Akamatsu sheds light on a puzzle pertaining to Bhartṛhari's definition of inference (*anumāna*) in the *Vākyapadīya*.

In this introduction, I shall provide a brief outline of the development of logic up to and including the period of early classical India and situate the content of each of the papers with respect to that period. In the first section, I set out a framework for such an outline, distinguishing between reasoning and logic, where logic is to be understood as the discipline which studies reasoning. In the next two sections, I outline the origins and growth of rational inquiry. Having set the stage for the appearance of the study of reasoning, I turn to the formulation of the Indian canonical syllogism which is the focus of logic in India. This can be divided into three stages: first, the appearance of the canonical syllogism; second, the formalization of the canonical syllogism; and third, developments in metaphysics which ensued its formalization.

1. REASONING AND LOGIC: PRACTICE AND FORM

Humans reason, that is, taking some things to be true, they conclude therefrom that other things are also true. If this is done in thought, one performs an inference; and if this is done in speech, one makes an argument. Indeed, inference and argument are but two sides of the same coin: an argument can be thought, and hence become an inference; an inference can be expressed, and hence become an argument.

Logic, at least as traditionally conceived, seeks to distinguish good reasoning from bad. More particularly, it seeks to identify the general conditions under which what one concludes is true, having taken other things to be true. These conditions can be sought in the nature of things. One asks, then, under what conditions do certain facts require some other fact. Insofar as facts are grasped in thought, one can also ask under what conditions does knowledge of some facts permit knowledge of another fact. Such conditions, once identified, would distinguish good inferences from bad inferences. Alternatively, insofar as facts are stated, one can ask as well under what conditions does the acceptance by someone of some facts require him or her to accept some other fact. These conditions, once identified, would distinguish good arguments from bad arguments.

Since an argument is an expression of an inference, and to that extent, expressed in a language, it is natural to use the forms of linguistic expressions to identify forms of inferences and arguments and thereby to distinguish forms of good inferences and arguments from forms of bad inferences and arguments.

We see then that the study of logic can be pursued from several points of view. It can be studied from the point of view of how facts are, an ontic point of view, from the point of view of what facts are known, an epistemic point of view, from the point of view of what facts are accepted, a dialectic point of view, or from the point of view of how facts are expressed, a linguistic point of view. Surprisingly, in spite of their deep grasp of linguistics, thinkers in classical India did not pursue the study of reasoning from a linguistic point of view. As Karl Potter has rightly emphasized, the study of reasoning in classical India was the study of the conditions under which some facts require other facts, or of the conditions under which knowledge of some facts permits knowledge of another fact, or of conditions under which acceptance by one person of some facts requires his or her acceptance of another fact. In other words, classical Indian thinkers were interested in reasoning primarily from the ontic, epistemic and dialectic points of view.

The fact that humans reason is no guarantee that those who do reflect on which reasoning is good and which is bad. Clearly, the activity of reasoning, on the one hand, and the activity of reflecting on which reasoning is good and which is not, on the other, are distinct, though naturally they are intimately related. How they are distinct and how they are related can be made clear by an analogy between logic and grammar. Both can be thought of as concerned with the identification of form exhibited in human behavior. The objects of study in grammar are the forms found in the use of language, while the objects of logic are the forms of reasoning. This analogy is strengthened by another similarity: both the use of language and reasoning are spontaneous human activities, whereas neither the pursuit of logic nor the pursuit of grammar is. Indeed, in the ancient world, we know of only three cultures which pursued the latter reflection: the Greek, the Indian and the Chinese.

It is worthwhile eliminating, at the outset, any doubt about the distinction between engaging in a human activity and reflection upon its form. It is well known that humans learn their mother tongue without instruction. Language instruction is a human institution of relatively recent advent – being non-existent for all linguistic communities before the coming of the classical civilizations, and until very recently, touching very few even among those encompassed by those civilizations. Just as the use of a language in a language community thrives without its having formulated a grammar for its language, so reasoning in a culture can thrive without its having formulated logic. Mathematics, the quintessential example of reasoning, has thrived for millennia without having paid the slightest attention to logic. Indeed, even today, few students of mathematics are trained in logic. In ancient Greece, the birthplace of formal logic and axiomatic mathematics, mathematicians and logicians were relatively unaware of one another's work. The proofs in Euclid, to the extent that they are formalized, cannot be adequately formalized either by the propositional logic of the Stoics or by the syllogistic of Aristotle. (See Muller 1972.) They require Classical Quantificational Logic for their formalization, a logic not formulated until the end of the 19th century.

The study of the history of logic investigates the forms of reasoning recognized as good or bad as well as the principles used to distinguish them, whether they are implicitly used or explicitly articulated. We shall look at logic in classical India in both ways and we shall see how reasoning was viewed ontically, epistemically, dialectically and linguistically.

If logic is the study of forms of reasoning, then the history of logic is the study of the development of the study of these forms. And if one is interested in the historical origins of logic, one is interested in how the study of these forms began, that is, in how people became aware that reasoning embodies form. Thus, in looking at the origins of logic, it is natural to look to practices in which reasoning played a role and which, as a result, were likely candidates for reflection. The obvious starting points for such practices are all forms of rational inquiry.

Rational inquiry comprises the search for reasons for publicly accepted facts, subject to public and rational scrutiny. This activity involves people both severally and collectively. It involves people severally insofar as people, individually, are the locus of inference. It involves people collectively insofar as arguments, the public manifestation of inferences, are sharpened by the scrutiny of others.

Though the origins in India of public debate (*pariṣad*), one form of rational inquiry, are not clear, we know that public debates were common in pre-classical India, for they are frequently alluded to in the early Brahmanical literature, for example in various Upaniṣads (*Chāndogya-upaniṣad* 5.3.1; *Bṛhadāranyaka-upaniṣad* 6.2.1), and in the Buddhist literature, for example, in over half of the thirty-four *sutta*s of the Buddhist *Dīgha Nikāya*, which are part of the *Suttapiṭaka*, one of the three 'baskets' of the Buddhist canon (Manné 1992). Better known, but much later examples of such engagements are the Buddhist works, *Milindapañha* and *Kathāvatthu*.

Public debate is not the only form of public deliberations in pre-classical India. Assemblies (*pariṣad* or *sabhā*) of various sorts, comprised of relevant experts, were regularly convened to deliberate on a variety of matters, including administrative, legal and religious matters. As reported by Solomon (1976, chapter 3), much of the legal vocabulary for such deliberations includes the well-known terms of debate and argument found in the philosophical literature, though, as shown by Karin Preisendanz in her contribution below, often with different, yet related senses.

By the 5th century BCE, rational inquiry into a wide range of topics was under way, including agriculture, architecture, astronomy, grammar, law, logic, mathematics, medicine, phonology and statecraft. Aside from the world's earliest extant grammar, Pāṇini's *Aṣṭādhyāyī*, however, no works devoted to these topics actually date from this pre-classical period. Nonetheless, scholars agree that incipient versions of the first extant texts on these topics were being formulated and early versions of them were redacted by the beginning of the common era. They include such texts as *Kṛṣiśāstra*, a treatise on agriculture, *Śilpaśāstra*, a treatise on architecture, *Jyotiṣaśāstra*, a treatise on astronomy, *Dharmaśāstra*, a treatise on law, *Carakasaṃhitā*, a treatise on medicine, and *Arthaśāstra*, a treatise on politics. (See both the contribution of Karin Preisendanz as well as that of Ernst Prets.)

The first five hundred years of the common era also saw the redaction of philosophical treatises in which proponents of diverse religious traditions put forth systematic versions of their world view. These latter works bear witness, in a number of different ways, to the intense interest in argumentation during this period. To begin with, the authors of many of these texts put forth arguments and, in doing so, explicitly appealed to such well-known logical principles as the principle of non-contradiction, the principle of excluded middle and the principle of double negation. Moreover, many of the arguments formulated in these texts correspond to such well recognized rules of inference as *modus ponens* (i.e., from α and $\alpha \rightarrow \beta$, one infers β), *modus tollens* (i.e., from $\neg\beta$ and $\alpha \rightarrow \beta$, one infers $\neg\alpha$), *disjunctive syllogism* (i.e., from $\neg\alpha$ and $\alpha \vee \beta$, one infers β), *constructive dilemma* (i.e., from $\alpha \vee \beta$, $\alpha \rightarrow \gamma$ and $\beta \rightarrow \gamma$, one infers γ), *categorical syllogism* (i.e., from $\alpha \rightarrow \beta$ and $\beta \rightarrow \gamma$, one infers $\alpha \rightarrow \gamma$) and *reductio ad absurdum* (i.e., if something false follows from an assumption, then the assumption is false). This last form of argument, termed *prasaṅga* in Sanskrit, was extremely common. Indeed, so common are such arguments in the works of the Buddhist philosopher Nāgārjuna (2nd century CE) that his follower, Buddhapālita (470-540), took all of Nāgārjuna's arguments to be *prasaṅga* arguments. As a result, Buddhapālita and his followers were, and are, referred to as *prasaṅgika*s, or absurdists.

2. PRINCIPLES OF LOGIC AND RULES OF INFERENCE

The principle of non-contradiction was well known in classical Greece before Aristotle. However, Aristotle was the first to discuss it in detail. Indeed, Aristotle devotes Book 3 of his *Metaphysics* to its discussion. Aristotle formulates the principle of non-contradiction both ontically and linguistically. For example, in *Metaphysics*, book 3, chapter 2, Aristotle gives an ontic formulation,

> ... that a thing cannot at the same time be and not be (996b29-30)

whereas in book 4, chapter 6, he gives a linguistic formulation,

> ... contradictory statements are not at the same time true. (1011b13)

Classical India also contains many statements, both ontic and linguistic, of the principle of non-contradiction, though no author seems to have made it the object of extensive discussion, as had Aristotle. The principle is often implicitly appealed to in the Buddhist canon, for example, in the *Samyutta Nikāya* (4.298; 4.299), where Nigaṇṭha Nātaputta, conversing with Citta, says at one point

> See how upright, honest and sincere Citta, the householder, is.

At another point, he says:

> See how Citta, the householder, is not upright, honest or sincere.

Citta, then, observes:

> If your former statement is true, your latter statement is false and if your latter statement is true, your former statement is false.

A linguistic formulation of a modal version of the principle is explicitly stated in the commentary, *Mahābhāṣya*, a commentary on Pāṇini's *Aṣṭādhyāyī* by the great Indian grammarian Patañjali (2nd BCE), who says:

> *vidhipratiṣedhayoḥ yugapad vacanānupapattiḥ*
> (Mbh ad A 1.1.44; Kielhorn ed., p. 103).
>
> It is impossible for a statement to express both an injunction and a prohibition simultaneously.

More common, however, are ontic statements of the principle. Thus, the Buddhist philosopher Nāgārjuna often invokes an ontic principle of noncontradiction, saying such things as

> *paraspara-viruddham hi sat ca asat ca ekataḥ kutaḥ*
> (*Mūlamadhyamakakārikā* 8.7cd).
>
> For how is it that which exists and that which does not exist, being mutually contradictory, are in the same place?

This is clearly reminiscent of Aristotle's ontic formulation of the principle of non-contradiction cited above.

Nor are these statements isolated. Vātsyāyana (5th century CE), whose commentary *Nyāyabhāṣya* is the earliest extant commentary on the *Nyāyasūtra*, says:

> *nitya-anityatva-virodhāt ca nityatvam a-nityatvam ca ekasya dharmiṇaḥ dharmau iti virudhyete na sambhavataḥ* (*Bhāṣya* to NS 5.1.36).
>
> Moreover, because of the exclusivity of being eternal and being non-eternal, eternality and non-eternality must be excluded as two properties of the very same property-possessor. (That is,) they cannot occur together.

Another principle endorsed by Aristotle is the principle of excluded middle (*Metaphysics*, book 3, chapter 2, 996b26-30; book 3, chapter 7, 1011b23-24), though he does call it into question in his discussion of future contingent sentences, treated in Chapter 9. In *Prior Analytics*, book 1, chapter 46, Aristotle gives an ontic formulation of the principle:

> Let A stand for "to be good", B for "not to be good" ... Then either A or B will belong to every thing. (51b36-40)

A linguistic version is also found at several places in the *Metaphysics*, including in book 4, chapter 7:

> There cannot be an intermediate between contradictories, but of one subject we must either affirm or deny any one predicate. (1011b23-25)

Bhartṛhari (6th century CE), the grammarian and philosopher of language, formulates an ontic version of the principle of excluded middle in his *Vākyapadīya*, where he says

> *sat asat vā api vastu syāt tṛtīyam na asti kiṃcana* (VP 3.9.85).
>
> A thing must be either existent or non-existent. There is no third.

Like Aristotle, classical Indian thinkers were aware of the possible limitation of the principle of excluded middle. Candrakīrti, for example, in his *Prasannapadā*, a commentary to Nāgārjuna's *Mūlamādhyamikakārikā*, points out that incompatible properties fail equally to apply to non-existent objects.

> *keṣāmcit tu ati-cira-abhyasta-tattva-darśanānām kiṃcit-mātra-anutkhāta-āvaraṇa-taru-mūlānām na eva a-tathyam na eva tathyam tat iti deśitaṃ tasya api kiṃcit-mātrasya āvaraṇasya prahāṇa-artham vandhyā-sutasya avadāta-śyānatā-pratiṣedhavat ubhayam etat pratiṣiddham* (cited by Staal 1975: 43; reprint, p. 50).
>
> But to some who have acquired a clear view of truth through very long practice and by whom the roots of the trees of obstruction have been unuprooted by only a little, it has been taught that it is neither true nor untrue; in order to destroy the least obstruction, both have been denied, just as one denies both whiteness and blackness of the son of a barren woman.

The last principle to be discussed is that of double negation. Here, the Stoics seem to have been the first among the Greeks to have identified the principle (Diogenes Laertius, book 7, chapter 69), formulating it linguistically to the effect that the negation of a negative proposition is equivalent to the original affirmative.

In classical India, the formulations again are ontic. Vātsyāyana says:

> *yāni khalu bhavanti teṣām abhāvaḥ vyāhataḥ* (*Bhāṣya* to NS 2.2.10).
>
> It is well known that the absence of those things which exist is excluded.

As stated above, well recognized rules of inference such as *modus ponens, modus tollens, disjunctive syllogism, constructive dilemma* and *categorical syllogism* are found in the arguments of text after text.

2.1 Form of argument

Awareness of the fact that the form of argument is crucial to its being good is found in a Buddhist work of the 3rd century BCE, Moggaliputta Tissa's *Kathāvatthu*, in which is found the refutation of some two hundred propositions over which the Sthaviravādins, one of the Buddhist schools, disagreed with other Buddhist schools. The treatment of each point comprises a debate between a proponent and an opponent. The refutations, of course, turn on demonstrating the inconsistency of a set of propositions. For example, in the passage below, the Sthaviravādin questions a Pudgalavādin with respect to the proposition of whether or not the soul is known truly and ultimately.

Sthaviravādin: Is the soul known truly and ultimately?

Pudgalavādin: Yes.

Sthaviravādin: Is the soul known truly and ultimately just like any ultimate fact?

Pudgalavādin: No.

Sthaviravādin: Acknowledge your refutation,

If the soul is known truly and ultimately, then indeed, good sir, you should also say that the soul is known truly and ultimately just like any ultimate fact.

What you say here is wrong: namely, that we ought to say (a) that the soul is known truly and ultimately; but we ought not to say (b) that the soul is known truly and ultimately just like any ultimate fact.

If the latter statement (b) cannot be admitted, then indeed the former statement (a) should not be admitted.

It is wrong to affirm the former statement (a) and to deny the latter (b).

One easily abstracts from this the following form,

Sthaviravādin:	Is A B?
Pudgalavādin:	Yes.
Sthaviravādin:	Is C D?
Pudgalavādin:	No.
Sthaviravādin:	Acknowledge your refutation,
	If A is B, then C is D.
	What you say here is wrong: namely, (a) that A is B but that C is not D.
	If C is not D, then A is not B.
	It is wrong that A is B and C is not D.

Indeed, this form is repeatedly instantiated throughout Book 1, Chapter 1.

Clearly, the author presumes it is self evident: first, that the propositions assented to are inconsistent, satisfying the following inconsistent propositional schemata of α , $\neg\beta$, $\alpha \rightarrow \beta$; second, that it is wrong to hold inconsistent propositions; and, third, that if $\alpha \rightarrow \beta$, then $\neg\beta \rightarrow \neg\alpha$ – that is, half of the equivalence of the principle of contraposition.

The earliest passages concerned with argument and inference are found in *Carakasaṃhitā*, a medical text, conjectured by some to have been redacted in its current form at the beginning of 1st century CE, on the one hand, and in the philosophical literature, both Brahmanical and Buddhist, on the other. Despite the enormous importance of the *Carakasaṃhitā*, it has never been critically edited. At present, Ernst Prets and Karin Preisendanz have undertaken to furnish a critical edition of those passages in it pertaining to inference and argument. Ernst Prets, in his contribution, reports on this text's commentaries, manuscripts and editions.

The best known Brahmanical text pertaining to inference is *Nyāyasūtra* by Gautama Akṣapāda (ca. 2nd CE), a treatise on rational inquiry, whose actual redaction is thought by some to date to the 3rd century CE. Another Brahmanical work touching upon inference is the *Vaiśeṣikasūtra*, a treatise of speculative ontology attributed to Kaṇāda (ca. 1st century CE), thought by some to have been redacted in its current form perhaps at the beginning of the

2nd century CE, though perhaps some of its passages date back to 2nd century BCE. And still another Brahmanical work, which survives only in fragments, collected by E. Frauwallner (1958), is a Sāṃkhya one, entitled *Ṣaṣṭitantra*, attributed by some to Pañcaśikha (ca. 2nd century BCE) and by others to Vṛṣagaṇa (ca. after the 2nd century CE).

The remaining texts are found in the Buddhist philosophical literature. The earliest text which contains passages pertaining to argument and inference and which has only recently been brought to the attention of scholars is the Spitzer Manuscript. The text, comprising about one thousand very small fragments, was discovered in 1906. It was first studied and transcribed by Moritz Spitzer. Recently, Eli Franco has studied and edited the fragments. Franco (2002) dates the text to the 3rd century CE. In his contribution, Franco discusses the fragments which pertain to the *pramāṇa*s, or means of epistemic cognition, revisiting some of his earlier conclusions.

Another Buddhist text, one of unknown authorship, whose original Sanskrit has been lost, but whose translations into Tibetan and Chinese have been preserved, is the *Sandhinirmocanasūtra*. This text, first translated into French by Étienne Lamotte (1935), contains in its tenth chapter a short section on reasoning. This section has been treated in detail by Chizuko Yoshimizu in her contribution.

The earliest identified Buddhist author to write on argument and inference is the idealist Asaṅga (ca. 4th century CE). One passage occurs in his *Abhidharmasamuccaya*, another occurs at the end of a chapter of his *Yogācārabhūmiśāstra* and a third occurs in a work which survives only in Chinese translation, *Shùn Zhèng Lùn* ("Treatise on According with What is Correct"). Shortly after him, Vasubandhu (ca. 5th century CE), another Buddhist idealist, thought to be the younger brother of Asaṅga, wrote at least three works on debate: the *Vādahṛdaya*, the *Vādavidhāna* and the *Vādavidhi*. No Sanskrit original survives of any of these, though Sanskrit fragments of the last have been collected by E. Frauwallner (1957). Finally, there are three works of unknown author and of unknown date which have survived only in Chinese translation: one is *Xǐan Chàng Shèng Jiào Lùn* ("Treatise which Reveals and Disseminates the Wise Teachings"), whose Sanskrit title G. Tucci gives as *Prakaraṇāryavācāśāstra* and E. Lamotte gives as *Āryadeśanāśāstra*; another is *Fāng Biàn Xīn Lùn* ("Core Treatise on Means"), translated back into Sanskrit by G. Tucci (1929), whose Sanskrit title Tucci renders as *Upāyahṛdaya*, while E. Frauwallner renders as it *Prayogasāra*; and the third is the *Rú Shíh Lùn* ("Treatise on Truth"), also translated back into Sanskrit by G. Tucci (1929) and given by him the Sanskrit title *Tarkaśāstra*.

With the notable exception of the *Vaiśeṣikasūtra* and the *Ṣaṣṭitantra*, which treat inference only as an epistemic process, the preponderance of the texts mentioned above is devoted to inference as argument in debate. These texts typically enumerate, define or classify public discussions, propositions as they are used in public discussions, parts of arguments, qualities which either enhance or detract from a discussant's performance and statements or actions by a discussant which warrant his being considered defeated, including the uttering of various fallacies.

These texts identify the form of argument used in debate. Thus, for example, the *Nyāyasūtra* (NS 1.1.32), like the *Carakasaṃhitā* (CS 2.8.31), defines an argument to have five parts: the proposition (*pratijñā*), the ground, or reason (*hetu*), the corroboration (called *dṛṣṭānta* in the *Carakasaṃhitā* and *udāharaṇa* in the *Nyāyasūtra*), the application (*upanaya*), and the conclusion (*nigamana*). The *Carakasaṃhitā* furnishes the following example:

pratijñā:	*nityaḥ puruṣaḥ*
proposition:	the soul is eternal
hetu:	*a-kṛtakatvāt*
ground:	because of being un-created
dṛṣṭānta:	*yathā ākāśam*
corroboration:	like space

upanaya:	*yathā ca a-kṛtakam ākāśam tat ca nityam tathā puruṣaḥ*
application:	as the sky is uncreated and it is eternal, so is the soul uncreated
nigamana:	*tasmāt nityaḥ*
conclusion:	therefore, the soul is eternal

This form of the argument clearly reflects the debate situation. First, one propounds a proposition, that is, one sets forth a proposition to be proved. One then states the ground, or reason, for the proposition one is propounding. Next, one corroborates with an example which illustrates the connection implicit between the property mentioned in the proposition and the property adduced as its ground. The immediately ensuing step, the application, spells out the similarity between the example and the subject of the proposition. Notice that this part of the argument retains the vestiges of the analogical reasoning which is no doubt its predecessor. Finally, one asserts the proposition.

As was obvious to these thinkers, not all arguments of this form are good arguments. Not surprisingly, these texts catalogue bad arguments. Grounds adduced in arguments catalogued as bad are referred to as non-grounds (*a-hetu*) or pseudo-grounds (*hetu-ābhāsa*). It is difficult to be sure what the basis for the classification was. In the case of the *Nyāyasūtra*, the author gives neither a definition nor an example. Even in cases where definitions and examples are given, as in the *Carakasaṃhitā*, the contemporary reader is not always sure what is intended. In all likelihood, included here are both cases where the premisses of the argument can be true but the conclusion false – formal fallacies – as well as cases where an argument, though formally valid, is nonetheless unpersuasive, since, for example, its ground (*hetu*) is as controversial as its conclusion.

These very same texts, as well as the *Vaiśeṣikasūtra*, touch on inference as an epistemic process. While the examples of inference furnished all have parts corresponding to a proposition (*pratijñā*) and to a ground (*hetu*), not all the texts are equally explicit in identifying the form of inference. In particular, both the *Caraka-saṃhitā* (CS 1.11.21-22) and the *Nyāyasūtra* (NS 1.1.5) define inference as knowledge of one fact on the basis of knowledge of another, leaving unmentioned any knowledge of a relation linking the two. Moreover, these texts classify inferences on the basis of characteristics completely extrinsic to logical features of the inferences adduced. Inferences appear to be classified according to the temporal order of the occurrences of the properties of the parts corresponding to a proposition (*pratijñā*) and to a ground (*hetu*).

Improved definitions, which mention not only the parts corresponding to a proposition (*pratijñā*) and to a ground (*hetu*) but also the relation between these two parts, are found in the *Ṣaṣṭitantra* and the *Vaiśeṣikasūtra*, where knowledge of the relation is explicitly included in their definitions of inference. However, the relation is not a formal one, but several from a miscellany of material relations. The *Ṣaṣṭitantra* enumerates seven such relations, while the *Vaiśeṣikasūtra* (VS 9.20) enumerates five: the relation of cause to effect, of effect to cause, of contact, of exclusion and of inherence. In each of these texts, the miscellany of material relations serves to classify inferences. Thus, although, in these two works, the parts of an inference have been made explicit, the formal connection among these parts remained implicit. Birgit Kellner's contribution to the session focuses on inference from exclusion (*virodhin*) found in the *Vaiśeṣikasūtra*.

Another author who is aware that sound inference must be based on a relation between the proposition and the ground is Vātsyāyana (5th century CE), the author of the *Nyāyabhāṣya*, the earliest extant commentary on the *Nyāyasūtra*. While the form of argument he uses retains the vestiges of its analogical antecedents, Vātsyāyana rejects the mere similarity and the mere dissimilarity, which underlie analogical reasoning, as underlying a sound syllogism. As Brendan Gillon shows in his contribution, Vātsyāyana seems to think that sound syllogisms are underpinned by the causation relation.

This identification of cause with ground leaves Vātsyāyana unclear about the difference between obversion and contraposition.

As Sh. Katsura (1986a: 165) has shown, the works of the Buddhist philosopher Vasubandhu (5th century CE) seem to be the earliest extant works which provide a formal characterization of the inference. Vasubandhu holds that inference has only three parts, a subject (*pakṣa*) and two properties, one the property to be established (*sādhya*) in the subject and another which is the ground (*hetu*). Exploiting an idea ascribed by his coreligionist Asaṅga in his *Shùn Zhèng Lùn* to an unknown school (thought by at least one scholar to be the Sāṃkhya school), he maintained that a ground in an inference is a proper one if, and only if, it satisfies three conditions – the so-called *trirūpahetu*, or the grounding property (*hetu*) in its three forms. The first form is that the grounding property (*hetu*) (*H*) occur in the subject of an inference (*pakṣa*) (*p*). The second is that the grounding property (*H*) occur in things similar to the subject insofar as they have the property to be established (*sādhya*) (*S*). And third, the grounding property (*H*) not occur in things dissimilar from the subject insofar as they lack the property to be established (*S*). These conditions can be viewed as a partial specification of the validity of inferences of this form:

thesis (*pakṣa*):	*p* has *S*.
ground (*hetu*):	*p* has *H*.
indispensability (*avinābhāva*):	Whatever has *H* has *S*.

The first condition corresponds to the premiss labelled ground in the schema above, while the second two correspond to the premiss labelled indispensability. In his *Vādavidhi*, Vasubandhu makes clear that the relation, knowledge of which is necessary for inference, is not just any in a miscellany of material relations, but a formal relation, which he designates, in some places, as *avinābhāva*, or indispensability – literally, not being without (cf. the Latin expression *sine qua non*) – and in others, as *nāntarīyakatva*, or immediacy – literally, being unmediated (Katsura 1986b: 5).

Then, Dignāga (late 5th century to early 6th century CE), building on the insights of his teacher, Vasubandhu, fully isolated the formal structure underlying the Indian syllogism (Steinkellner 1993). First, distinguishing between inference for oneself and inference for another, he made explicit what had previously been only implicit, namely, that inference, the cognitive process whereby one increases one's knowledge, and argument, the device of persuasion, are but two sides of a single coin. Second, he changed the formulation of the corroboration to make its logical character more salient. In particular, as Katsura (1986b: 11-12) has noted, Dignāga replaced the singular statements in which the grounding property and the property to be established are said to belong to some recognized instance and in which the grounding property and the property to be established are said not to belong to a recognized instance with corresponding universal statements: namely, that everything which has the grounding property has the property to be established; and that everything which does not have the property to be established does not have the grounding property. Thus, for example, where Vātsyāyana argues

pratijñā: proposition:	*a-nityaḥ śabdaḥ* sound is non-eternal
hetu: ground:	*utpatti-dharmakatvāt* because of having the property of arising
udāharaṇa: corroboration:	*utpatti-dharmakam sthāli-ādi dravyam a-nityam* a substance, such as a pot, having the property of arising, is non-eternal
upanaya: application:	*tathā ca utpatti-dharmakaḥ śabdaḥ* and likewise, sound has the property of arising
nigamana: conclusion:	*tasmāt utpatti-dharmakatvāt a-nityaḥ śabdaḥ* therefore, sound is non-eternal because of having the property of arising

Dignāga argues as follows:

pakṣa:	*a-nityaḥ śabdaḥ*
thesis:	sound is non-eternal
hetu:	*prayatnajatvāt*
ground:	because it results from effort
dṛṣṭānta:	*yat prayatnajam tat anityam dṛṣṭam yathā ghaṭaḥ*
corroboration:	whatever results from effort is observed to be non-eternal, like a pot

(This is cited in Katsura 1986b: 11-12.) In short, Dignāga's syllogism has the following:

pakṣa (thesis):	*p* has *S*.
hetu (ground):	*p* has *H*.
dṛṣṭānta (corroboration):	whatever has *H* is observed to have *S*, like *d*.

(where *d* is an instance of something recognized to have both *H* and *S*.) As is clear from inspection, syllogisms of this form are valid.

Having thus identified within the classical Indian syllogism a valid form, Dignāga pressed into service the Sanskrit particle *eva* ("only") (Katsura 1986a: 163; 1986b: 6-10) to ensure that the *trirūpahetu*, the truth conditions for inference identified by Vasubandhu, accurately characterize the validity of the form of Dignāga's syllogism.

Lastly, and most strikingly, Dignāga gave an alternative and nearly equivalent characterization of the truth conditions of his syllogism, which he called the *hetucakra*, or "wheel of reasons". The so-called wheel of reasons is a three by three matrix, which distinguishes proper from improper grounds and is equivalent to the last two forms of the three forms of a proper ground (*trirūpahetu*). The near equivalence between the *trirūpahetu* and the *hetucakra* confirms that Dignāga was fully aware of the formal character of the syllogism for which he gave the truth conditions. The matrix comprises, on the one hand, the three cases of the grounding property (*H*) occurring in some, none, or all of substrata where the property to be established (*S*) occurs, and, on the other, three cases of the grounding property (*H*) occurring in some, none, or all of the substrata where the property to be established (S) does not occur. Letting S be the substrata in which S occurs and $\overline{S}$ be the substrata in which S does not occur, one arrives at the following table.

H occurs in:	all S all $\overline{S}$	all S no $\overline{S}$	all S some $\overline{S}$
H occurs in:	no S all $\overline{S}$	no S no $\overline{S}$	no S some $\overline{S}$
H occurs in:	some S all $\overline{S}$	some S no $\overline{S}$	some S some $\overline{S}$

Dignāga identified the top and bottom cases of the middle column as those cases rendering the statements of corroboration true.

Dignāga's works set the framework within which subsequent Buddhist thinkers addressed philosophical issues pertaining to inference and debate. Thus, Śankarasvāmin (ca. 6th century CE) wrote a brief manual of inference for Buddhists, called the *Nyāya-praveśa*, based directly on Dignāga's work. Not long thereafter, Dharmakīrti (ca. 7th century CE), the great Buddhist metaphysician, also elaborated his views on inference and debate within the framework found in Dignāga.

Dignāga's treatment of the classical Indian syllogism brought to light an important problem. The syllogism, conceived as an inference, is that whereby one who knows the truth of its premisses may also come to know the truth of its conclusion. The second premiss is known, of course, either through perception or through another inference. But how is the first premiss known? It cannot be known by inference, since the first premiss is a universal statement and the conclusions of syllogisms are particular statements. However, to know the truth of the first premiss by perception would seem to require that one know of each thing which has H, whether or not it also has S. Yet if one knew that, one would already know by perception the syllogism's conclusion. As a result, inference would be a superfluous means of knowledge.

The earliest classical Indian philosopher thought to have recognized the problem of how one comes to know the first premiss of the classical Indian syllogism – essentially, the problem of induction – seems to have been Dignāga's student, Īśvarasena (Steinkellner 1997: 638). He appears to have thought that knowledge of the syllogism's first premiss is grounded in nonperception (*anupalabdhi*). That is, according to Īśvarasena, knowledge that whatever has *H* has *S* comes from the simple failure to perceive something which has *H* but which does not have *S*. (See Steinkellner 1993, where he draws on Steinkellner 1966.)

However, this suggestion does not solve the problem, for reasons laid out in detail by Īśvarasena's student, Dharmakīrti, in the *svārthānumāna* chapter of his *Pramāṇavārttika*. (See verses 13 through 25.) As Dharmakīrti makes abundantly clear, the simple failure to perceive something which has *H* but which does not have *S* is no guarantee that whatever has *H* has *S*; after all, while one has never encountered something which has *H* and does not have *S*, what guarantee is there that something which has *H* and does not have *S* is not among the things which one has yet to encounter? Dharmakīrti's answer was that the truth of the first premiss is guaranteed by either of two relations obtaining between properties: causation relation (*tadutpatti*) and the identity relation (*tādātmya*). Unfortunately, as one might suspect, Dharmakīrti's solution does not work. (See Gillon 1991 for details.)

Dignāga not only had a profound influence on the Buddhist thinkers who followed him, he also influenced his non-Buddhist contemporaries and their followers. It would be wrong to conclude that every adoption of ideas similar to those used by Dignāga in his works should be attributed to him. After all, we cannot be certain that Dignāga's contemporaries did not arrive at similar ideas independently or that they might not have got their ideas from sources common to them and Dignāga. In any event, Praśastapāda (ca. 6th century CE), an adherent of the Vaiśeṣika school, and a near contemporary of Dignāga, also defined inference in a way which not only made clear its formal nature but also used the quantificational adjective *sarva* ("all") to make the formal connection precise. Another thinker of this period is Bhartṛhari (6th CE). Though a grammarian interested in the metaphysical foundations of language, he has an interest in inference. His view of inference (*anumāna*), formulated in his famous work, *Vākyapadīya*, has been misunderstood by later critics. Akihiko Akamatsu shows, in his contribution to the session, how these later critics misunderstood essential epistemic aspects of his definition.

It was not long, however, before the advocates of both Nyāya and Mīmāṃsā adapted to the formal view of inference. On the one hand, one finds that the Mīmāṃsā thinker, Kumārila Bhaṭṭa (ca. early 7th century CE), adopted, without special comment, the formal perspective. On the other hand, one also finds that, though the Nyāya thinker, Uddyotakara (ca. late 6th century CE) argued vigorously against many of Dignāga's views, he nonetheless advocated a view which presupposed the formalization found in Dignāga's works. Thus, Uddyotakara classified grounds (*hetu*) as: concomitant (*anvaya*), where nothing distinct from particular substratum p (in the inferential schema) fails to have the property *S*; exclusive (*vyatireka*), where nothing distinct from p (in the inferential schema) has the property *S*; and both concomitant and exclusive, where some things distinct from p have the property *S* and some fail to have the property *S*. This classification becomes the standard classification for the adherents of Nyāya during the scholastic period.

While Brahmanical thinkers accepted the insight of the Buddhists that the canonical inference is underpinned by indispensability, they refrained from modifying the form of syllogism they used. Rather, the Brahmanical thinkers retained the form of inference found in Vātsyāyana's *Nyāyabhāṣya*. However, they understood the steps of corroboration and application to convey the indispensability relation.

pratijñā (proposition):	*p* has *S*.
hetu (ground):	*p* has *H*.
udāharaṇa (corroboration):	*d* has *H* and *d* has *S*.
upanaya (application):	As *d* has *H* and has *S*, so *p* has *H* and has *S*.
nigamana (conclusion):	*p* has *S*.

In addition, in spite of the metaphysical differences which distinguished the various schools of thought, both Buddhist and Brahmanical, all thinkers came to use a naive realist's ontology to specify the states of affairs used to study the syllogism. According to this view, the world consists of individual substances, or things (*dravya*), universals (*sāmānya*) and relations between them. The fundamental relation is the one of occurrence (*vṛtti*). The relata of this relation are known as substratum (*dharmin*) and superstratum (*dharma*) respectively. The relation has two forms: contact (*samyoga*) and inherence (*samavāya*). So, for example, one individual substance, a pot, may occur on another, say the ground, by the relation of contact. In this case, the pot is the superstratum and the ground is the substratum. Or, a universal, say treeness, may occur in an individual substance, say an individual tree, by the relation of inherence. Here, treeness, the superstratum, inheres in the individual tree, the substratum. The converse of the relation of occurrence is the relation of possession.

Another important relation is the relation which one superstratum bears to another. This relation, mentioned above as indispensability (*avinābhāva*), and later known as pervasion (*vyāpti*), can be defined in terms of the occurrence relation. One superstratum pervades another just in case wherever the second occurs the first occurs. The converse of the pervasion relation is the concomitance relation.

As a result of these relations, the world embodies a structure: if one superstratum, designated as *H*, is concomitant with another superstratum, designated as *S*, and if a particular substratum, say p, possesses the former superstratum, then it possesses the second.

This structure is the one which underlies the classical Indian syllogism.

3. CONCLUSION

This very brief outline of logic found in India during the classical and preclassical period is intended to provide the general reader only with the bare minimum needed to assist him or her with following the discussions contained in the contributions of this volume. For a more comprehensive treatment of logic in India, the reader may wish to consult the following: Bochenski 1956, §§ 50-54, Ganeri 2001, Randle 1930, Solomon 1976, Staal 1988 or Vidyabhusana 1921.

ACKNOWLEDGEMENTS

I wish to express my gratitude to Shoryu Katsura for his comments and corrections to an earlier version of this introduction. Thanks are also due to the Finnish Cultural Foundation for having supported the publication of the papers of the Helsinki conference.

REFERENCES

BOCHENSKI, I. M. 1956. *Formale Logik*. München: Verlag Karl Alber. English translation: Ivo Thomas (trans.), *A History of Formal Logic*. 2nd edition. Notre Dame, Indiana: University of Notre Dame Press, 1970. (Reprinted by Chelsea Publishing Co., New York.)

FRANCO, Eli 2002. Towards a reconstruction of the Spitzer Manuscript – The dialectical portion. *Wiener Zeitschrift für die Kunde Südasiens* 46: 171-224.

FRAUWALLNER, Erich 1957. Vasubandhu's Vādavidhiḥ. *Wiener Zeitschrift für die Kunde Süd- und Ostasiens und Archiv für Indische Philosophie* 1: 104-146.

—— 1958. Die Erkenntnislehre des klassischen Sāṃkhya-Systems. *Wiener Zeitschrift für die Kunde Süd- und Ostasiens und Archiv für Indische Philosophie* 2: 84-139.

GANERI, Jonardon (ed.) 2001. *Indian Logic. A Reader*. Richmond: Curzon.

GILLON, Brendan S. 1991. Dharmakīrti and the problem of induction. In: Ernst Steinkellner (ed.), *Studies in the Buddhist Epistemological Tradition Proceedings of the Second International Dharmakīrti Conference, Vienna, 11-16 June, 1989*: 53-58. Wien: Verlag der Österreichischen Akademie der Wissenschaften.

KATSURA, Shoryu 1986a. On Trairūpya Formulae. In: *Buddhism and Its Relation to Other Religions. Essays in Honour of Dr. Shozen Kumoi on His Seventieth Birthday*: 161-172. Tokyo: Heirakuji-Shoten.

—— 1986b. On the origin and development of the concept of *vyāpti* in Indian logic. *Hiroshima Tetsugakkai* 38: 1-16.

LAMOTTE, Étienne 1935. *Saṃdhinirmocanasūtra: L'explication des mystères. Texte Tibétain édité et traduit*. Louvain: Université de Louvain.

MANNÉ, Joy 1992. The Digha Nikāya debates. *Buddhist Studies Review* 9(2): 117-136.

Mbh = *Patañjali Mahābhāṣya*. Edited by Franz Kielhorn. Pune: Bhandarkar Oriental Research Institute, 1880. (4th edition revised by R. N. Dandekar, 1985.)

MULLER, Ian 1972. Greek mathematics and Greek logic. In: John Corcoran (ed.), *Ancient Logic and its Modern Interpreters*: 35-70. Dordrecht: D. Reidel Publishing Co.

RANDLE, H. N. 1930. *Indian Logic in the Early Schools. A Study of the Nyāyadarśana in its Relation to the Early Logic of Other Schools*. Oxford: Oxford University Press.

SOLOMON, Esther A. 1976. *Indian Dialectics. Methods of Philosophical Discussion*, I-II.. Ahmedabad: B. J. Institute of Learning and Research.

STAAL, J. F. 1975. *Exploring Mysticism. A Methodological Essay*. Berkeley: The University of California Press. (Reprinted by Penguin Books, Harmondsworth, 1976).

—— (ed.) 1988. *Universals. Studies in Indian Logic and Linguistics*. Chicago: The University of Chicago Press.

STEINKELLNER, Ernst 1966. Bemerkungen zu Īśvarasenas Lehre vom Grund. *Wiener Zeitschrift für die Kunde Südasiens* 10: 73-85.

—— 1993. Buddhist logic: The search for certainty. In: Takeuchi Yoshinori (ed.), *Buddhist Spirituality. Indian, Southeast Asian, Tibetan, and Early Chinese*: 213-218. New York: Crossroad.

—— 1997. Kumārila, Īśvarasena, and Dharmakīrti in dialogue: A new interpretation of Pramāṇavārttika I 33. In: Petra Kieffer-Pulz & Jens-Uwe Hartmann (eds), *Bauddhavidyāsudhākarah. Studies in Honour of Heinz Bechert on the Occasion of His 65th Birthday*. (Monographien zu den Sprachen und Literaturen des indo-tibetischen Kulturraumes, 30): 625-646. Swisttal-Odendorf: Indica et Tibetica Verlag.

TUCCI, Giuseppe 1929. *Pre-Dinnāga Texts on Logic from Chinese Sources.* (Gaekwad Oriental Series, 49.) Baroda.

VIDYABHUSANA, Satis Chandra 1921. *A History of Indian Logic. Ancient, Medieval and Modern.* Calcutta: Calcutta University. (Reprinted by Motilal Banarsidass, Delhi, 1971.)

Reasoning as a Science, its Role in Early Dharma Literature, and the Emergence of the Term *nyāya*

KARIN PREISENDANZ

THE CULTURAL BACKGROUND OF THE DEVELOPMENT OF LOGIC IN INDIA

Previous research on the early development of Indian logic and its cultural background has placed a great deal of emphasis on the evidence provided by the early classical Āyurvedic tradition. To be sure, the probably already pre-classical tradition of debate with its inherent concern about convincing and correct procedures of proof contains important seeds for the development of logic, and its treatment found a special place in the *Carakasaṃhitā*. I will discuss in detail elsewhere the diametrically opposed positions of the pioneering Indian scholars in this area, namely, Satishchandra Vidyabhusana and Surendranath Dasgupta, as regards the relationship between, on the one hand, the medical tradition, and, on the other, the early theories about debate and reflections on the proto-logical concepts embedded in it as exemplified by the *Carakasaṃhitā*.[1] In this connection I take a middle position between their rather extreme views and attempt to demonstrate the particular importance of debate – responsible for an intense intellectual interest in it – in the medical context, drawing on the diverse evidence provided by the *Carakasaṃhitā* itself. This interest, I argue, not only led to some specific-

[1] Cf. Preisendanz, forthcoming.

ally *medical* theoretical treatment of the types of debate, their constitutive elements and their structure by Āyurvedic scholars,[2] but also occasioned the integration of some theoretical framework of debate into the text of the *Carakasaṃhitā*, which consisted in the listing of various components of debate in the widest sense.[3] This framework seems to have been designed in another intellectual setting, probably the milieu of those ancient Indian savants of different scholarly pursuits who, just like the Āyurvedic scholars, were concerned with establishing a procedural structure and firm rules and guidelines for the mutual scholarly controversies as carried out by them in debate; it was then explicated, not altogether unconvincingly, within the framework of the medical tradition's own special concepts concerning the details of debate and exemplified for practical purposes within the medical context.

Another discourse in which early logical concepts could develop was, of course, the epistemological one, foremost in the context of inference as a means of knowledge. Here too a strong connection to the medical tradition can be made out on the evidence of the *Carakasaṃhitā*. The various means of knowledge involved in, and required for, a reliable diagnosis of the appropriate and successful treatment of diseases, received due attention in the work,[4] and the important role of inference in the widest sense of the word for medical practice was duly recognized.[5] Here also the early classical

---

[2] Cf. CaS Vimānasthāna 8.15-26 and 67.

[3] Cf. CaS Vimānasthāna 8.27-66.

[4] Cf. CaS Vimānasthāna 4.3-4 (on three instruments of detailed knowledge of specifics of diseases [*rogaviśeṣavijñāna*]), 8.79-82 and 8.83-132 (on the various objects of the twofold or threefold means of examination [*parīkṣā*] used in diagnosis). Cf. also the examples relating to the medical field of embryology adduced in the general characterization of inference and "combination" (*yukti*), both constituting means of examination (*parīkṣā*), in Sūtrasthāna 11.21, 23 and 32.

[5] Cf. the basic role of the signs (*liṅga*) or symptoms of diseases expressed, e.g., in CaS Sūtrasthāna 1.24, which implies the necessity of their correct interpretation in the sense of an inference of the underlying disease. In the *Kauśikasūtra* (KS 25.2), *liṅgin* seems to be used as a special term to denote "disease" (cf. the commentator Dārilabhaṭṭa who glosses *liṅgin* with *vyādhi*); cf. Dasgupta 1932: 293.

Āyurvedic scholars were situated in a broader intellectual setting which may have partially overlapped with that in which debate was an issue,[6] or had some strong affinity to it, namely, the setting of those scholars with various fields of specialisation who strove to come to grips with what constitutes a proper examination of the objects and issues of their special interest, with a focus on the means to conduct such an examination.[7] As in the case of the dialectical-eristic discourse, the Āyurvedic tradition must also have participated in the epistemological discourse of the early classical period (1st to 3rd centuries) by contributing its own ideas[8] and have integrated concepts developed by other thinkers belonging to the relevant intellectual milieu. The strong Āyurvedic concern with examination (*parīkṣā*) is documented in the *Carakasaṃhitā* by the several different contexts in which examination, its means and its objects are presented and in which the act of examination is referred to and enjoined.[9] On the stylistic level this concern involves the usage of a strikingly large variety of forms and derivates of the verbal root √*īkṣ* with the preverb *pari-*, but also with *vi-*, with *ava-*, the latter sometimes combined with *anu-* and *sam-*, and with *sam-* combined with *abhi-*, to mention the most frequent variations on the theme. Like the concern with debate, this concern with examination, together with the terminological emphasis on "viewing from all sides", i.e., comprehensive viewing (*pari-*√*īkṣ*), indicates

---

[6] Cf. the listing of what may be six sources of knowledge in CaS Vimānasthāna 8.27 and their further treatment in 8.38-42.

[7] Cf. the treatment of four sources of knowledge, called "means of examination" (*parīkṣā*) and "means of valid cognition" (*pramāṇa*), in the context of the ascertainment of the "other world" (*paraloka*) in CaS Sūtrasthāna 11.7, 17-25 and 27 (for the designation as *pramāṇa*s cf. 11.33).

[8] Cf. especially the notion of a means of knowledge called *yukti* ("combination").

[9] Besides the contexts already mentioned above (i.e., diagnosis and metaphysical-soteriological inquiry), one may mention the contexts of debate, of finding a suitable expert tradition or doctrinal edifice (*śāstra*) in the area of medicine, the right teacher and the right student, of discerning a quack from a proper physician, of medical etiquette and a physician's appropriate behavior in general, and of therapy.

an intellectual milieu that the early classical Āyurvedic scholars shared with scholars of the later, classical philosophical tradition of Nyāya as consolidated in the *Nyāyasūtra* and, in addition, with the authors of the religio-philosophical treatises assembled in the Vārṣṇeyādhyātma group of chapters found in the Mokṣadharma section of the *Mahābhārata.*

In the last-mentioned treatises, emphasis is put on "examination with reasons", amplified by references to intellectual vision (*jñāna-cakṣus*), consideration (*vimarśa*) and reasons (*hetu*); the last two terms are again shared with the *Nyāyasūtra* and with the *Carakasaṃhitā*, which also mentions *jñānacakṣus*.[10] Indeed, although examination – in the sense of the means of examination – as understood in the *Carakasaṃhitā* is of various types, including especially perception, inference, "combination" (*yukti*) and tradition, and although the act of thorough examination has accordingly to be understood as combining various means of examination, a strong emphasis on intellectual examination involving inference and, possibly, "combination" is implied by the term *parīkṣā*, other derivations of *pari-√īkṣ* and related formations, and with it the use of reasons. Thus, both notions, i.e., the notion of examination in the specific sense of examination with reasons as well as the notion of the main means of examination characterized by reasoning, lead us to another, equally important historical context for the development of logic, namely, the "science" or art of reasoning described and highly praised in Kauṭilya's *Arthaśāstra* as the well-known "investigating (science)" (*ānvīkṣikī* [*vidyā*]).[11] Similar to the arts of debate and comprehensive examination, *ānvīkṣikī* (*vidyā*) understood as a method, an interpretation we owe especially to Paul Hacker's observations,[12] can be applied to various "sciences", that is, areas of knowledge (*vidyā*),[13] inasmuch as – as it is formulated

[10] Cf. Preisendanz 2000: 239-240.

[11] Cf. the famous passage AŚ 1.2.11-12.

[12] Cf. Hacker 1958: 58, 64-65, 71-73.

in the *Arthaśāstra* and unmistakenly echoed in a verse of the Vārṣṇeyādhyātma – one "investigates with reasons" their respective chief issues as well as their strengths and weaknesses;[14] it is therefore certainly justified to call *ānvīkṣikī* (*vidyā*) "the lamp of all sciences".[15] Such an interpretation does not, however, rule out that *ānvīkṣikī* (*vidyā*) was also considered to be a "science" proper with its own subject matter like the other three sciences mentioned in this context, namely, the Vedic science that has the triple sacred tradition as its subject matter (*trayī*), the science of material acquisition (*vārttā*) and the science of government (*daṇḍanīti*); that is, the designation *ānvīkṣikī* (*vidyā*) may at the same time refer to a science concerned with understanding the process of reasoning and its constituents as its special object, *and* to a scientific methodology of reasoning developed in and on the basis of this science.[16]

REASONING IN CLASSIFICATIONS OF TYPES, METHODS AND AREAS OF KNOWLEDGE

The four sciences (*vidyā*) treated in the relevant chapter of the *Arthaśāstra* (called *vidyāsamuddeśa*) and in subsequent Arthaśāstra and Arthaśāstra-related literature[17] have sometimes been called the

---

[13] Cf. also Halbfass' remark, relating to *ānvīkṣikī* (*vidyā*), that it was "a method ... to be used by various branches of learning" (Halbfass 1988: 284).

[14] Cf. Preisendanz 2000: 240.

[15] Cf. Preisendanz 2000: 226-228, treating *ānvīkṣikī* in the context of its great significance for Vātsyāyana when determining the place of the philosophical Nyāya tradition in the cultural and intellectual world of classical India.

[16] Similarly, one speaks of mathematics as a science (i.e., the systematic treatment of magnitude, relationships between figures and forms, and relations between quantities expressed symbolically) and a methodology (i.e., mathematical procedures and operations) applicable to a number of other sciences.

[17] For the Arthaśāstra-related literature, cf. the sections outlining the duties and functions of a king in the Dharmaśāstra works addressed below and the Rājadharmānuśāsanaparvan of the Śāntiparvan where the huge treatise of 100,000 verses composed by God Brahman to restore order after the decline of the *kṛtayuga* had set in is specifically said to also comprise the four sciences; cf. MBh 12.59.33: *trayī cānvīkṣikī caiva vārttā ca bharatarṣabha* I *daṇḍanītiś ca vipulā vidyās tatra nidarśitāḥ* II (cf. also Hazra 1960: 33; Thakur 1975: 40;

"royal" sciences, as opposed to the well-known fourteen (or eighteen) "orthodox" or "Brahminical" sciences (*vidyā*) or areas ("places/footholds") of knowledge (*vidyāsthāna*)[18].[19] However, the lists partially overlap and both contain items which may be considered purely secular as well as items associated with the religious sphere: it is therefore more appropriate to speak of a royal *classification* with an emphasis on the secular sciences which are of special relevance to the ruling order[20] as opposed to a Brahminical *classification* with its own non-exclusive focus on the sciences which pertain to the religious tradition, its appropriate transmission and interpretation as well as to the concrete enactment of its injunctions and norms.[21] The context provided by the classification of the four *vidyās* points at the concrete setting of the royal court with its specific daily routines where the art of reasoning accompanied by reflections on the "logic" implied in it (*ānvīkṣikī* [*vidyā*]) must have been fostered, whereas the context of the classification of the fourteen (/eighteen) *vidyā*(*sthāna*)s with its corresponding item (*tarka*, *nyāya*, *nyāyavistara*) indicates a more general intellectual setting

Narain 1979: 381). As regards the didactic-narrative literature related to the Artha- and Nītiśāstra and developing around the *Pañcatantra* and *Hitopadeśa*, to name the two most famous exponents of this genre, the introduction to the *Pañcatantra* clearly evidences a strong influence by the concept of the triad of human aims: it mentions, next to the teachings on grammar (*vyākaraṇa*), those on socio-religious norms (*dharma*), on material and political gain (*artha*), and on sexual and other physical pleasures (*kāma*) as the doctrinal edifices (*śāstra*) which should form components of the princely curriculum (cf. PT p. 2,14-16), whereas the introduction to the *Hitopadeśa*, with its focus on the *Hitopadeśa* itself as the subject of instruction, mentions only *nītiśāstra* as the essential teaching for young princes (cf. HU pp. 4,21, 26; 5,1, 11, and the conclusion p. 105,14: *rājyavyavahārāṅga*). On a large array of sources on the fields of royal education cf. Kane, HDh III, pp. 48-51.

[18] For various lists of these fourteen (eighteen) sciences or areas of science cf. below.

[19] Cf., e.g., Hacker 1958: 67-68, 73, 30.

[20] In the case of the classifications of the Auśanasas and Bārhaspatyas as referred to in the *Arthaśāstra*, this would be an exclusive emphasis.

[21] Cf. also the stress on the different nature of this classification, not necessarily of the sciences themselves, in Hacker 1958: 67.

for reasoning, a setting which may to a large degree contain the just mentioned concrete setting owing to the prominent position of the intellectual Brahminical order in higher state administration; it may also overlap with the general intellectual milieu of those scholars which I assume to have been involved in the art of examination (*parīkṣā*) and debate, i.e., their practise and the reflection on them.

As compared to the four *vidyā*s, the Brahminical classification of fourteen (/eighteen) *vidyā*(*sthāna*)s and its wider context have received comparatively little attention in studies on the cultural background of the art of reasoning in India and on the cultural self-understanding of the Nyāya philosophical tradition.[22] The 9th-century Naiyāyika Jayanta refers to this classification in the introduction to his *Nyāyamañjarī* by way of quoting two well-known verses. The second of these verses occurs with a few insignificant variants in the Purāṇic literature, in the *Viṣṇupurāṇa*, *Vāyupurāṇa* and *Bhaviṣyapurāṇa*, and lists the auxiliaries (*aṅga*) of the Vedas, the four Vedas themselves, Mīmāṃsā, the vastness of *nyāya* (*nyāyavistara*), the "[stories] pertaining to the past" (*purāṇa*) and the teachings on socio-religious norms (*dharmaśāstra*) as the fourteen sciences;[23] the first three *pāda*s of the verse are utilized with

---

[22] Cf., however, the observations in Hacker 1958: 67-69.

[23] Cf. NM Vol. I, p. 8,7-8: *aṅgāni vedāś catvāro mīmāṃsā nyāyavistaraḥ* | *purāṇaṃ dharmaśāstraṃ ca vidyā hy etāś caturdaśa* ||. This reading of the verse corresponds to the version found in VP 3.6.27 as published by the Venkateshvara Steam Press, Bombay (cf. also Vidyabhusana 1920: 42), and reprinted in *Viṣṇu-mahāpurāṇa*; in this Purāṇa, the following verse brings the number up to eighteen with medicine (Āyurveda), archery or weaponry in general (Dhanurveda), music (Gāndharvaveda) and state craft (Arthaśāstra) (cf. also, e.g., Pollock 1985: 502; 1989: 23), a list which was – as Halbfass already notes (cf. Halbfass 1988: 40, with reference to Rajamanickam 1972) – probably first mentioned in Western scholarship on India by Roberto de Nobili in his *Informatio* (for both verses cf. also MBh Vol. XIII [Rājadharma Part 1], Appendix I, No. 13, lines 7-10). Wilson (1980: 411) read a text of the *Viṣṇupurāṇa* in which the verse starts with *aṅgāni caturo vedāḥ* (cf. also Hazra 1959: 33, n. 49), as in its *Bhaviṣyapurāṇa* version (BhP Brāhmaparvan 2.6). The *Vāyupurāṇa* inverts the two items in the second half of the verse and has *tu* instead of *hi*: *dharmaśāstraṃ purāṇaṃ ca vidyās tv etāḥ* ... (VāP Pūrvārdha 61.78) (cf. also Ruben 1926: 351; Kane, HDh II.1, p. 355); the inversion is also found in the quotation of the verse in Mitra-

slight variation in the *Kāmandakīyanītisāra* to explicate the precise content of Kauṭilya's *trayī* in an attempt to merge the Brahminical

---

miśra's *Vīramitrodaya* (VM p. 15,9-10) on YS 1.3 (cf. also Hazra 1959: 33, n. 49; 1960: 25). According to Kane (HDh II.1, p. 355, n. 862), Aparārka refers to the verse (and the following verse, cf. Kane, HDh III, p. 10, n. 7) in his commentary on the *Yājñavalkyasmṛti* (p. 6), which is not available to me (cf., however, Hazra 1960: 21, n. 26, who quotes the relevant portion of Aparārka's comments on YS 1.3 [cf. below] where *hi* in the last *pāda* is missing). The verse as quoted by Jayanta is also quoted by Mallinātha on RV 5.21 (p. 115,23-24), where fourteen sciences are referred to (cf. Kane, HDh II.1, p. 355; Hacker 1958: 67), but erroneously attributed to the *Manusmṛti*. For another verse, consisting of six *pāda*s, which lists the eighteen sciences, cf. the *Garuḍapurāṇa* (GP 1.224.21): *purāṇaṃ dharmaśāstraṃ ca vedās tv aṅgāni yan mune* I *nyāyaḥ śaunaka mīmāṃsā āyurvedārthaśāstrakam* II *gāndharvaś ca dhanurvedo vidyā hy aṣṭādaśa smṛtāḥ* II. Cf. also the the eighteen components of the "lower science" (*aparā vidyā*) in the *Agnipurāṇa* (AP 1.1.15cd-17c) (... *mīmāṃsā dharmaśāstraṃ purāṇakam* II *nyāyavaidyakagāndharvaṃ dhanurvedo 'rthaśāstrakam* I *apareyam* [scil. *vidyā*] ...) (cf. Horsch 1966: 70; Pollock 1985: 514). – The enumeration of the fourteen sciences may be compared with the list in VP 5.1.36-37 where God Brahmā praises Viṣṇu: "You are the Ṛgveda, Yajurveda, Sāmaveda and the Atharvan, phonetics, ritual and etymology, prosody and astronomy, and traditional narratives (*itihāsa*) and stories pertaining to the past (*purāṇa*), [and] also grammar, O Lord; you are Mīmāṃsā [and] *nyāyaka*, [and] the teachings on socio-religious norms (*dharmaśāstra*), O imperceptible one (lit.: who is beyond perception) (*adhokṣaja*)." Here, *itihāsa* and *purāṇa*, referred to by means of a dual *dvandva*-compound, probably have to be understood as one item, although the number 14 is not mentioned in this context. Thakur states, without further reference, that Nyāya is also counted among the *vidyāsthāna*s in the *Padmapurāṇa* (cf. Thakur 1975: 43, maybe in dependence on the unspecified reference in Vidyabhusana 1913: xiv [1930: xvii], which is taken from the excerpt in Aufrecht's *Catalogue of Sanskrit MSS. in the Bodleian Library at Oxford* quoted in Muir 1873: 27); he may have had in mind PP 1.1.48 where an abbreviated list of only twelve items (48ab: *aṅgāni caturo vedān purāṇanyāyavistaram* ...) specifies what is meant by "the whole expert tradition" (*akhilaṃ śāstram*, cf. 48c; this verse division is much more meaningful than the one in the edition published in the Gurumandal Series). Here, *purāṇa* may stand for both *purāṇa* and *itihāsa*, whereas *nyāyavistara* may imply Mīmāṃsā as well as Dharmaśāstra. Eighteen areas of knowledge (*vijjaṭṭhāna*) are mentioned already in Jātaka No. 50 (Dummedhajātaka) (J I, p. 259,13), but not detailed (cf. also the eighteen crafts [*sippa*] replacing the eighteen areas of knowledge in the same context in Jātaka No. 181 [Asadisajātaka] [J II, p. 87,9] and Jātaka No. 336 [Brahāchattajātaka] [J III, p. 115,19]); on the various numbers and lists of crafts in Buddhist literature, cf. Horsch (1966: 58-59), who mistakenly subsumes the passage in the Dhummedhajātaka under this topic.

list with the fourfold royal classification.[24] Jayanta identifies his own philosophical tradition Nyāya with the "vastness of *nyāya*" and refers to it repeatedly with the term *nyāyavistara* in his introduction, although the claim for an identification of his own school with *nyāyavistara* is also made by Kumārila in his *Tantravārttika*: obviously referring to the same verse, the latter understands *nyāyavistara* as an apposition to or an attribute qualifying the Mīmāṃsā owing to the fact that the Mīmāṃsā tradition represents the collection of a huge amount of arguments (*yukti*) which could not have been brought forth by a single person but are rather founded on the activities, such as sensory perception and inference, of many scholars within a common uninterrupted chain of traditional transmission.[25]

---

[24] Cf. KNS 2.13: *aṅgāni vedāś catvāro mīmāṃsā nyāyavistaraḥ* I *dharmaśāstraṃ purāṇaṃ ca trayīdaṃ sarvam ucyate.* Cf. also Jacobi 1911: 739; Ruben 1926: 351. A related verse quoted by Madanasiṃha in his *Madanaratnapradīpa* and ascribed by him to Pitāmaha, which serves to identify the fourteen sciences as expert traditions of *dharma* (cf. YS 1.3 discussed below p. 36ff.), still bears traces of a re-working of the Purāṇic verse under discussion; cf. Hazra 1960: 24: *sāṅgā vedās tu catvāro mīmāṃsā smṛtayas tathā* I *etāni dharmaśāstrāṇi purāṇaṃ nyāyadarśanam* II.

[25] Cf. TV Vol. I, p. 80,8-10. This may be compared with Rāghavānanda's interpretation as evidenced in his commentary on MS 12.106 where he comments on the term *tarka* with a view to the enumeration found in the first verse quoted by Jayanta, namely, YS 1.3: *tarkeṇa mīmāṃsayā purāṇanyāyamīmāṃsetyādi mīmāṃsāsañjñakas tarka ity ukteḥ* (MS Vol. VI, p. 318,9-10) (cf. also below p. 38 for Viśvarūpa's preferred interpretation of the compound *purāṇanyāyamīmāṃsā-*). – In this interpretation, the missing science required to arrive at the number 14 is to be extracted from the mention of the "[stories] pertaining to the past" (*purāṇa*), namely, *itihāsa*. By implication, such an interpretation of YS 1.3, with the reading *-tarkamīmāṃsā-* instead of *-nyāyamīmāṃsā-* (cf. below), may also have to be presupposed for the author of the *Yuktidīpikā*. In his explanation of the two possible grammatical interpretations of the word *āptaśruti* in SK 5 he distinguishes between (1) impersonal, independent tradition, i.e., the hearing (cf. *śravaṇaṃ śrutiḥ*) itself is trustworthy (cf. the grammatical explanation *āptā cāsau śrutiś ca*), and, by implication, (2) dependent personalized tradition, i.e., hearing from trustworthy persons (cf. the explanation of the compound as *āptebhyaḥ śrutiḥ*), as a means of valid cognition (*pramāṇa*). The first type, although not further clarified, would certainly comprise the four Vedas, whereas the tradition of the second type is explained as the statements of the *smṛtis*, i.e., the compositions (*nibandhana*) of Manu and others (= *dharma-*

The first verse quoted by Jayanta in the present context is found in the beginning of the *Yājñavalkyasmṛti* and lists the fourteen *vidyāsthāna*s in the following order: the "[stories] pertaining to the past", reasoning (*tarka*), Mīmāṃsā, the teachings on socio-religious norms, the auxiliaries and the Vedas.[26] According to Jayanta, they are called *vidyāsthāna*s, that is, "places" or "locations" in the sense of supports (*āśraya*) and means (*upāya*) of knowledge, inasmuch as they provide the knowledge about the means by way of which one achieves those human aims (*puruṣārtha*) which cannot be experienced directly (*adṛṣṭa*), namely, heaven and liberation.[27] Some of the *vidyāsthāna*s, amongst which the Vedas figure most prominently, instruct us directly in these means, others, namely, the auxiliaries and the Mīmāṃsā, which is virtually a part of the Veda, contribute indirectly to their knowledge.[28] The "vastness of *nyāya*" (*nyāyavistara*), however, in the sense of the vast extent and depth of reasoning and identified by Jayanta with the Nyāya philosophical tradition, is the supportive pillar of all the other *vidyāsthā-*

śāstra), the auxiliaries of the Veda (*vedāṅga*), reasoning (*tarka*), traditional narratives (*itihāsa*) and stories pertaining to the past (*purāṇa*), augmented by the utterings of learned persons (*śiṣṭa*) and those proficient in the various arts (*nānāśilpābhiyukta*) (cf. YD p. 87,4-12). The only term which could refer to the indispensable Mīmāṃsā in this enumeration is *tarka*. Under the assumption of his acceptance of the almost canonical number of fourteen sciences and his reference to YS 1.3, the author would have taken *tarka* and *mīmāṃsā* as referring to one item and understood the term *purāṇa* in YS 1.3 to point to traditional narratives (*itihāsa*) as a further, related item; the utterings of learned persons, even though they are frequently mentioned as sources of knowledge, and of those proficient in the various arts could not have been intended by him as the missing item because they can hardly be considered to constitute a "place of knowledge", the topic of YS 1.3.

[26] Cf. NM Vol. I, p. 8,5-6: *purāṇatarkamīmāṃsādharmaśāstrāṅgamiśritāḥ* | *vedāḥ sthānāni vidyānāṃ dharmasya ca caturdaśa* ||.

[27] Cf. NM I p. 4,15-5,2 (*adṛṣṭe tu svargāpavargamātre ... śāstram eva prakāśaḥ ... tac ca caturdaśavidham ...*) and p. 7,15-8,1: *vedanaṃ vidyā, tac ca na ghaṭādivedanam api tu puruṣārthasādhanavedanam. vidyāyāḥ sthānam āśraya upāya ity arthaḥ* (cf. also Pollock 1985: 508 and 1989: 22-23, and the paraphrase in Jha 1994: 1-2).

[28] Cf. NM I p. 5,3-6,4 (cf. the paraphrases in Mishra 1966, II: 10-11 and Jha 1994: 2-3).

nas[29] and therefore the most excellent among them for the reason that it protects the authority (*prāmāṇya*) of the Vedas.[30] The "vastness of *nyāya*" or Nyāya tradition achieves this in a special way since it is also said to decide upon the Vedic authority,[31] to firmly determine,[32] establish[33] and prove it.[34] Using the term *nyāyavistara* of the Purāṇic verse discussed above Jayanta in this way also identifies "reasoning" (*tarka*, the relevant term in the quoted Smṛti verse) with his own philosophical tradition, where reasoning – *nyāya*, *tarka* and *anumāna* – is expounded.[35]

The verse YS 1.3 as quoted by Jayanta is found in this form in the *Bṛhadyogiyājñavalkya*, a compilation of verses from the Dharmaśāstras and from *yoga*-related literature, including numerous verses taken from the *Manusmṛti* and the *Bhagavadgītā*.[36] Also a late quotation of this verse in Nyāya-Vaiśeṣika literature, in Viśvanātha Pañcānana's 17th-century *Nyāyavṛtti*,[37] reads *tarka* as

---

[29] Cf. with this Rājaśekhara's claim in his *Kāvyamīmāṃsā* that poetics (*alaṅkāraśāstra*), as the fifteenth *vidyāsthāna*, is the foundation of all other *vidyāsthānas* (cf. the quotation in Bhattacharyya 1956: 49, n. 5, and Pollock 1989: 24).

[30] Cf. NM I p. 7,6-13: (... *vedaprāmāṇyarakṣāhetutvāt.*).

[31] Cf. NM I p. 10,1: *nanu vedaprāmāṇyanirṇayaprayojanaś cen nyāyavistaraḥ* ... (cf. also the paraphrase in Shah 1992: 10).

[32] Cf. NM I p. 11,3: *nanv akṣapādāt pūrvaṃ kuto vedaprāmāṇyaniścaya āsīt* (cf. the paraphrase in Jha 1994: 4 and the remarks in Shah 1992: 13) and p. 635,3: *vedaprāmāṇyaniścayahetuś ca nyāyavistaraḥ.*

[33] Cf. NM I p. 23,2-3: *nyāyaś ca vedaprāmāṇyapratiṣṭhāpanapūrvakatvena puruṣārthopayogitvam upayāti.*

[34] Cf. NM I p. 28,10: ... *upadeṣṭavyāḥ padārthāḥ* ... I ... *vedaprāmāṇyasiddhaye* II and p. 639,18: *vedaprāmāṇyasiddhyarthaṃ hīdaṃ śāstram ārabdham.* Cf. also Shah's critical exposition of this issue in Shah 1992: 7-8 and 10-13.

[35] Cf. NM I p. 8,10-12 (cf. also Mishra 1966: 11; Halbfass 1988: 284; Shah 1992: 7).

[36] Cf. BṛYY 13.3, translated in Gharote & Bedekar 1982. The compilation of this work must have been concluded before Vācaspati Miśra I's time; for further details on this work, cf. Kane, HDh I.1, pp. 449-457.

[37] Cf. NVṛ I p. 62,22. Viśvanātha, who belongs to the Navadvīpa "school" of Navya-Nyāya, is also credited with the authorship of the *Bhāṣāpariccheda* together with its commentary *Siddhāntamuktāvalī*; however, on the basis of manuscript evidence D. C. Bhattacharya has claimed that this ascription is faulty and the two works were written by Kṛṣṇānanda, the teacher of Bhavānanda, who

the second item here, which is understood by Viśvanātha, as by Jayanta before him, as the term referring to the Nyāya philosophical tradition. The transmitted text of the *Yājñavalkyasmṛti*, however, reads *purāṇa**nyāya**mīmāṃsā.*[38] In spite of this presumably unambiguous term, the Dharmaśāstra tradition does not unanimously agree with Jayanta in the identification of the respective "location of knowledge" designated as *nyāya* in this reading. Viśvarūpa, the late classical or early medieval commentator,[39] is aware of the fact that some scholars understand that Akṣapāda's Nyāya tradition is intended here,[40] but his own preferred interpretation is to take the terms *nyāya* and *mīmāṃsā* as referring together to *one* science, that is, the Mīmāṃsā.[41] For Jayanta, though, the identification of the second *vidyāsthāna* (for him: "support/means of knowledge") with a single traditional "system", namely, the Nyāya philosophical tradition, is beyond doubt, as is the equation of the terms *nyāya* and *tarka* in the sense of "reasoning",[42] an equation he subsequently stresses and which is frequently found in the relevant classical and medieval scholarly works. Many modern scholars have followed him in this respect.[43] However, even though *nyāya* and *tarka* may

lived about a hundred years earlier (cf. Bhattacharya's *Baṅge Navya-Nyāya Carcā* according to Matilal 1977: 109).

[38] Cf. YS 1.3: *purāṇa**nyāya**mīmāṃsādharmaśāstrāṅgamiśritāḥ* I *vedāḥ sthānāni vidyānāṃ dharmasya tu* caturdaśa* II. * *ca* according to Stenzler 1849, the other editions used in this paper and the quotation in PBh p. 1,11-12 (cf. also Weber 1850: 2; Horsch 1966: 70). Cf. also Vidyabhusana 1913: xiv [1930: xvii] and 1920: 38, 43 on this verse. See further Hazra 1960: 7.

[39] Kane (HDh I.1., § 61, pp. 553-565) arrives at the rather extensive period of 750-1000 for Viśvarūpa's date.

[40] Cf. also, from a much later period, Mitramiśra who specifies that the teaching consisting of five *adhyāya*s and founded by Akṣapāda is meant here; cf. VM p. 9,26-27. This is to be compared with PBh p. 6,7 (with reference to YS 1.3): *nyāya ānvīkṣikī pañcādhyāyī gautamena praṇītā* (referred to also in Hacker 1958: 76).

[41] Cf. BK p. 9,11-14. This means, of course, that *purāṇa* should be interpreted to further refer to *itihāsa*; cf. Rāghavānanda's commentary on MS 12.106 referred to in footnote 25.

[42] Cf. also Vijñāneśvara's equation *nyāyas tarkavidyā* in MA p. 2,26 on YS 1.3 (according to Kane, HDh I.2, § 71, pp. 599-616, to be dated to 1100-1120).

be synonymous in classical literature (roughly from the Gupta period onwards),[44] this should not be taken for granted for the preceding literary period. In order to evaluate the alternative reading *tarka* in YS 1.3 and the appropriateness of the general equation of *nyāya* with "logic" I shall present in the following some evidence from the Dharmaśāstra literature, with a focus on the Dharmasūtras, with regard to the role and function of reasoning and the terms employed to refer to reasoning; it is here that the royal and Brahminical concerns with reasoning overlap and a concrete intellectual setting which must have specifically stimulated the development of theories about exact and truthful reasoning becomes obvious, namely, that of legal procedures at the royal court.

REASONING IN THE DHARMASŪTRAS

Many of the references to reasoning in the relevant corpus of literature are found in the context of *rājadharma*. According to the *Gautamadharmasūtra*, the king should be educated in the Vedas (*trayī*) as well as in the "investigating science" (*ānvīkṣikī*), i.e., two of Kauṭilya's four sciences.[45] Under the assumption that the "triple

---

[43] Cf., e.g., Keith 1919: 11; Lingat 1973: 148 (*nyāya* = "system of formal logic"); Thakur 1975: 42-43. As regards the identification with Nyāya, Ruben, by spelling the relevant word *nyāya*, not Nyāya, seems to disagree (cf. Ruben 1926: 351); cf. also the clear statement relating to *ānvīkṣikī* (*vidyā*) in Halbfass 1988: 284.

[44] Cf. Hacker 1958: 76: "*tarka* ist aber ein Synonym von *nyāya*"; cf. also Halbfass 1988: 284 where – in the context of the lists of fourteen sciences – *ānvīkṣikī* is mentioned as a further synonym.

[45] Cf. GDhS 11.3 (= 2.2.3): *trayyām ānvīkṣikyāṃ cābhivinītaḥ* (scil. *rājā*) (cf. also Dahlmann 1895: 226; Vidyabhusana 1913: xiv [1930: xvii] and 1920: 7, 37; Winternitz 1929: 3-4; Kane, HDh III, p. 46; Hacker 1958: 64; wrongly given as a reference to a passage mentioning the four *vidyā*s in Narain 1979: 381, n. 7). *ānvīkṣikī* is here explained as *nyāyavidyā* by Maskarin (ca. 900-1100 according to Kane, HDh I.1, p. 37), alternatively as *ātmavidyā*, probably referring to passages such as KNS 2.7a (*ānvīkṣiky ātmavijñānam*) and 2.11, and MS 7.43 (cf. below, footnote 90) (pointed out in Kane, HDh III, p. 48; Hacker 1958: 74-75; Narain 1979: 584; cf. GDhSMBh p. 177,10-11). In GDhSM (p. 108,18), the later commentator Haradatta repeats only the first identification provided by Maskarin (cf. also Kane, HDh III, p. 48). Haradatta, who is also credited with a commen-

science" covers inter alia *dharma* and *adharma*,[46] it becomes evident immediately afterwards in which area the knowledge of both sciences may be applied: this is the proper determination of *dharma* which constitutes one of the king's important roles, foremost within the framework of legal procedures where he presides, is responsible for the appropriate composition of the assembly of advisors, and decides himself on the case. Reasoning (*tarka*) is the means recommended to him with respect to (i.e., for) coming to the right settlement in a law suit:[47] after deliberation (*abhyūhya*) by means of *tarka* he should bestow a conclusion[48] "according to the (actual) state (of affairs) / situation" or "as befits the case", that is, advance the case to a decision according to the truth or to the side of the

---

tary on the *Āpastambadharmasūtra*, has been dated by Kane (HDh I.2, § 87, pp. 742-749) to 1100-1300, considerably earlier than the 15th century given by Bühler in the introduction to his edition of the *Āpastambadharmasūtra*; however, on the basis of the different standards of the two commentaries, Olivelle has recently argued that Haradatta commenting upon the *Āpastambhadharmasūtra* and dated by Kane is different from the commentator of the same name on the *Gautamadharmasūtra* (cf. Olivelle 1999: 116).

[46] Cf. e.g., AŚ 1.2.11: *dharmādharmau trayyām* ... .

[47] Cf. GDhS 11.23: *nyāyādhigame tarko 'bhyupāyaḥ*. The precise interpretation of the expression *nyāyādhigama* is problematic; cf. below p. 49f. – Cf. also the reference to this passage in Vidyabhusana 1913: xiv [1930: xvii] and 1920: 8, 37, Kane, HDh II.2, p. 967, Lingat 1973: 6, 70 (who speaks of "analogy and inference" in this context) and 159, n. 35 ("reasoning"), and Wezler 1999: 148 (read "11" for "19").

[48] For my understanding of the elliptic *gamayet* (cf. footnote 50) which lacks its direct object, cf. *niṣṭhāṃ gamayet* in GDhS 11.25, with *niṣṭhā* understood as direct object. Alternatively, one may assume that in both phrases the legal case is the unexpressed direct object of the causative verbal action and *niṣṭhā* the – in the first phrase unexpressed – aim of the underlying verbal action, in this case a motion (i.e., "should bring [the case] to a close"). Elsewhere Maskarin speaks about the setting up or installing (*sthāpayet*) of legal procedures (*vyavahāra*) (cf. GDhSMBh p. 184,13) which presumably refers to the first step in the proceedings; if this expression should refer to the settling of cases, i.e., their definite determination, this would imply that the final step in the sequence of events relating to the king's task to conduct legal procedures would be anticipated here, which I think is rather improbable. However, other occurrences of the phrase *yathāsthānaṃ gamayet* in Dharma literature suggest that the causative verb is used in the meaning of "to bestow, grant, impart", with the explicit or implicit direct object in the accusative case. Cf. the next footnote.

party which is in the right (*yathāsthānam*)[49].[50] In a more general way, the *Vāsiṣṭhadharmasūtra* speaks of the king (or minister) deliberating on offences (*aparādhohin*) in such a way that he is impartial towards all living beings and as befits the case (?).[51]

---

[49] The difficult expression *yathāsthānam* (cf. footnote 50) is paraphrased with *yathātattvam* by Maskarin (GDhSMBh p. 186,14 on 11.24 = the edition's 11.26), a contextually adequate interpretation which can also be reconciled with the literal meaning of the compound suggested by me above. Haradatta's explanation also seems to attempt to do justice to the wording: "on the side where the matter [stands]" (?) (cf. GDhSM p. 114,17-18 on 11.24 = the edition's 2.2.24: *yatra pakṣe 'rthas tatra*). Two further occurrences of the phrase *yathāsthānaṃ gamayet* in the *Gautamadharmasūtra* corroborate the interpretation "he/one should bestow according to the state of (affairs) / situation", i.e., impart something as befits the specific case. Cf. GDhS 10.46 (said of the king; quoted in Vijñāneśvara's *Mitākṣarā* [MA p. 160,14 on YS 2.38 = the edition's 2.36]): *corahṛtam avajitya yathāsthānaṃ gamayet* ("After he has recovered what has been taken by thieves he should bestow [it] as befits the specific case", i.e., find out its rightful owner or, in his absence, a dependent of his and return it to him [cf. GDhSMBh p. 169,7: ... *yathārhato 'rpayet* ...]; cf. also the interpretation of this injunction in MS 8.40ab and YS 2.38ab), and GDhS 22.31-32 (said of an adulterer): *dravyalābhe cotsargaḥ. yathāsthānaṃ vā gamayet* ("And, in case [the adulterer] has obtained any property [from the adulterous wife of a scholar], [it should] be given away, or he should bestow it as befits the specific case", i.e., find out from whom the woman had received the object in question and return it to him or another suitable person); in the latter case, Haradatta again attempts to account for the wording with his contextually conditioned explanation *yatra sthāne labdhaṃ tadā* ... (cf. GDhSM p. 231,28 on the edition's 3.4.32). The adverb *yathāsthānam* in the suggested meaning "as befits the case" is also used in BDhS 1.9.11 in the context of purification of the ground by various means; the means has to be chosen as befits the case on account of the specific ritual flaw to be removed by this action (*bhūmes tu saṃmārjanaprokṣaṇopalepanāvastaraṇollekhanair yathāsthānaṃ doṣaviśeṣāt prāyatyam*). Govindasvāmin's paraphrase *yathādeśam* is conditioned by the context. – A corresponding usage of *yathāsthānam* can be found in VS 1.13cd-14 in a cosmogonic context: Viṣṇu redistributes the waters on the surface of the previously submerged earth as befits the specific case, i.e., directs the waters to their specific earlier places on the earth such as the ocean, rivers, ponds and lakes (... *yathāsthānaṃ vibhajyāpas tadgatā madhusūdanaḥ* II *sāmudryaś ca samudreṣu nādeyīś* [recte: *nādeyāś*] *ca nadīṣu ca* I *palvaleṣu ca pālvalyaḥ saraḥsu ca sarobhavāḥ* II). However, it has to be noted that the verse portions constitute the latest stratum of the *Viṣṇusmṛti* (cf. Lingat 1973: 25-27).

[50] Cf. GDhS 11.24: *tenābhyūhya yathāsthānaṃ gamayet*. – Both *sūtra*s are quoted in Vijñāneśvara's *Mitākṣarā* (MA p. 143) on YS 2.20.

According to the *Gautamadharmasūtra* deliberation (*ūha*) also characterizes the learned and cultured persons (*śiṣṭa*) who are involved in legal decisions. At least ten such persons, all without any

---

[51] Cf. VDhS 16.5: *samaḥ sarvabhūteṣu yathāsanam aparādhohy ādyavarṇayor vidyāntataḥ. yathāsanam*, which already occurs in 16.4, is considered to be a (hopeless) corruption by Böhtlingk (1885: 485). I would like to suggest here the conjecture *yathāsthānam*, as in GDhS 11.24 (cf. footnote 49); such a conjecture would fit the translation given for this corrupt compound in Böhtlingk's shorter *Sanskrit-Wörterbuch* (Böhtlingk 1883-86, s.v.: "je an der betreffenden Stelle"). Olivelle tentatively interprets *yathāsanam* as "according to social position" and – following the Benares "edition" of 1858 – separates *sūtra* 16.5 into two phrases, the second one starting with *yathāsanam aparādho hi.* However, if *hi* has its usual causal function here or indicates that some thing or fact is quite obvious, I fail to find a satisfactory meaning for the sequence of the two resulting sentences. Also, the syntax, as implied by Olivelle's translation, would be rather unusual: *hi*, signaling the beginning of a new sentence, would not be placed before, but right after the supposed subject *aparādhaḥ*, with the preceding adverb *yathāsanam* understood as the predicate of this sentence. In my understanding, *yathāsthānam* ("as befits the case") would adverbially qualify the noun *aparādhohin.* According to Olivelle's note on this difficult *sūtra*, one of the mss. filmed by the NGMPP (siglum Kb) and the Benares edition continue the sentence with *ayaṃ* (instead of *ādya-*); this pronoun would provide a reference back to the king (or minister) as subject of the complete sentence. Further, if *vidhānataḥ* is read, as in the second ms. filmed by the NGMPP (siglum Ka) (for further details cf. Sänger 2000: 184) and the Calcutta edition, instead of *vidyāntataḥ* (cf. again Olivelle's note; according to Führer, the unreliable ms. J.O. 913 also reads *vidhānataḥ*), the main statement of the sentence would be specified to the effect that the king's (or minister's) described impartial deliberation "according to the state (of affairs) / situation" or "as befits the case" is in accordance with the injunction(s) for the two (involved) social classes or in accordance with their manner of procedure (*varṇayor vidhānataḥ*); such a specification would be meaningful because the minister, who is mentioned next to the king (ideally a *kṣatriya*), may indeed be a Brahmin. – Like other interpreters before me, I cannot make much sense of the preceding *sūtra* 4 whose beginning I would tentatively analyze parallel to the problematic phrase in 5, i.e., *yathāsanam* (*yathāsthānam*?) *aparādhohy ante nāparādhaḥ*. The repetition of the phrase may point to a scribal error and subsequent further corruption: a scribe may have prematurely copied the phrase *yathāsanam* (*yathāsthānam*?) *aparādhohy* contained in 5 before copying the sentence starting with *samaḥ sarvabhūteṣu*; if the resulting reduplication of the former phrase was not sufficiently marked (or not at all detected) in the process of "proof-reading" and therefore included in further copies of the text, the first truncated phrase may have been supplemented at a later time to form a complete sentence of its own. – For the ten *aparādha*s, listed with this term, e.g., in two verses ascribed to Nārada, but not found in the extant *Nāradasmṛti*, cf. Kane, HDh III, p. 264, and Lingat 1973: 238.

interest in personal gain, are called upon to make a recommendation in cases in which *dharma* has not been realized.[52] The ten scholars, who are named a *pariṣad*, include four specialists in the Vedas, three persons characterized by their life style as exceptional Brahminical householders (*āśramin*),[53] and three persons who are knowledgeable about different specific corpora of norms (*pṛthag-dharmavid*).[54] In the *Āpastambadharmasūtra*, the mature persons (*vṛddha*), endowed with knowledge and a good family background,

---

[52] Cf. GDhS 28.48: *anājñāte* (scil. *dharme*) *daśāvaraiḥ śiṣṭair ūhavadbhir alubdhaiḥ praśastaṃ kāryam.* Maskarin relates deliberation (*ūha*) to a training of the mind attained by studying the teachings of the Mīmāṃsā, etc.: *ūhavadbhir ūhāpohasamarthair mīmāṃsādiśāstrakṛtabuddhibhir ity arthaḥ* (cf. GDhSMBh p. 453,13-14 on 28.48 = the edition's 28.49). For the pair *ūha* and *apoha*, cf. also Haradatta's *ūhāpohakuśala* on *ūhavat* in this *sūtra* (GDhSM p. 290,17 on 28.48 = the edition 3.10.46) and on *medhāvin* in ĀDhS 2.29.5 = the edition's 2.11.29.5 (see below) (cf. Uj p. 373,6: *medhāvina ūhāpohakuśalāḥ*; cf. also p. 196,1 in ĀDhS(B); on Haradatta cf., however, footnote 45). Contrary to Olivelle's paraphrase (Olivelle 2000: 210), Gautama refers to the designation of these ten persons as an assembly (*pariṣad*) only in the following *sūtra*. Cf. also Kane, HDh II.2, p. 966 on this *sūtra*; Kane paraphrases *ūhavat* with "clever in discussion".

[53] I follow Olivelle's understanding of the original meaning of *āśrama* (cf. Olivelle 1993: 16-24) and his well-reasoned argumentation against an interpretation of the term *āsramin* (and *āśramastha* in BDhS 1.1.7-8 and VDhS 3.20, cf. below, p. 46f.) relating to the three *āśrama*s in the sense of the alternative or subsequent life styles discussed in the Dharmasūtra literature (cf. Olivelle 1993: 210-214). According to the latter interpretation, the term may refer to persons characterized by the three life styles which would allow them to participate in a committee in the first place (on the *āśrama*s, cf. GDhS 3.1f.) (cf. the references to this interpretation and its variations in Olivelle 1993: 210-214). A *vaikhānasa* is excluded because he should not enter a village (3.33), not to mention larger settlements, where presumably legal procedures were conducted. A *bhikṣu*, however, may not stay in a village for more than one night when it is not the rainy season (3.21; cf. also Kane, HDh II.2, p. 934); this rule implies that during the rainy season he may or should reside permanently in one place (cf. 3.13 and Lingat 1973: 20, 47), not excluding a village, and thus may be available for longer stretches of time to serve in a committee. Cf. e.g., Kane, HDh II.1, p. 416, and Vol. II.2, p. 968, for a corresponding interpretation relating the term *āśramin* to three *stages* of life.

[54] Cf. GDhS 28.49: *catvāraś caturṇāṃ pāragā vedānāṃ prāguttamāt traya āśramiṇaḥ pṛthagdharmavidas traya ity etān daśāvarān pariṣad ity ācakṣate.* Cf. Kane, HDh II.2, p. 968, Lingat 1973: 15, and especially Olivelle 1993: 210-214 for further details of this *sūtra*.

who are involved as advisors or judges in legal controversies are more generally said to possess understanding (*medhāvin*);[55] however, it is specified that if there is doubt they discern or examine on the basis of signs (*liṅgataḥ*),[56] which may point to an early type of inferential thinking in the widest sense.

Among the classical means of valid cognition, the one most closely connected with reasoning and related to logic, namely, inference (*anumāna*), is indeed mentioned in the Dharmasūtra literature in connection with the learned and cultured persons (*śiṣṭa*). According to the *Baudhāyanadharmasūtra* their tradition constitutes the third norm (*dharma*),[57] next to the norm as evident in the four Vedas and manifest in the Smṛti. In a verse quoted from another source to supplement the characterization of these persons

[55] Cf. ĀDhS 2.29.5 (= ĀDhS(B) 2.11.29.5): *vivāde vidyābhijanasampannā vṛddhā medhāvino dharmeṣv avinipātinaḥ* (cf. also Kane, HDh III, p. 271). Friedrich's translation as "Gelehrte" is rather undifferentiated (cf. Friedrich 1993: 205).

[56] Cf. ĀDhS 2.29.6 (= ĀDhS(B) 2.11.29.6): *sandehe liṅgato daiveneti vicitya. daivena* may be considered a gloss on *liṅgataḥ*, specifying the nature of the sign; however, it is highly improbable that in all cases of doubt divine means or ordeals (*daiva*) (cf. also 2.11.3, addressed in Lingat 1973: 69, 93) (on both *sūtra*s cf. Lariviere 1981: 1-2) were resorted to. Kane (HDh III, p. 355) understands that inference and ordeal are meant as alternative means ("or"), whereas Olivelle (2000: 115) coordinates the two means ("and") (cf. also Lariviere 1981: 1-2); this presupposes that *iti* concludes here an enumeration of two items (without explicit mention of a term under which both items could be subsumed, e.g., *upāya*, following upon *iti*) which are not connected by a conjunction. According to Hazra, who extensively treats ĀDhS 2.29.6 (Hazra 1968: 29-38), the enumeration should be a complete one (Hazra 1968: 38). Bühler translates *iti* as if it would stand for *-ādi* (Bühler 1879: 170: "by inference, ordeals, and the like"), following Uj p. 373,11-12 on the edition's 2.11.6: *itiśabdaḥ prakāre* ("The word *iti* refers to the kind/sort") (cf. also Hazra 1968: 29-30). For Hazra's ingeniously argued position that the word *liṅga* in ĀDhS 2.29.6 refers to the human means of judicial proof (as opposed to the divine means, i.e., ordeals) which have to be examined before they can be used in the decision of a doubtful case (*liṅgataḥ* = *liṅgāt* = *liṅgāni parīkṣya*), cf. Hazra 1968: 35-36.

[57] Cf. BDhS 1.1.4 (= BDhS(H) 1.1.1.4): *tṛtīyaḥ* (scil. *dharmaḥ*) *śiṣṭāgamaḥ*. On the further characterization of the *śiṣṭa*s in this context, cf. Kane, HDh II.2, p. 971.

given so far with regard to their moral standing, *anumāna* is said to be something they are knowledgeable about (*tadanumānajña*). The context suggests that "inference" is some kind of instrument by means of which the *śiṣṭa*s gain relevant knowledge. The object of inference (*tad-*) is not stated explicitly; it may be that which is *dharma*, or statements relating to *dharma* in the Śruti that are at the basis of the tradition of the Smṛti and of the *śiṣṭa*s' own tradition in cases where a relevant explicit statement of the Śruti cannot be found.[58] Such an inferential activity in the widest sense could easily be imagined to be performed by a Mīmāṃsaka engaged in scriptural exegesis and officially involved in legal procedures. Further causes or means (*hetu*) of cognition mentioned in the verse are the Śruti itself and direct, sensory perception (*pratyakṣa*);[59] thus, three

---

[58] My second interpretation of the anaphoric *tad-* in *tadanumānajña*, which can hardly refer back to *veda* in the second *pāda* of this verse, follows Govindasvāmin's *Vivaraṇa*. According to this interpretation the imported verse provides the contextually required explication of BDhS 1.1.4 (*tṛtīyaḥ śiṣṭāgamaḥ*) and at the same time clarifies the contextually thematic link between 1.1.4 and the two *sūtra*s 1.1.1 (*upadiṣṭo dharmaḥ prativedam*) and 1.1.3 (*smārto dvitīyaḥ*) because in its own characterization of the *śiṣṭa*s in 1.1.5 the author himself does not address in which way their tradition enumerated in 1.1.4 constitutes a/the third *dharma* and in which way this third *dharma* and the two first-mentioned *dharma*s are related; cf. BDhSV p. 3,13-14: *ata evānumānajñās te bhavanti, smārtaśiṣṭāgamayoḥ śrutyanumānavida ity arthaḥ*. Cf. also Olivelle 1993: 84-85 on the differentiation between *pratyakṣaśruti* and *anumitaśruti* and on the expression *ānumānika* in ĀDhS 1.4.8 (*śrutir hi balīyasy ānumānikād ācārāt*), meaning "from which [corresponding statements in the Śruti] are inferred" (cf. also Lingat 1973: 16). For a completely different interpretation of *tadanumānajña*, cf. Kane, HDh II.2, p. 971, maybe following Bühler (1882: 144), who understands *tad-* as referring to the *śiṣṭa*s' knowledge of the Vedas together with their appendages, in the sense of a *basis* for inference ("who know how to draw inferences *from that*" [my emphasis]). Lingat's paraphrase of the relevant expression suggests a similar grammatical understanding: "... should know how to draw all the consequences which flow from the Vedic injunctions for conduct to be followed" (cf. Lingat 1973: 196).

[59] I am uncertain about Olivelle's grammatical understanding of the former part of the compound; he translates "are able to adduce as proofs express vedic texts" (cf. Olivelle 2000: 197). Should one understand *śrutipratyakṣa-*, as the first member of an undisputed *bahuvrīhi* compound, to mean "something perceptible, [namely] the Śruti" (cf. Govindasvāmin's explanation of the compound: "for whom the perceptible cause (i.e., reason/proof) [of *dharma*] is the Śruti"

of the later means of valid cognition (*pramāṇa*) can be identified in this verse.[60]

Another characteristic of reasoning is addressed in the Dharmasūtra literature in connection with the committee or assembly called *pariṣad* or *parṣad*, which is closely related or even identical in its function to the group of at least ten *śiṣṭa*s mentioned in the *Gautamadharmasūtra* (cf. above, p. 42f.).[61] This committee is specified in a verse that is quoted in the *Baudhāyana*-[62] and *Vāsiṣṭhadharma*-

---

[BDhSV p. 3,24-4,1 on the edition's 1.1.1.6: *śrutir eva pratyakṣaṃ kāraṇam asya dharmasyeti yeṣāṃ darśanam iti vigrahaḥ*]) or "perception, [namely] of the Śruti"? Bühler's translation seems to assume an analysis as "something perceptible *from* the Śruti" (cf. Bühler 1882: 144: "are able to adduce proofs perceptible by the senses from the revealed texts"). For a completely different interpretation of the expression *śrutipratyakṣahetavaḥ*, cf. Kane, HDh II.2, p. 971: "who tend to make people realize the teaching of the Veda". It is highly improbable, though, that the *śiṣṭa*s themselves would be called *hetu*s, i.e., that the relevant compound is a *karmadhāraya* compound.

[60] Cf. BDhS 1.1.6 (= BDhS(H) 1.1.1.6): *dharmeṇādhigato yeṣāṃ vedaḥ saparibṛṃhaṇaḥ* I *śiṣṭās tadanumānajñāḥ śrutipratyakṣahetava iti* II. This verse is also used in the *Manusmṛti*, in a form modified to fit the context which lacks the component of *anumāna* relevant in the context of this paper: *dharmeṇādhigato yais tu vedaḥ saparibṛṃhaṇaḥ* I *te śiṣṭā brāhmaṇā jñeyāḥ śrutipratyakṣahetavaḥ* II (MS 12.109). It is quoted from this latter source by Haradatta (GDhSM p. 290,15-16 on GDhS 28.48 = the edition's 3.10.46) and Maskarin (GDhSMBh p. 453,11-12 on 28.48 = the edition's 28.49); cf. also Ānandagiri's *Ṭīkā* on *Bṛhadāraṇyakopaniṣadbhāṣya* ad 9.3.2 (BUBhṬ p. 547,24-25). *pāda*s b-d of MS 12.109, on the other hand, are identical with VDhS 6.43b-d (cf. also the reference in Kane, HDh II.2, p. 971). The changed context of the verse in the *Manusmṛti* and *Vāsiṣṭhadharmasūtra* may suggest an alternative interpretation of the compound *śrutipratyakṣahetu* here as "having as [their chief] means [of knowledge] something perceptible, [namely] the Śruti" or "... perception, [namely] of the Śruti"; cf. also footnote 59 above.

[61] On the *pariṣad* as an archaic institution which was already obsolete at least by the time of the *Manusmṛti*, cf. Lingat 1973: 17 and Olivelle 1993: 212.

[62] Cf. BDhS 1.1.7-8 (= BDhS(H) 1.1.1.7-8): *tadabhāve daśāvarā pariṣat. athāpy udāharanti – cāturvaidyaṃ vikalpī ca aṅgavid dharmapāṭhakaḥ* I *āśramasthās trayo viprāḥ parṣad eṣā daśāvarā* II. In the first *pāda*, six of Hultzsch's mss. read *cāturvedyaṃ*; ms. Cs (which also contains Govindasvāmin's commentary) has *cāturvedyaṃ ca vikalpī cāṅgavid. cāturvaidyam* ("proficiency in the four Vedas", derived from *cāturvidya*; cf. also *traividya* in MS 7.43 [cf. footnote 90 below]) has to be understood metaphorically, referring collectively to four

sūtras[63] and also found in the *Parāśarasmṛti*:[64] one of its at least ten members has to be a *vikalpin*, that is, a person who is considering alternatives. Govindasvāmin associates this role with a Mīmāṃsaka,[65] whereas according to Aṅgiras' explanation – contained in his lost Smṛti[66] as quoted by Mādhavācārya, the 14th-century commentator on the *Parāśarasmṛti*[67] – of the various roles of the ten members of this assembly the *vikalpin* is a twice-born who knows the means of valid cognition (*pramāṇa*).[68]

The above survey shows that reasoning played a considerable role in the context of determining *dharma* and arriving at the right decision and that this context therefore may have formed another intellectual and cultural context for the early development of logic in India whose evidence precedes, by centuries, the *Carakasaṃhitā*, the chief witness for the medical context; further, it will have

---

persons who are individually or jointly proficient in the four Vedas. A number of mss., including some of the commentary, unmetrically read *pariṣad* instead of *parṣad*.

[63] Cf. VDhS 3.20: *cāturvidyo* (*cāturvaidyam*?) *vikalpī ca aṅgavid dharmapāṭhakaḥ* | *āśramasthās trayo mukhyāḥ parṣad eṣā daśāvarā* ||. In the first *pāda*, Führer's edition has *cāturvidyam* (cf. *traividyam* in YS 1.9, quoted below in footnote 98), and – similarly as in the quotation of this verse in BDhS 1.1.8 – instead of *parṣad eṣā* some mss. and editions substitute the more regular *pariṣad* by reading *pariṣat syāt* and – unmetrically – *pariṣad eṣā*. – Cf. Lingat 1973: 15, 75-76 and especially Olivelle 1993: 211-213 on this verse and its variant form in the *Baudhāyanadharmasūtra*. On the meaning of *āśramastha* according to Olivelle, cf. above, footnote 53.

[64] Cf. PS 8.27. Cf. also Kane, HDh II.2., p. 968. Kane dates this Smṛti to 100-400 (cf. Kane, HDh I.1, § 35, pp. 459-465).

[65] Cf. BDhSV p. 4,3-4: *vikalpī mīmāṃsakaḥ*. Bühler (1882: 20, 144) and Lingat (1973: 148) follow this interpretation. Cf. similarly Kane, HDh II.2, p. 968: "one who knows the Mīmāṃsā", and Olivelle 1993: 211: "an expert in vedic exegesis".

[66] Cf. Kane, HDh I.1., § 39 (pp. 507-509) on Aṅgiras and his Smṛti which survives only in a reconstructed form.

[67] Kane, HDh II.2, p. 968, n. 2206, relies on a corresponding quotation by Aparārka which is not accessible to me.

[68] Cf. Mādhavācārya's commentary on the *Parāśarasmṛti*, Vol. 2, p. 277,3 and 7: *tatra cāturvedyādiśabdārthān aṅgirā vivṛṇoti* – ... *trayāṇāṃ yaḥ pramāṇajñaḥ sa vikalpī bhaved dvijaḥ* |.

become evident that there was a variety of terms connected with the mental activity of reasoning, one of them being *tarka*, the term which denotes one of the fourteen "places of knowledge" enumerated in the verse from the *Yājñavalkyasmṛti* discussed above (cf. p. 36ff.). One might therefore expect that also the term *nyāya*, transmitted as a variant reading for *tarka* in this verse and found in the compound *nyāyavistara* in the above-mentioned popular Purāṇic verse on the areas of knowledge" (cf. p. 33f.), would appear in this or a similar meaning in the Dharmasūtras. However, this is not the case. Most of the occurrences of the term *nyāya* in this literary corpus clearly demonstrate that the term is used there in the sense of "right manner" or "proper way", that is, referring to what is appropriate within a specific set of rules or norms. In the *Āpastambadharmasūtra* it is said that one should practise application or exercises (*yoga*) relating to the Self "in accordance with the right manner" (*nyāyasaṃhita*).[69] The king, according to the *Gautama-*

[69] See ĀDhS 1.22.1 = ĀDhS(B) 1.8.22.1: *adhyātmikān* (v.l. *ādhyātmikān*; cf. also HDhS 1.6.20.1 according to ms. Bü. 257 and commentary, against ms. M. 38 which reads *adhyātmikān*) *yogān anutiṣṭhen nyāyasaṃhitān* (v.l. *nyāyasahitān*) *anaiścārikān*; cf. also ĀDhS 1.23.6 = 1.8.23.6, referring to positive qualities which are designated as themes/points of agreement (*samayapada*) with regard to all styles of life (*āśrama*): ... *tāny anutiṣṭhan vidhinā* (v.l. *vidhānā*) ... . Although a contrastive relationship may indeed be intended between the two following predicates (*anaiścārika*, "not at will"; cf. Böhtlingk & Roth 1855-75 s.v. *niścāraka* "Eigenwille"), Friedrich's modern idiomatic translation (cf. Friedrich 1993: 119) "die Methode haben" does not seem to fit the intention here, whereas the translation offered by Bühler and adapted by Olivelle seems to be rather unfounded (cf. Bühler 1879: 75: "which are attended by the consequent (destruction of the passions)" and Olivelle 2000: 59: "that have definite consequences"). Haradatta paraphrases *nyāya* with *upapatti* in the meaning of "appropriateness" (cf. Uj p. 162,9-11): ... *nyāyasaṃhitān upapattisamanvitān. upapadyante hi te nyāyataḥ krodhādīnāṃ doṣādīnāṃ nirghāte* ("... according to the right manner, [i.e.] endowed with appropriateness, because they are appropriate in the right manner with regard to the destruction of flaws such as anger, etc."), to be preferred to the reading of this passage of the *Ujjvalā* as extracted in ĀDhS(B) p. 139,5-6: *upapadyate hi nyāyataḥ krodhādīnāṃ doṣāṇāṃ nirghātaḥ*. This statement has a correspondence in the commentary on the *Adhyātmapaṭalavivaraṇa* (considered as an authentic work of Śaṅkara by Hacker in Hacker 1968-69: 135) (p. 425,20-21 in APV, and p. 130,19-20 in Pandeya's edition of the *Āpastamba-*

dharmasūtra, should protect the four social classes and all persons following the four styles of life in the right manner (*nyāyataḥ*);[70] he should also appoint as *purohita* a Brahmin who conducts himself in the right manner (*nyāyavṛtta*).[71] In the context of the regulation of inheritance, we find the opposite term *anyāyavṛtta* clearly referring to improper conduct: a son, even if he has been born from a wife belonging to the same social class as the father, does not receive his share in the case of improper conduct.[72]

I would also like to recall the above passage in the *Gautamadharmasūtra* referring to *tarka* as a means to be used by the king (cf. p. 40).[73] There I had paraphrased *nyāyādhigame* as "with respect to (i.e., for) coming to the right settlement in a law suit". Maskarin's brief explanation as "in the determination of what is connected with *nyāya*" is ambiguous,[74] as is Haradatta's similar

---

dharmasūtra with *Ujjvalā*): *nyāyasaṃhitān upapattisamanvitān. te hi krodhādi*[*ṣu*](?) *doṣanirghātaṃ prati samarthā upapadyante nyāyataḥ.*

[70] Cf. GDhS 11.9: *varṇāśramāṃś ca nyāyato 'bhirakṣet.* Maskarin explains *nyāyataḥ* with *lokaśāstrāviruddhena mārgeṇa* (GDhSMBh p. 178,17-18). Haradatta seems to separate the two aspects of this explication; he interprets the expression as *yathāśāstram* (GDhSM p. 109,25 on the edition's 2.2.9, with further explication), to be followed by the alternative interpretation *yathā deśādidharmāṇāṃ bhaṅgo na bhavati* [*y*]<*t*>*athā* ... (p. 109,27-28).

[71] Cf. GDhS 11.12: *brāhmaṇaṃ ca puro dadhīta ... nyāyavṛttam ...* . Here Maskarin stresses that the *purohita*'s conduct among the people should not be in contradiction (to their norms?) (GDhSMBh p. 180,15 on the edition's 11.14: *aviruddhalokācāropetaḥ*); cf. also Haradatta who paraphrases the expression with *lokāviruddhācāra* ("whose conduct is not in contradiction with [the norms of] the people") (GDhSM p. 110,22 on the edition's 2.2.12).

[72] Cf. GDhS 28.40: *savarṇāputro 'py anyāyavṛtto na labhetaikeṣām.* Maskarin, with a reference to Vasiṣṭha, briefly glosses *anyāyavṛtta* with *durvṛttaḥ patita iti yāvat* (GDhSMBh p. 450,22-451,1 on the edition's 28.41), whereas Haradatta, referring to Āpastamba, understands that with improper conduct a specific case of misdemeanor is meant here, namely, the squandering of parental property in an adharmic manner, such as on prostitutes (GDhSM p. 288,26-29 on the edition's 3.10.38). Cf. Kane, HDh III, p. 608, on lapse of conduct as a reason to exclude a person from the division of property.

[73] Cf. GDhS 11.23: *nyāyādhigame tarko 'bhyupāyaḥ.*

[74] Cf. GDhSMBh p. 186,6 on the edition's 11.25: *nyāyayuktasyādhigame 'vadhāraṇe ...* .

gloss.[75] Both interpretations seem to assume that *nyāya* here means something like "reasonableness" or "reasoned thinking", namely, within the specific framework of *dharma* or specifically regarding *dharma*, which would in the final analysis amount to the determination of what is just (and true[76]). However, the other occurrences of *nyāya* in the Dharmasūtras adduced here make such an underlying meaning of *nyāya* improbable. As a literal understanding of *nyāyādhigama* I would rather suggest "finding the proper way" or "getting to the right manner", namely, in/of establishing in a discerning manner (*vyavasthā*) what is *dharma*;[77] alternatively, one could interpret the first member of the compound, *nyāya-*, as standing for an adverbial *nyāyena* or *nyāyataḥ*[78] qualifying *adhigama* in the meaning of "understanding", the whole compound then meaning "with respect to (i.e., for) understanding [what is *dharma*] in the right manner".[79] Both interpretations amount to Olivelle's translation as "reaching a correct judgment"[80] which obviously relies on the meaning "judgment" ("Urteilsspruch") given for *nyāya* by Böhtlingk and Roth – with ambiguous, certainly not unproblematic references.

A usage of the term *nyāya* in the further, derived sense of "method" or "rule" can be found in the *Baudhāyanadharmasūtra*: one should live from milk alone according to the method used in or

---

[75] *nyāyayuktasyārthasyādhigame 'vadhāraṇe* ...; cf. GDhSM p. 114,10 on the edition's 2.2.23.

[76] Cf. Bühler's free rendering "for arriving at the truth" (Bühler 1879: 236).

[77] Cf. *dharmavyavasthā* at the conclusion of the preceding sentence (GDhS 11.22). One might object that this could be an interpolation inasmuch as the term may be considered to include the final judgment and its occurrence would therefore be premature in the sequence of a legal procedure described here; on the other hand, *dharmavyavasthā* could also be understood as preceding the actual procedure towards a legal decision in the sense of the settlement of the specific dharmic presuppositions relating to the case.

[78] Cf. the preceding *sūtra* 11.9.

[79] Cf. the compound *nyāyavṛtta* in the preceding *sūtra* 11.12. Cf. similarly also Wezler 1999: 155, n. 74: "attaining [the truth] methodically".

[80] Cf. Olivelle 2000: 147.

the rule applying to the *upasad*-ritual (*upasannyāyena*),[81] i.e., from a minute amount which fits on the tip of an awl.[82]

Finally, in the *Āpastambadharmasūtra*, we hear about the convention or agreement (*samaya*) of those who know the right manner (*nyāyavid*) in connection with the designation of the auxiliary sciences (*aṅga*).[83] In a further passage of the same work those who know the proper way or method, obviously of scriptural exegesis, are called *nyāyavid*.[84] One may therefore assume that the first occurrence of the term also has to be understood in this sense,[85] and not as context-specifically relating to the right manner of designating the constituent parts of the Vedic corpus.[86] The classical appellation of the Mīmāṃsakas as *nyāyavidaḥ* is clearly foreshadowed in this usage,[87] as is their less frequent appellation *naiyāyika*.[88]

---

[81] Cf. BDhS 3.10.11: *upasannyāyena payovratatā ... iti medhyāni.*

[82] Cf. Govindasvāmin's commentary BDhSV p. 349,7 on the edition's 3.10.12: *upasannyāya ārāgrā parovarīyasī*(?) *vā.*

[83] Cf. ĀDhS 2.8.13 = ĀDhS(B) 2.4.8.13: *aṅgānāṃ tu pradhānair avyapadeśa iti nyāyavitsamayaḥ*, that is, the auxiliary sciences are not designated according to the specific Vedas to which they belong. The version in HDhS 2.1.4.14 reads *ca* instead of *tu.*

[84] Cf. ĀDhS 2.14.13 = ĀDhS(B) 2.6.14.13: *athāpi nityānuvādam avidhim āhur nyāyavidaḥ ....*

[85] Cf. also Olivelle's contextually appropriate free translation with "experts in exegesis" and "exegetical experts" (Olivelle 2000: 87 and 95), following Bühler's equally free translation of the term in ĀDhS 2.14.13 ("those who are acquainted with the interpretation of the law") (Bühler 1879: 136).

[86] Friedrich's translations "die den Nyāya kennen" (cf. Friedrich 1993: 165) and "Kenner des Nyāya" are naively anachronistic and nonsensical.

[87] Cf., e.g., Śaṅkara in BSBh p. 443,21 ad BS 3.4.22 and Viśvarūpa in BK p. 62,22 on YS 1.53 (*nyāyavidaś ca yājñikāḥ* ..., with reference to MSū 1.3.16) and p. 87,24 on YS 1.87 (with reference to MSū 6.8.17). Cf. also Bühler's translation of *nyāyavid* in the first *Āpastambadharmasūtra* passage "those who are learned in Mīmāṃsā" (Bühler 1879: 121), which assumes that the *nyāyavid* are belonging to a clearly defined tradition or "system".

[88] Cf. Viśvarūpa in BK p. 66,9 on YS 1.58 where he uses the appellation *naiyāyikāḥ* when referring to Śabara's comments on MSū 3.2.3.

REASONING IN THE DHARMAŚĀSTRAS

The evidence of the Dharmaśāstras, which can only be briefly addressed here, presents a similar picture.[89] The *Manusmṛti* also mentions *ānvīkṣikī* among the four sciences (*vidyā*) to be mastered by the king,[90] and in the *Yājñavalkyasmṛti* he is said to be trained in these very sciences.[91] A verse of the *Manusmṛti* states, similar to

---

[89] Cf. in general Lingat 1973: 6-7 on "reason and logic" as a means of determining *dharma* according to the Dharmaśāstras.

[90] Cf. MS 7.43: *traividyebhyas trayīṃ vidyā[ṃ]<d> daṇḍanītiṃ ca śāśvatīm* | *ānvīkṣikīṃ cātmavidyāṃ vārttārambhāṃś ca lokataḥ* ||, a verse found also as MP 215.54 (with the reading *tv ātmavidyāṃ vārttārambhāś ca*; cf. also MP(W) 215.53cd-54ab, with the additional variant *trayīvidyāṃ*) and AP 225.21cd-22ab (which reads *cārthavidyāṃ*!) (cf. the references in Kane, HDh III, p. 51). It is quoted by Maskarin (GDhSMBh p. 177,13-14) and Haradatta (GDhSM p. 108, 21-22 on the edition's 2.2.3) in their commentaries on GDhS 11.3, by Vijñāneśvara (MA p. 108,11-12) and Mitramiśra (VM p. 351,11-12) on YS 1.311, in both cases with the variant readings *tadvidaḥ* for *śāśvatīm* (in MA according to v.l. 2), and *cātmavidbhyo* for *cātmavidyāṃ*, and by Viśvanātha in NVṛ (I p. 63,21-22) on NSū 1.1.1. Cf. the references in Vidyabhusana 1913: xiv [1930: xvii] and 1920: 4, 7, 38; Mishra 1966: 9; Thakur 1975: 40; Narain 1979: 581, n. 7, and 583, n. 9. In his second interpretation, Medhātithi understands *ātmavidyā* as a specification of *ānvīkṣikī*, and not as a fifth science; this is most probably closest to the intention of the author (cf. also Bhāruci's MŚV p. 33,7-10), against Kullūka's interpretation (MAM p. 32,13-15). Other, heretic types of (application of) *ānvīkṣikī* by *ātman*-denying Buddhist and Cārvāka scholars, etc., are thus excluded (cf. MBhā p. 31,33-32,1). Similarly Sarvajñanārāyaṇa determines the relevant science as Nyāya, Sāṅkhya, etc., which are conducive to liberation (MAV p. 32,8-9) (see also Govindarāja's MṬ p. 32,32-33). Cf. also Halbfass 1988: 283-284 in critical response to Hacker 1958: 75, with n. 19, who, like Dahlmann before him with regard to Epic occurrences (cf. Dahlmann 1895: 226-227), understands *ānvīkṣikī* as an adjective qualifying *ātmavidyā*. On Medhātithi's second interpretation and related comments, cf. already Winternitz 1929: 5.

[91] Cf. YS 1.306: *svarandhragoptānvīkṣikyāṃ daṇḍanītyāṃ tathaiva ca* | *vinītas tv atha vārttāyāṃ trayyāṃ caiva narādhipaḥ* ||. Viśvarūpa's qualification of *ānvīkṣikī* as *samastāsāndṛṣṭikanirūpaṇakṣamā hetuvidyā* ("the science of reasons, capable of examining everything imperceptible") (BK p. 182,20-21; against Kane, HDh III, p. 47, n. 58, and Hacker 1958: 76 who may have used a different edition) may allude to *ātmavidyā* as a qualification of *ānvīkṣikī* in MS 7.43 (cf. footnote 90). Vijñāneśvara's addition in MA p. 108,8 (*ānvīkṣikyām ātmavidyāyām*, on the edition's 1.311; cf. also Kane, HDh III, p. 48; Winternitz 1929: 4; Hacker 1958: 76) is certainly dependent on the latter. It is therefore surprising that Mitramiśra, who just like Vijñāneśvara quotes MS 7.43 in his commentary,

the *sūtra* about *tarka* in the *Gautamadharmasūtra* (cf. p. 40 above), that in the context of finding the right judgment the king should "find out",[92] i.e., locate, the footprint, that is, the track, of *dharma* by means of *anumāna*, just as a hunter locates the track of game that has already been hit by means of blood which has fallen onto the ground.[93] *anumāna* seems to be used here, just like in the *Baudhāyanadharmasūtra* (cf. p. 44 above), in a less technical, wider sense of the term as "inferential thinking" or "deduction". In general, next to sensory perception and the doctrinal edifice (*śāstra*) concerning *dharma*, which is composed of various traditions (*vividhāgama*), *anumāna* is one of the means by which "purity" of *dharma* can be achieved.[94] Of course, as Bṛhaspati is purported to have stressed, in the context of coming to a legal judgment, *anumāna* is not necessarily the strongest means; e.g., in property disputes, *anumāna* provides weaker evidence than that given by witnesses, written documents, etc.[95] Elsewhere, in another verse of the *Manusmṛti*, *anumāna* in the sense of a more formal inference may be

---

glosses *ānvīkṣikī* with *tarkavidyā* (VM p. 351,7-8 on the edition's 1.311; cf. again Hacker 1958: 76). However, he read MS 7.43 with the variant reading *ānvīkṣikīṃ cātmavidbhyaḥ* (cf. again footnote 90) and must therefore have followed those commentators on this verse who separate *ānvīkṣikī* from *ātmavidyā* and explain the former science as *tarkavidyā*.

[92] Cf. Wezler 1999: 153, n. 45.

[93] Cf. MS 8.44: *yathā nayaty asṛkpātair mṛgasya mṛgayuḥ padam* I *tathānumānena nayed dharmasya nṛpatiḥ padam* II. On this verse and the precise role of *anumāna* in legal procedure cf. Hazra 1968: 30-31. Cf. also the similar verse NS 1.32: *yathā mṛgasya viddhasya vyādho mṛgapadaṃ nayet* I *kakṣe śoṇitaleśena tathā dharmapadaṃ nayet* II. In this verse, though, the means by which the king acts is not specified. Maskarin (GDhSMBh p. 186,7 on the edition's 11.25) erroneously ascribes MS 8.44 to Nārada.

[94] Cf. MS 12.105: *pratyakṣaṃ cānumānaṃ ca śāstraṃ ca vividhāgamam* I *trayaṃ suviditaṃ kāryaṃ dharmaśuddhim abhīpsatā* II. Cf. also Vidyabhusana 1920: 23; Mishra 1966: 11-12; see Wezler 1999: 145-146 especially on Medhātithi's comments on *anumāna* in this verse and the problematic state of transmission of his commentary.

[95] Cf. the *Bṛhaspati-* and *Kātyāyanasmṛti* as quoted in later sources (cf. Kane, HDh III, p. 306, with n. 433; Lingat 1962: 496): *anumānād guruḥ sākṣī sākṣibhyo likhitaṃ guru* I *avyāhatā tripuruṣī bhuktir ebhyo garīyasī* II). On *anumāna* according to Bṛhaspati, cf. also Kane, HDh III, p. 355.

intended: there the king who is presiding over the legal procedure is enjoined to figure out the internal state (i.e., the truthfulness or untruthfulness) of the quarrelling parties and the witnesses by means of external signs (*liṅga*), that is, by means of the appearance of voice, facial colour and movements, by means of their eyes and by means of gestures.[96] Furthermore, in the legal context of the – by now definitely archaic[97] – assembly of at least ten members, which is also briefly treated by Manu, one person is enumerated who deals with reasons (*hetuka*, *haituka*) – obviously taking the place of a specialist in the fourth Veda, i.e., the *Atharvaveda*, originally referred to in the version of the verse as found in two Dharmasūtras and the *Parāśarasmṛti* (cf. above, p. 46f.) –, next to whom there is another expert characterized by reasoning (*tarkin*) – obviously replacing (for mere metrical reasons in this case) the *vikalpin* mentioned in the relevant Dharmasūtra verse.[98] Also the presiding judge, according to a verse ascribed to the *Nāradasmṛti*, should be proficient in the "investigating [science], etc.",[99] similar

---

[96] Cf. MS 8.25: *bāhyair vibhāvayel liṅgair bhāvam antargataṃ nṛṇām* I *svaravarṇeṅgitākāraiś cakṣuṣā ceṣṭitena ca* II. See also Wezler 1999: 144-145 on this verse and Medhātithi's comments on it. Cf. further the following verse MS 8.26, quoted by Maskarin (GDhSMBh p. 186,12-13) on GDhS 11.26: *ākārair iṅgitair gatyā ceṣṭayā bhāṣitena ca* I *netravaktravikāraiś ca gṛhyate 'ntargataṃ Dharmasutra with Maskarivaktravikārābhyāṃ* and *punaḥ* instead of *manaḥ*).

[97] Cf. footnote 61 above.

[98] Cf. MS 12.111: *traividyo haitukas tarkī nairukto dharmapāṭhakaḥ* I *trayaś cāśramiṇaḥ pūrve pariṣat syād daśāvarā* II. Cf. also Vidyabhusana 1913: xiv [1930: xvii] and 1920: 8, 22, 38, Kane, HDh II.2, p. 868, Lingat 1973: 15, 17, 148, 159 and especially Olivelle 1993: 211 and 213-214 on this verse (on *āśramin* cf. above, p. 43, with footnote 53). On *traividyo* cf. Bühler 1886: 510, n., and Derrett 1975: Vol. II, p. 437, n. 1. With a view to the parallel verses mentioned above and to YS 1.9 (... *parṣat traividyam eva vā* I), one should probably read *traivaidyam* or *traividyam* (cf. especially Vijñāneśvara's explanation MA 4,23-24 on YS 1.9: *tisro vidyā adhīyanta iti traividyāḥ, teṣāṃ samūhas traividyam*). Rāghavānanda, Nandana and Bhāruci read *hetuka* instead of *haituka*.

[99] Cf. Kane, HDh III, p. 271, n. 351: *aṣṭādaśapadābhijñas tadbhedāṣṭasahasravit* I *ānvīkṣikyādikuśalaḥ śrutismṛtiparāyaṇaḥ* II *yathā śalyaṃ bhiṣak kāyād uddharet yantrayuktibhiḥ* I *prāḍvivākas tathā śalyam uddhared vyavahārataḥ* II. Only the second verse, with the reading *vidvān* instead of *kāyāt*, is preserved in the extant *Nāradasmṛti* (Mātṛkā 3.15).

to the king who will make the final decision on the basis of his judgment. Finally, the role of *yukti*, literally: "combination", i.e., the consideration of a number of different facts towards their factual and logical coherence,[100] is stressed in a verse ascribed to the *Bṛhaspatismṛti*: a legal decision should not be made in mere reliance on the doctrinal edifice relating to *dharma*; when reflection (*vicāra*) takes place without consideration of all involved facts as to their coherence (*yukti*), this leads to a loss of *dharma*.[101] A related, difficult verse of the *Nāradasmṛti* also refers to *yukti* in the sense of consideration of the circumstantial evidence.[102]

---

[100] Cf. footnote 4 on this special means of knowledge in the epistemology of the *Carakasaṃhitā*.

[101] Cf. the quotation in various medieval sources given in Kane, HDh III, p. 867, n. 1684: *kevalaṃ śāstram āśritya na kartavyo hi nirṇayaḥ* I *yuktihīne vicāre tu* (v.l. *hi*) *dharmahāniḥ prajāyate* II (cf. e.g., the *Vyavahāramayūkha* [VMa p. 7,2-3] with the introduction *nyāyam anālocayato doṣam āha bṛhaspatiḥ*); cf. also Kane, op. cit., p. 357, with n. 549, where Māṇḍavya's famous case is given as an example (... *yuktiṃ vinā vicāreṇa māṇḍavyaś cauratāṃ gataḥ* II) (cf. also Lingat 1962: 502, n. 18), and Vol. II.2, p. 967. See also Lingat (1962: 502, n. 18; 1973: 250) on this verse who translates *yuktihīna* as "without taking account of the circumstances of the case" ("sans qu'il ait été tenu compte des circonstances de la cause"). The relevant term *yukti* is missing in the problematic version as found in the *Smṛticandrikā* (SC p. 24,20-21) and Vācaspati Miśra II's *Vyavahāracintāmaṇi* (cf. Lingat 1962: 502, n. 18): *śāstraṃ kevalam āśritya kriyate yatra nirṇayaḥ* I *vyavahāraḥ sa vijñeyo dharmas tenāpahīyate* II.

[102] Cf. NS Mātṛkā 1.34: *dharmaśāstravirodhe tu yuktiyukto 'pi dharmataḥ* I *vyavahāro hi balavān dharmas tenāvahīyate* (cf. also Kane, HDh III, p. 867, following the reading of the Pune manuscript). Lariviere translates (1989, II: 11): "When there is disagreement between a dharma text and custom, it is right to apply common sense, for custom prevails over dharma." The variant form of the first half of this verse, also quoted in the *Vyavahāracintāmaṇi* (... *yuktiyukto vidhiḥ smṛtaḥ*), is rendered by Lingat (1973: 161, n. 40) as follows: "Where there is a conflict between two precepts of the *śāstras*, it is the injunction which is obtained by reasoning (*yukti-yukto*) which should be respected"; cf. also his earlier translation (Lingat 1962: 502, n. 18): "... la décision qui convient est celle qui repose sur l'examen des circonstances." Regardless of the precise meaning of the verse, Lingat's earlier translation of *yukti* should be preferred to his later one and that by Lariviere. On *yukti* in the juridical context cf. also Lingat 1962: 502, n. 18; for further occurrences of the term *yukti* in Dharmaśāstra literature which cannot be discussed here, cf. Kane, HDh III, p. 354.

Restrictions of space and the scope of the present paper do not allow me to enter into further details here, but I would like to add that in those parts of the Dharmaśāstras where suspicion towards the independent use of reasoning becomes noticeable, the usage of the term *tarka* and references to *hetu*, such as in *hetuśāstra* and, in a negative sense, *haituka*, clearly dominate.[103] And similar to the situation as ascertained above for the Dharmasūtras, *nyāya* and *anyāya* are generally used in the sense of "proper way" or "right manner" in the Smṛtis. For example, the *Yājñavalkyasmṛti* speaks of the king's protection of his subjects in the right manner (*nyāyena*)[104] and of his employment of the "punishing rod" (*daṇḍa*) in the proper way (*nyāyataḥ*),[105] and outside the context of *rājadharma* of a householder who has attained his wealth in the right manner.[106] In

---

[103] Cf., e.g., the remarks in Lingat 1973: 159. This topic will have to be dealt with in a separate paper.

[104] Cf. YS 1.331b: ... *nyāyena paripālayan* I. Vijñāneśvara explains *nyāyena* as *śāstroktamārgeṇa* (MA p. 114,26 on the edition's 1.335), Mitramiśra as *śāstrānumatavartmanā* (VM p. 366,12 ad loc.). Cf. also Stenzler 1849: "wenn er den gehörigen Schutz ertheilt". Hazra's rendering of *nyāyena* as "with justice" (cf. Hazra 1960: 14) imports a legal connotation which may not have been intended here. YS 1.331b may be compared with MS 7.2cd: *sarvasyāsya yathānyāyaṃ kartavyaṃ parirakṣaṇam* I (cf. Lingat 1973: 209, n. 11: "according to the rule"). Medhātithi also explains that the "right manner" to be complied with (cf. Bühler 1886: 216: "duly") is constituted by or consists in the *śāstra*, more specifically, the *dharmaśāstra* (cf. MBh 2,27: *nyāyaḥ śāstraṃ dharmaśāstrarūpam* ...).

[105] Cf. YS 1.351a (*sa na netum ataḥ śakyo lubdhenākṛtabuddhinā* I) in the form transmitted together with Vijñāneśvara's and Vīramitra's commentaries (i.e., 1.355a): *sa* (scil. *daṇḍo*) *netuṃ nyāyato 'śakyo lubdhenākṛtabuddhinā*). Vijñāneśvara merely provides the paraphrase *nyāyānusāreṇa* (MA p. 118,26), whereas Mitramiśra, just as in the case of the occurrence of the adverbial *nyāyena* in YS 1.331 (cf. footnote 104 above), explains what is meant by "in the proper way", i.e., "in accordance with the [relevant] doctrinal edifice(s)" (VM p. 376,11: *śāstrānusāreṇa*). Indeed, *nyāyataḥ* has to be understood with reference to the adverbial *yathāśāstram* in the subsequent verse. Here, Hazra's rendering "with justice" (Hazra 1960: 14) is more appropriate than in the case of 1.331b; cf. also Stenzler 1849: "gerecht". Cf. further the expression *nyāyadaṇḍa* ("one who wields the punishing rod in the proper way") in VS 3.96a, a verse which relates to the same context: *svarāṣṭre nyāyadaṇḍaḥ syāt*. Nandapaṇḍita explicates the *bahuvrīhi* compound *nyāyadaṇḍa* as follows (KV p. 72,3-4): *svarāṣṭre ye 'parādhinas teṣu nyāyena deśakālādyaucityena daṇḍo yasya*.

the *Nāradasmṛti* there is reference to deeds of other kings which have departed from the proper way (*nyāyāpeta*) and have been done out of ignorance; these, performed improperly (*anyāyavihita*), should be "set right" again (*punar nyāye niveśayet*) by the king.[107] There are further occurrences of negated forms of the term *nyāya*; e.g., the *Yājñavalkyasmṛti* predicts dire consequences for a king who increases his own wealth by taking from his kingdom in an improper way (*anyāyena*).[108] It has to be noted, though, that a problematic verse of the *Yājñavalkyasmṛti*, which is transmitted with a number of variants, may demand a different understanding of *nyāya* in the special sense of "methodical thinking" or "reasoning";[109] this

---

[106] Cf. YS 3.196a (recte 206): *nyāyārjitadhanaḥ* ...; the verse as transmitted in the *Mitākṣarā* and in the *Vīramitrodaya* (= 3.205) reads *nyāyāgatadhanaḥ* (MA p. 400, 5: *satpratigrahādinyāyenopārjitadhanaḥ*; VM p. 904,4 ad loc.: *nyāyena satpratigrahādinā*.) Stenzler translates "auf rechtmässige Weise".

[107] Cf. NS 18.9: *nyāyāpetaṃ yad anyena rājñājñānakṛtaṃ ca yat* | *tad apy anyāyavihitaṃ punar nyāye niveśayet* ||. I doubt that Lingat is right when he speaks in this context of "unreasonable" transactions (cf. Lingat 1973: 225) or judgments "contrary to reason" (cf. Lingat 1973: 256). Lariviere's translation of *nyāyāpeta* (or *anyāyavihita*?) with "unjust" (Lariviere 1989, II: 196) is free, but closer to the literal meaning of the term *nyāya* and can be derived from an equation of the "proper way" or "right manner" with the *śāstra* (cf. also Jolly 1876: 111: "contrary to justice", although I am not certain which of the two relevant adjectives is translated here). Cf. also the verse quoted from the *Kātyāyanasmṛti* adduced by Lingat (1962: 497-498; 1973: 225) which speaks of behaviour that is considered "contradictory from the point of view of the right manner" or as being "in contradiction with the right manner" (*viruddhaṃ nyāyataḥ*) (cf. Lingat 1962: 497: "contraire à l'équité"), and not contrary to reason or logic (as assumed in Lingat 1973: 225).

[108] Cf. YS 1.336: *anyāyena nṛpo rāṣṭrāt svakośaṃ yo 'bhivardhayet* | *so 'cirād vigataśrīko nāśam eti sabāndhavaḥ* ||. Mitramiśra explains the improper way as the punishment of those who should not be punished, the excessive collection of taxes, etc. (VM p. 368,17 on the edition's 1.340: *anyāyenādaṇḍyadaṇḍanādhikakaragrahaṇādinā*). Cf. Stenzler 1849: "unrechtmässig". Hazra (1960: 14) gives only a paraphrase of the expression ("by wronging his subjects"). Cf. also the use of *anyāyena* referring to the holding of property in *Nāradasmṛti* 1.91a according to Jolly's edition of the longer version of this Smṛti, a verse found in Asahāya's commentary on NS 1.78 (*anyāyenāpi yad bhuktam* ...) (cf. Jolly 1876: 25 in his earlier translation of the shorter version's verse 4.20: "unlawfully"; Lingat 1973: 162. n. 41: "irregularly").

meaning of the term *nyāya* could have developed from a generalisation of references to the "proper way" or "right manner" relating context-specifically to thinking, i.e., be derived from references to the "method" or "methodical procedure" of thinking. Alternatively, *nyāya* may here refer, along similar lines, to exegesis in the sense of the "proper way" or "method" of interpreting the scriptures which is nothing but a special type of thinking; that is, *nyāya* may refer here to exegetical reasoning.[110]

CONCLUSION

The evidence of the above survey of the Dharmasūtras and the brief glimpse into the major Dharmaśāstras suggest that the term *nyāya*, often lightly translated as "logic" (or even "syllogism"), has to be considered as having acquired a new distinctive meaning in the classical period, namely, referring to the "proper way" or "right manner" specifically of thinking, and further to a "method" or "methodical procedure",[111] namely, of thinking; thus it came to refer to right thinking or methodical thinking, i.e., the process of reasoned thinking or reasoning. It is here that a special reference to logic and logical thinking could attach itself. The term *nyāya* consequently came to rival the previously used terms *ānvīkṣikī* (referring to the science of and method of investigation with reasons),

---

[109] Cf. YS 2.21: *smṛter virodhe nyāyas tu balavān vyavahārataḥ* I *arthaśāstrāt tu balavad dharmaśāstram iti sthitiḥ* II. The general context is the same as that of the two verses from *Bṛhaspati-* and *Nāradasmṛti* referred to in connection with the term *yukti*; cf. above p. 55. A discussion of this verse will have to be undertaken in a further study of the term *nyāya*.

[110] Cf. the remarks on *nyāyavid* above, p. 51.

[111] According to P 3.3.37 (*parinyor nīṇor dyūtābhreṣayoḥ*) the suffix *ghañ* (cf. 3.3.16), which refers to the instrument (*karaṇa*) or substratum (*adhikaraṇa*) (cf. 3.3.120, with 3.3.118 and 117), is added to the root √*i* in combination with the preverb *ni-* in the sense of "non-deviation/non-aberration". *nyāya* is thus the means used to arrive at a certain goal without fail or deviation, i.e., the proper way or right manner, and may consequently also refer to a method or rule/ maxim. Similarly, the word *pariṇāya*, the means by which one moves around tokens or figures in a board game, refers to a move in such a game.

tarka, *ūha*, *anumāna* (in a general sense) and *yukti*; the terms *anumāna* and especially *tarka*, also frequently used in other pre-classical and early classical sources, now assumed more specific, technical meanings in the developing philosophical traditions even though their old general meaning (neutral as well as derogatory, especially in the case of *tarka*) was evidently preserved in the non-philosophical literature. In the traditional Brahminical enumeration of the "places of knowledge" as found in the *Yājñavalkyasmṛti* the original reading *tarka* could therefore be replaced by the variant reading *nyāya*, referring to methodical thinking as exemplified by logical or exegetical reasoning, whereas in the wording of the presumably later Purāṇic enumerations of areas of knowledge the terms *nyāya*, *nyāyavistara* or *nyāyaka* were right away preferred over the older term *tarka*, which by then must have lost its general and unambiguous, value-free meaning of "reasoning".

The transition to the dominance of *nyāya* in the above sense may have occurred around the beginning of the classical period. In this connection I would like to point to the first chapter of the already mentioned Vārṣṇeyādhyātma group of chapters in the Mokṣadharma which contains a plethora of references to reasoned examination and reflection. In a mythological context, methodical thinking (*nyāya*), not *tarka*, occurs there on an equal standing with a large number of traditional sciences.[112] These include the Vedas, the auxiliary sciences, the traditional narratives (*itihāsa*), the teachings relating to government and politics (*nītiśāstra*), music (*gāndharvaveda*), archery or weaponry in general (*dhanurgraha*), the stories about the deeds of gods and sages (*devarṣicarita*), and medicine (*cikitsita*). In conclusion many basic models or sets of rules of methodical thinking (*nyāyatantra*) are referred to which indicates that there existed a special topical science of reasoning; nevertheless, it is also clearly implied that the sages who pro-

---

[112] Cf. Preisendanz 2000: 240-242. For further treatments of the section on the sciences not mentioned in this paper cf. Dasgupta 1932: 276; Horsch 1966: 69; Narain 1979: 381.

nounced the above-mentioned sciences used these various models of *nyāya* when devising and teaching their specific sciences and that they also employed them in scholarly debate.[113] This obviously provides a typological parallel to the case of the *ānvīkṣikī* (*vidyā*) as referring to a science and method. However, further close and careful study of the term and of related terms referring to reasoning in the Epics, especially the *Mahābhārata*, as well as in the *Arthaśāstra*, is needed to throw more light on the emergence of the term *nyāya*.[114]

REFERENCES

Texts and abbreviations

ĀDhS =*Āpastambadharmasūtra*. In Olivelle 2000.

ĀDhS(B) = *Āpastambīyadharmasūtram. Āpastamba's Aphorisms on The Sacred Law of the Hindus*. Ed. George Bühler. 3rd edition. (Bombay Sanskrit Series, 44 & 50.) Bombay 1932.

AP = *The Agnimahāpurāṇam*. Delhi 1985. (Reprint of the Venkateshvara Steam Press edition, Bombay.)

APV = *Adhyātmapaṭalavivaraṇa*. In: *Minor Works of Śrī Śaṅkarācārya*. Ed. by H. R. Bhagavat. 2nd edition. (Poona Oriental Series, 8.) Poona 1952.

AŚ = *The Kauṭilīya Arthaśāstra*. Ed. by R. P. Kangle. (University of Bombay Studies: Sanskrit, Prakrit and Pali, 1.) Bombay 1960.

BDhS =*Baudhāyanadharmasūtra*. In Olivelle 2000.

BDhS(H) = *Das Baudhāyana-Dharmasūtra*. Ed. by E. Hultzsch. 2nd edition. (Abhandlungen für die Kunde des Morgenlandes, 16.2.) Leipzig 1922.

BDhSV = *Vivaraṇa* of Govindasvāmin. In: *The Bodhāyana-Dharma-Sūtra with the Commentary of Govindasvamin*. Ed. by L. Srinivasacharya. (Government Oriental Library Series Bibliotheca Sanskrita, 34.) Mysore 1907.

BhP = *Bhaviṣyamahāpurāṇam*. Delhi 1984 (Reprint of the Venkateshvara Steam Press edition, Bombay.)

---

[113] Cf. MBh 12.203.20: *nyāyatantrāṇy anekāni tais tair uktāni vādibhiḥ* | *hetvāgamasadācārair yad uktaṃ tad upāsyate* ||. For a translation, cf. Preisendanz 2000: 241.

[114] I am indebted to my husband, Prof. Eli Franco, for his valuable criticism and comments on the present and earlier versions of this paper. Thanks are also due to my colleague Dr. Anne MacDonald for her careful reading and pertinent suggestions.

BK = *Bālakrīḍā* of Viśvarūpa. In YS.

BṛYY = *Bṛhadyogiyājñavalkya*. Ed. by Swami Kuvalayananda & Raghunatha Shastri Kokaje. Lonavla 1951.

BS = *Brahmasūtra*. In BSBh.

BSBh = *Brahmasūtrabhāṣya* of Śaṅkara. Delhi, n.d.

BUBhṬ = *Bṛhadāraṇyakopaniṣadbhāṣyaṭīkā* of Ānandagiri. In: *Bṛhadāraṇyakopaniṣad.* (Anandashrama Sanskrit Series, 15.) Poona, n.d.

CaS = *Carakasaṃhitā*. Ed. by Gangasahaya Pandeya. 2nd edition. (Kashi Sanskrit Series, 194.) Varanasi 1983. (Remake of the edition by Yadavji Trikamji, 3rd edition, Bombay 1941.)

GDhS = *Gautamadharmasūtra*. In Olivelle 2000.

GDhSM = *Mitākṣarā* of Haradatta. In: *The Gautama-Dharma-Sūtra with the 'Mitākṣarā' Sanskrit Commentary of Haradatta*. Ed. by Umesh Chandra Pandey. (Kashi Sanskrit Series, 172.) Varanasi 1966.

GDhSMBh = *Maskaribhāṣya*. In: *Goutama-Dharmasutra with Maskari Bhashya*. Ed. by L. Srinivasacharya. (Government Oriental Library Series Bibliotheca Sanskrita, 50.) Mysore 1917.

HDh Cf. Kane 1968, 1973, 1974a, 1974b, 1975.

HDhS = Various readings of the *Hiraṇyakeśidharmasūtra* to *sūtra*s of the ĀDhS as recorded in Appendix I of ĀDhS(B).

HU = *Hitopadeśa* of Nārāyaṇa. Ed. by M. R. Kale. 6th edition. Delhi 1967.

J I = *The Jātaka together with its Commentary*, I. Ed. by V. Fausbøll. London 1877.

J II = *The Jātaka together with its Commentary*, II. Ed. by V. Fausbøll. London 1879.

J III = *The Jātaka together with its Commentary*, III. Ed. by V. Fausbøll. London 1883.

KNS = *The Nītisāra of Kāmanda with the Commentary Jayamaṅgalā of Śaṅkarārya*. Ed. by T. Ganapati Sastri. Trivandrum 1912.

KS = *The Kauśika Sūtra of Atharva Veda*. Ed. by Maurice Bloomfield. Delhi 1972. (Reprint of 1889.)

KV = *Keśavavaijayantī* of Nandapaṇḍita. In VS.

MA = *Mitākṣarā* of Vijñāneśvara. In: *Yājñavalkyasmṛti. With the Commentary Mitākṣarā of Vijñāneśvara*. Ed. by Narayan Ram Acharya. Delhi 1985. (Reprint of the Nirnaya Sagar Press edition.)

MAM = *Manvarthamuktāvalī* of Kullūka. In MS.

MAV = *Manvarthavivṛti* of Sarvajñanārāyaṇa. In MS.

MBh = *The Mahābhārata*. Critical edition by Vishnu S. Sukthankar et al.. Poona 1933-66.

MBhā = *Manubhāṣya* of Medhatithi. In MS.

MP = *Matsyapurāṇa*. (Anandashrama Sanskrit Series, 54.) Poona 1981.

MP(W) = *The Matsyamahāpurāṇam*. Delhi 1983. (Text rearranged by Nag Sharan Singh together with Wilson's translation.)

MS = *Manu-Smṛti*. Ed. by Jayantakrishna Harikrishna Dave. 6 vols. Bombay 1972-85. For *adhyāya* 8: *Mānava-Dharma-Śāstra*, II. Ed. by Vishvanath Narayan Mandlik. Bombay 1886. (Reprint: New Delhi 1992.)

MSū = *Mīmāṃsāsūtra*. In: *Mīmāṃsādarśana*, II, IV, V. Ed. by Kashinath Vasudev Shastri Abhyankar & Ganesh Shastri Joshi. 2nd edition. (Anandashrama Sanskrit Series, 97.) Poona 1970, 1972, 1973.

MŚV = *Manuśāstravivaraṇa* of Bhāruci. In MS.

MṬ = *Manuṭīkā* of Govindarāja. In MS.

NM = *Nyāyamañjarī* of Jayantabhaṭṭa, I. Ed. by K. S. Varadacharya. (University of Mysore Oriental Research Institute Series, 116.) Mysore 1969.

NS = *Nāradasmṛti*. Ed. in Lariviere 1989.

NSū = *Nyāyasūtra*. In NVṛ.

NVṛ = *Nyāyavṛtti* of Viśvanātha Pañcānana. In: *Nyāyadarśanam*, I. Ed. by Taranatha Nyaya-Tarkatirtha & Amarendramohan Tarkatirtha. (Calcutta Sanskrit Series, 18.) Calcutta 1936.

P = Pāṇini's *Aṣṭādhyāyī*. Ed. in: Otto Böhtlingk, *Pāṇini's Grammatik*. 2nd edition. Leipzig 1887.

PBh = *Prasthānabheda* of Madhusūdana Sarasvatī. Printed as an appendix in: *Sarvadarśanasaṅgraha* of Mādhava. 4th edition. (Anandashrama Sanskrit Series, 51.) Poona 1977. Cf. also Weber 1850.

PP = *The Padmamahāpurāṇam*. Delhi 1984. (Reprint of the Venkateshvara Steam Press edition, Bombay.)

Padma Puranam, I. (Gurumandal Series, 18.) Calcutta 1957.

PS = *Parāśarasmṛti ... with the Gloss by Mādhavācārya*. Ed. by Chandrakanta Tarkalankara, II-III. Calcutta 1899. (Reprint: Calcutta 1973.)

PT = *Pañcatantra* of Viṣṇuśarman. Ed. by M. R. Kale. 1st edition. Bombay 1912.

RV = *Raghuvaṃśa* of Kālidāsa, with Mallinātha's commentary. Ed. by Narayan Ram Acharya. 11th edition. Bombay 1948.

SC = *Smṛticandrikā* of Devaṇṇabhaṭṭa. Ed. in: J. R. Gharpure, *Hindu Law Texts*. Bombay 1919.

TV = *Tantravārttika*, I = *Mīmāṃsādarśana*, II. Ed. by Kashinath Vasudev Shastri Abhyankar & Ganesh Shastri Joshi. 2nd edition. (Anandashrama Sanskrit Series, 97.) Poona 1970.

Uj = *Ujjvalā* of Haradatta. In: *The Āpastamba-Dharma-Sūtra with the 'Ujjvalā' Commentary of Śrī Haradatta Miśra*. Ed. by Umesh Chandra Pandeya. (Kashi Sanskrit Series, 93.) Varanasi 1969.

VāP = *The Vāyumahāpurāṇam*. Delhi 1983. (Reprint of the Venkateshvara Steam Press edition, Bombay.)

VDhS = *Vāsiṣṭhadharmasūtra*. In Olivelle 2000.

VDhS(F) = *Śrīvāsiṣṭhadharmasūtram. Aphorisms on the Sacred Law of the Āryas as Taught in the School of Vasishṭha*. Ed. by A. A. Führer. Bombay 1883.

VM = *Vīramitrodaya* of Mitramiśra. In: *Yājñavalkya Smṛti*. Ed. by Narayana Shastri Khiste & Jagannatha Shastri Hoshinga. 2nd edition. (Chowkhamba Sanskrit Series, 62.) Varanasi 1997.

VMa = *The Vyavahāramayūkha of Bhaṭṭa Nīlakaṇṭha*. Ed. by P. V. Kane. (Bombay Sanskrit and Prakrit Series, 80.) Bombay 1926.

VP = *The Viṣṇumahāpurāṇam*. Delhi 1985. (Reprint of the Venkateshvara Steam Press edition, Bombay.)

VS = *Viṣṇusmṛti with the Commentary Keśavavaijayantī of Nandapaṇḍita*. Ed. by Pandit V. Krishnamacharya. (Adyar Library Series, 93.) Madras 1964.

YD = *Yuktidīpikā. The Most Significant Commentary on the Sāṅkhyakārikā*. Ed. by Albrecht Wezler & Shujun Motegi. (Alt- und Neu-Indische Studien, 44.) Stuttgart 1998.

YS = *Yājñavalkyasmṛti*. In: *The Yājñavalkyasmṛti with the Commentary Bālakrīda of Visvarūpāchārya*. Ed. by T. Ganapati Shastri. Trivandrum 1921-22. (Reprint: New Delhi 1982.)

Secondary literature

BHATTACHARYYA, Sivaprasad 1956. The neo-Buddhist nucleus in Alaṅkāraśāstra. *Journal of the Asiatic Society* 22(1): 49-66.

BÖHTLINGK, Otto 1883-86. *Sanskrit-Wörterbuch in kürzerer Fassung*. St. Petersburg.

—— 1885. Bemerkungen zu Führer's Ausgabe und zu Bühler's Übersetzung des Vāsiṣṭhadharmaśāstra. *Zeitschrift der Deutschen Morgenländischen Gesellschaft* 39: 481-488.

BÖHTLINGK, Otto & Rudolf ROTH 1855-75. *Sanskrit-Wörterbuch*. St. Petersburg.

BÜHLER, Georg (trans.) 1879. *The Sacred Laws of the Āryas as Taught in the School of Apastamba, Gautama, Vasishtha and Baudhayana*, I. (Sacred Books of the East, 2.) Oxford. (Reprint: Delhi 1965.)

—— (trans.) 1882. *The Sacred Laws of the Āryas As Taught in the School of Apastamba, Gautama, Vasishtha and Baudhayana*, Part II. (Sacred Books of the East, 14.) Oxford. (Reprint: Delhi 1965.)

—— (trans.) 1886. *The Laws of Manu*. (Sacred Books of the East, 25.) Oxford. (Reprint: Delhi 1988.)

DAHLMANN, Joseph 1895. *Das Mahābhārata als Epos und Rechtsbuch*. Berlin.

DASGUPTA, Surendranath 1932. *A History of Indian Philosophy*, II. Cambridge.

DERRETT, J. Duncan M. (ed. & trans.) 1975. *Bhāruci's Commentary on the Manusmṛti*, I-II. (Schriftenreihe des Südasien-Instituts der Universität Heidelberg, 18.) Stuttgart.

FRIEDRICH, Elvira 1993. *Das Āpastamba-Dharmasūtra – Aufbau und Aussage*. (Europäische Hochschulschriften, Reihe 27: Asiatische und Afrikanische Studien, 31.) Frankfurt.

GHAROTE, M. L. & V. A. BEDEKAR (trans.) 1982. *Bṛhadyogiyājñavalkya*. Lonavla.

HACKER, Paul 1958. Ānvīkṣikī. *Wiener Zeitschrift für die Kunde Süd- und Ostasiens* 2: 54-83.

—— 1968-69. Śaṅkara der Yogin und Śaṅkara der Advaitin. *Wiener Zeitschrift für die Kunde Süd- und Ostasiens* 12-13 (Festschrift Erich Frauwallner): 119-148.

HALBFASS, Wilhelm 1988. *India and Europe. An Essay in Understanding*. Albany.

HAZRA, R. C. 1959. Dharma – Its early meaning and scope. *Our Heritage* 7: 15-35.

—— 1960. Dharma – Its early meaning and scope. Part II. *Our Heritage* 8: 8-34.

—— 1968. The judicial Pramāṇas (means of proof) known to or mentioned in the extant Dharma-Sūtras of Gautama and others. *Our Heritage* 16: 1-56.

HORSCH, Paul 1966. *Die vedische Gāthā- und Śloka-Literatur*. Bern.

JACOBI, Hermann 1911. Zur Frühgeschichte der indischen Philosophie. In: *Sitzungsberichte der Königlich Preußischen Akademie der Wissenschaften* 1911: 732-743. Berlin.

JHA, Ganganath 1994. *Sāḍholāl Lectures on Nyāya*. 2nd edition. Delhi.

JOLLY, Julius (trans.) 1876. *Naradiya Dharmasastra, or The Institutes of Narada*. London.

KANE, P. V. 1968. *History of Dharmaśāstra*, I.1. 2nd edition. Poona.

—— 1973. *History of Dharmaśāstra*, III. 2nd edition. Poona.

—— 1974a. *History of Dharmaśāstra*, II.1. 2nd edition. Poona.

—— 1974b. *History of Dharmaśāstra*, II.2. 2nd edition. Poona.

—— 1975. *History of Dharmaśāstra*, I.2. 2nd edition. Poona.

KEITH, Arthur Berriedale 1919. *Indian Logic and Atomism*. Oxford.

LARIVIERE, Richard W. (ed. & trans.) 1981. *The Divyatattva of Raghunandana Bhaṭṭācārya. Ordeals in Classical Hindu Law*. New Delhi.

—— (ed. & trans.) 1989. *The Nāradasmṛti*, I-II. Philadelphia.

LINGAT, Robert 1962. Les quatre pieds du procès. *Journal Asiatique* 250: 489-503.

—— 1973. *The Classical Law of India*. Translated from the French, with additions, by J. Duncan M. Derrett. Berkeley.

MATILAL, Bimal Krishna 1977. *Nyāya-Vaiśeṣika*. (A History of Indian Literature, 6.2.) Wiesbaden.

MISHRA, Umesh 1966. *History of Indian Philosophy*, II. Allahabad.

MUIR, J. 1873. *Original Sanskrit Texts on the Origin and History of the People of India, their Religion and Institutions*. III: *The Vedas: Opinions of their Authors and of Later Indian Writers on their Origins, Inspiration, and Authority*. 2nd edition. London. (Reprint: New Delhi 1976.)

NARAIN, Harsh 1979. *ānvīkṣikī* as dialectic. In: *Ludwik Sternbach Felicitation Volume*, II: 579-592. Lucknow.

OLIVELLE, Patrick 1993. *The Āśrama System. The History and Hermeneutics of a Religious Institution*. New York.

—— 1999. Sanskrit commentators and the transmission of texts. *Journal of Indian Philosophy* 27: 551-574.

—— (ed. & trans.) 2000. *Dharmasūtras. The Law Codes of Āpastamba, Gautama, Baudhāyana, and Vasiṣṭha*. Delhi.

POLLOCK, Sheldon 1985. The theory of practice and the practice of theory in Indian intellectual history. *Journal of the American Oriental Society* 105(3): 499-519.

—— 1989. The idea of Śāstra in traditional India. In: Anna Libera Dallapiccola (ed.), *Shastric Traditions in Indian Arts*, I: 17-26. Stuttgart.

PREISENDANZ, Karin 2000 [= 2001]. Debate and independent reasoning vs. tradition: On the precarious position of early Nyāya. In: Ryutaro Tsuchida & Albrecht Wezler (eds.), *Harānandalaharī. Volume in Honour of Professor Minoru Hara on his Seventieth Birthday*: 221-251. Reinbek.

—— forthcoming. The Carakasaṃhitā and the early history of Nyāya: Some critical remarks.

RAJAMANICKAM, S. 1972. *On Indian Customs*. Palayamkottai.

RUBEN, Walter 1926. Zur Frühgeschichte der indischen Philosophie. In: Willibald Kirfel (ed.), *Beiträge zur Literaturwissenschaft und Geistesgeschichte Indiens* (Festschrift Hermann Jacobi): 346-357. Bonn.

SÄNGER, Anke 2000. Drei frühe Editionen des Vāsiṣṭhadharmaśāstra. *Berliner Indologische Studien* 13/14: 175-200.

SHAH, Nagin J. 1992. *A Study of Jayanta Bhaṭṭa's Nyāyamañjarī. A Mature Sanskrit Work on Indian Logic*, I. Ahmedabad.

STENZLER, Adolf Friedrich (ed. & trans.) 1849. *Yājñavalkya's Gesetzbuch*. Berlin.

THAKUR, Anantalal 1975. Gautama. In: V. Raghavan (ed.), *Founders of Philosophy*: 39-54. Delhi.

VIDYABHUSANA, Satish Chandra (ed. & trans.) 1913. *The Nyāya Sūtras of Gotama*. Allahabad.

—— 1920. *A History of Indian Logic*. Calcutta.

—— (ed. & trans.) 1930. *The Nyāya Sūtras of Gotama*. Allahabad. (= Reprint of Vidyabhusana 1913.)

WEBER, Albrecht (trans.) 1850. Madhusūdana-Sarasvatī's encyclopädische Uebersicht der orthodoxen brahmanischen Literatur. *Indische Studien* 1: 1-24.

WEZLER, Albrecht 1999. Medhātithi on Sāmānyato Dṛṣṭam [Anumānam]. *Journal of Indian Philosophy* 27: 139-157.

WILSON, Horace Hayman (trans.) 1980. *The Viṣṇu Purāṇa. A System of Hindu Mythology and Tradition*, I-II. Enlarged and rearranged reprint by Nag Sharan Singh. Delhi.

WINTERNITZ, M. 1929. Ānvīkṣikī und Ātmavidyā. *Indologica Pragensia* 1: 1-8.

On the Proof Passage of the *Carakasaṃhitā*: Editions, Manuscripts and Commentaries

Ernst Prets

Without any doubt the *Carakasaṃhitā* – being primarily a treatise on internal medicine (*kāyacikitsā*), but also dealing with all topics of early Indian medicine – also represents one of the richest early sources for the history of Indian philosophy in general, epistemology, dialectics, logic, early Indian education, cultural and social history, as well as cultural anthropology. As already pointed out many times, in the eighth chapter of the third book of the *Carakasaṃhitā*, the Vimānasthāna, we come across a section discussing the method of debate (*saṃbhāṣāvidhi*). It depicts, in a very lively manner, the "parley of specialists" (*tadvidyasaṃbhāṣā*)[1] with its two sub-forms, the "friendly parley" (*sandhāyasaṃbhāṣā* or *anulomasaṃbhāṣā*) and the "hostile parley" (*vigṛhyasaṃbhāṣā*).[2] It has already been emphasized that after this vivid description of debate practice, the following text changes stylistically and terminologically, continuing with a list of forty-four basic topics of debate (*vādamārgapada*)[3] followed by brief definitions and short examples, pointing to an adapted compilation of definitions from an earlier source that concerned debate.[4]

---

[1] CS Vimānasthāna 8.15f.

[2] Cf. Roth 1872; Kang 1998; Prets 2000: 369ff.; and TPhSI 2 s.v.

[3] CS Vimānasthāna 8.27. For interpretations of the individual topics cf. Solomon 1976: 78-87; TPhSI 1 and 2 s.v.; and Prets 2000: 371ff.

[4] CS Vimānasthāna 8.28-65.

The importance of this passage and its relation to the section in the *Nyāyasūtra* that refers to dialectical and logical terms was realized quite early[5] and its technical terminology was contrasted with other early texts.[6] However, the authors who were engaged in the analyses of the *saṃbhāṣāvidhi* did not work through the text very critically nor in great detail. For various reasons none of them analyzed the text using appropriate philological criteria with the exception of Hakuju Ui, who tried – obviously after having recognized that deviating readings of the passage existed – to prepare a sort of critical edition for his own purposes.[7] The ambiguity of the transmitted text can already be seen by the fact that the study of this subject matter in the secondary literature is based on varying textual evidence.[8] Even the list of the topics of debate referred to by these authors diverges, as for example in the positioning of "example" (*dṛṣṭānta*), listed by some following "answer" (*uttara*),[9] and by others between "reason" (*hetu*) and "application" (*upanaya*)[10] as

---

[5] Cf. e.g. Vidyabhusana 1920: 31-35; Dasgupta 1922: 377ff.

[6] Cf. Tucci 1929: xvi-xxii.

[7] Ui 1925 used copies of six editions of the *Carakasaṃhitā* for the compilation of a "critical" text. Ui mentions only editor, place of edition and year of edition. Four of these editions could be identified: CS 1877, CS 1878/79 (= 2nd edition of CS 1868) CS 1896 (= 2nd edition of CS 1877; in comparison to the first edition which is based on a manuscript of the Kashmiri recension, the second edition is based on manuscripts of the eastern recension; cf. the discussion of recension below), and CS 1897-98. The other two editions could not be identified with certainty. One of these two editions, that by Harinath Sankar, Calcutta without date, may be the edition by Yashodanandan Sarkar, Calcutta 1894 or the edition by Harinatha Visharada that includes the *Āyurvedadīpikā*, Calcutta 1892-1919. The other edition, Calcutta 1882, of which Ui does not mention the editor, may be the edition including translation by Avinashacandra Kaviratna Kaviraj, Calcutta 1884/85. But these suggestions regarding the two unidentified editions are only speculative.

[8] Cf. e.g. Vidyabhusana 1920, Dasgupta 1922 or Frauwallner 1984: 70 with Solomon 1976, TPhSI 1 and 2 s.v., Kang 1998: 133, or Prets 2000: 371, fn. 9.

[9] CS 1877, p. 300,13-16: *imāni khalu padāni vādamārgajñānārtham adhigamyāni | ... hetuḥ upanayo nigamanam uttaraṃ dṛṣṭāntaḥ siddhāntaḥ ...*

[10] CS Vimānasthāna 8.27: *imāni tu khalu padāni bhiṣagvādamārgajñānārtham adhigamyāni ... hetuḥ, dṛṣṭāntaḥ, upanayaḥ, nigamanam, uttaraṃ, siddhāntaḥ ...*

the sequence is found in the members of proof (*avayava*) in the *Nyāyasūtra*.[11]

It is remarkable that in the list of debate topics many of the *Carakasaṃhitā* editions of the 19th century, "example" (*dṛṣṭānta*) is listed following "answer" (*uttara*) and before "accomplished doctrine" (*siddhānta*),[12] whereas most of the editions of the 20th century display the other reading, i.e., "example" between "reason" and "application" in the sequence of proof terms.[13] It should also be mentioned that all manuscripts considered in our study so far support the former reading.[14] In contrast to other, later editions and the 19th-century edition of the *Jalpakalpataru* of Gaṅgādhara Kavirāja that support the latter reading,[15] earlier editions of the *Carakasaṃhitā* together with the *Āyurvedadīpikā* of Cakrapāṇidatta (about AD 1100) also support the former reading.[16]

A problem to be taken even more seriously is seen in connection with the manner of proof, in which of the two, as yet, recognised readings of the editions, the formulation of example (*dṛṣṭānta*) and application (*upanaya*) would lead to different conclusions regarding the early manner of proof, a fact already pointed out by Oetke.[17] In the manuscripts and all the editions which have – according to the manuscripts – "example" (*dṛṣṭānta*) following

---

[11] Cf. NSū 1.1.32: *pratijñāhetūdāharaṇopanayanigamanāny avayavāḥ*.

[12] Cf. e.g. CS 1877 above, CS 1884/85, CS 1897-98.

[13] Cf. e.g. CS above; although according to his introduction (cf. p. 17) the editor of the CS used the Lahore manuscripts (cf. Ch, below footnote 31) for his edition, which is confirmed by some variant readings found in the footnotes of the CS, he did not record the deviating order of the items of the list as found in this manuscript. It is remarkable that all other editors who present the position of *dṛṣṭānta* between *hetu* and *upanaya* do not point out the existence of an alternative order elsewhere.

[14] Cf. e.g. Ch (DAV College, Chandigarh, Lalchand Research Library, Ms. no. 2315) fol. 164^r,4f.: ... *pratijñā sthāpanā pratiṣṭhāpanā hetuḥ upanayo nigamanam uttaraṃ dṛṣṭāṃtaḥ siddhāntaḥ* ...

[15] Cf. CS 1878/79 (with JKT) and CS 1927-33 (with ĀD and JKT).

[16] Cf. e.g. CS 1892-1919 (with ĀD) and CS 1922 (with ĀD).

[17] Cf. Oetke 1994: 38 and 81f.

"answer" (*uttara*) in the list and definition section, the example in the proof (*sthāpanā*) and the counterproof (*pratiṣṭhāpanā*) verbally exemplifies both properties: the property to be proved (*sādhya*) and the proving property (*sādhana*), and is accordingly also followed by a different reading of the application (*upanaya*).[18] In contrast to this reading, in Gaṅgādhara's edition[19] and in most of the later editions the example mentions only the exemplifying object without adducing the two respective properties, whereas these properties are explicitly formulated in the application.[20]

Although there are more than forty editions of the *Carakasaṃhitā* dating from the middle of the 19th century up to the last few years,[21] and new editions are even now in progress, a critical edition of the text has yet to be made. Contrary to all expectations, several editions of the *Carakasaṃhitā* are seemingly not based on new material at all. They present rather – and this situation can already be seen from the beginning of the 20th century – secondary or even tertiary compilations of texts previously edited. Only very few of these editions offer variations of the manuscripts and thus could theoretically be called critical. The few critical remarks are rather incidental, as is also the case in the perhaps most-quoted

---

[18] Cf. e.g. CS 1877, p. 301,6-15: *sthāpanā ... yathā nityaḥ puruṣa iti pratijñā, hetur akṛtakatvād iti, dṛṣṭāntaḥ – akṛtakam ākāśaṃ tac ca nityam, upanayo yathā cākṛtakam ākāśan tathā puruṣaḥ, nigamanan tasmān nitya iti. pratiṣṭhāpanā ... yathānityaḥ puruṣa iti pratijñā, hetur aindriyakatvāt, dṛṣṭānto ghaṭaḥ aindriyakaḥ sa cānityaḥ, upanayo yathā ghaṭaḥ tathā puruṣas tasmād anitya iti.* Cf. the same textual reading with minor variants in Ch fol. 164ᵛ,4-7. In this way also CS 1892-1919 (with ĀD), CS 1922 (with ĀD), CS 1970.

[19] Cf. CS 1878/79.

[20] CS Vimānasthāna 8.31f. (with ĀDī): *sthāpanā ... yathā – nityaḥ puruṣa iti pratijñā; hetuḥ – akṛtakatvād iti; dṛṣṭāntaḥ – yathākāśam iti; upanayaḥ – yathā cākṛtakam ākāśaṃ tac ca nityaṃ tathā puruṣa iti; nigamanam – tasmān nitya iti. pratiṣṭhāpanā ... yathā – anityaḥ puruṣa iti pratijñā, hetuḥ – aindriyakatvād iti, dṛṣṭāntaḥ – yathā ghaṭa iti, upanayo yathā ghaṭa aindriyakaḥ sa cānityaḥ, tathā cāyam iti, nigamanaṃ – tasmād anitya iti.* Cf. the same textual reading with minor variants in CS 1878/79 (with JKT), CS 1920-22 (with CU), CS 1927-33 (with ĀD and JKT) and CS 1983-88.

[21] Cf. Meulenbeld 1999, 1B: 3-6.

edition of the *Carakasaṃhitā*, namely Trikamji's edition of 1941, upon which translations of the *Carakasaṃhitā* are based today.[22]

The irregularity of the texts of the *saṃbhāṣāvidhi* in its various editions as shown in the above examples also continues in the thirty-six manuscripts containing the Vimānasthāna that have been considered in our study thus far. In addition to this, there are more than a hundred other variant readings in the usual editions alone, to which must be added those variants that are seen in the manuscripts and in the oldest surviving commentary, Cakrapāṇidatta's *Āyurvedadīpikā*.

Consequently, the decision was made to undertake the project of a critical edition and annotated translation of the eighth chapter of the Vimānasthāna of the *Carakasaṃhitā* with the collaboration of Karin Preisendanz and funded by the Austrian Science Fund.[23] It has been decided to take all available manuscripts and editions, as well as the preserved commentaries into account.

Before going into the details of the subject matter of proof and counterproof, some remarks on the collection of manuscripts and the manuscript situation with regard to the *Carakasaṃhitā* in general should be added: At the moment the project is aware of about two hundred existing manuscripts of the *Carakasaṃhitā* and its commentaries, in part consisting only of chapters of the text or even smaller sections. The collection of manuscripts which has been drawn together in Vienna amounts to about ninety manuscripts, partly on microfilm, partly photocopied and partly in digital form, of which thirty-seven contain the relevant section of the Vimānasthāna. Unfortunately, only one manuscript of Cakrapāṇidatta's *Āyurvedadīpikā* containing the complete text of Vimānasthāna 8 (CĀ) is available and regrettably this copy of the manuscript is largely illegible in relevant portions.[24]

---

[22] Cf. e.g. CS 1976-97 and CS 1981-94.

[23] Fonds zur Förderung der wissenschaftlichen Forschung, Project no. P 14451, direction: Karin Preisendanz.

[24] National Library, Kolkata, Ms. no. RDS 78.

One has also to take into account that most of the manuscripts are rather late copies dating from the 17th to the 19th century. From the 12th century we have a copy of one manuscript written in early Devanagari script,[25] but which unfortunately does not contain the Vimānasthāna, but only Cikitsasthāna 3 up to the end of the *Carakasaṃhitā*. Some relevant manuscripts have been located in Indian manuscript libraries, as for example the manuscripts in the Maharaja Sawai Man Singh II Museum, City Palace, Jaipur[26] that are mentioned by Yogindra Nath Sen in his edition,[27] but due to various reasons they could not yet be procured for the project.

Generally speaking, the thirty-six manuscripts containing the Vimānasthāna, which are written in Sharada and different kinds of Bengali and Devanagari scripts, are of heterogeneous quality with régard to the scribal habits, the occurrence of scribal errors, the legibility, etc.

As to the preliminary stemmatological results, one has to go somewhat into details. The first results of the critical work have clarified somewhat the differentiation of recensions. As early as the beginning of the last century Cordier[28] had noticed "that the text of the *Carakasaṃhitā* must have been subject of considerable variations, as is obvious from quotations found in commentaries."[29] Ann Glazier, who for a time worked on a critical edition of Caraka's Śārīrasthāna, but unfortunately discontinued her endeavour, com-

---

[25] Ms. no. 1-1648, Reel no. A 46/6 of the Nepal-German Manuscript Preservation Project (184 folios [cikitsāsthāna 3 – jvaracikitsita, to the end], old Devanagari [according to catalogues: Newari], palm leaf, date: *saṃvat* 303, i.e. AD 1183).

[26] Mss. nos. 2068, 2069, 2107.

[27] Yogindra Nath Sen mentions two Mss. from Jaipur in the introduction of his edition (CS 1920-22): "Jaipur manuscript, copied in 1643 of the Saṃvat era, i.e AD 1700 [most probably either AD 1586/1586 or 1721/22]; character Devanagri; fairly correct" and "Jaipur manuscript, very old, without date; character Devanagri; correct but incomplete, from the beginning up to the end of Gulma Nidana only".

[28] Cordier 1902: 528-530 (= Roşu 1989: 546-548).

[29] Meulenbeld 1999, 1A: 96.

pared passages of the Cikitsāsthāna of the mentioned manuscript from the 12th century to a Sharada manuscript from Pune (P1)[30] and the manuscript from Lahore (Ch).[31] Based on Cordier's observations, she found convincing evidence for the existence of a Kashmiri recension. This conclusion is supported by the commentary of Cakrapāṇidatta, who mentions the deviating readings of the Kashmiri version on several occasions. In any case, the crucial criterion for the distinction of these two recensions is the different order of the chapters (*adhyāya*) in the Cikitsāsthāna from the ninth to the twenty-fifth chapter.[32] On closer examination it turns out that not only do the Sharada manuscript and the Lahore manuscript display this deviating composition, but so do five other manuscripts from manuscript libraries in Jammu (J1, J2, J3),[33] Udaipur (U),[34] Alwar (A)[35] also do, as well as a Devanagari manuscript (C7)[36] from the library of the Asiatic Society of Bengal, Calcutta. At the beginning of Vimānasthāna 8 one finds similar variant readings in both the Sharada manuscript and the other five manuscripts which are not found in any of the other manuscripts – although they are not directly interdependent with the exception of one Jammu manuscript (J2) that is a direct copy of the Sharada manuscript. Surprisingly, one Bengali manuscript, containing only fragments of the Vimānasthāna (C6),[37] also supports these variations.

---

[30] Bhandarkar Oriental Research Institute, Pune, Ms. no. 555 of 1875-76.

[31] DAV College, Chandigarh (Lalchand Research Library), Ms. no. 2315.

[32] The ninth *adhyāya* of the Kashmiri recension is the fourteenth of the eastern recension, the tenth *adhyāya* of the Kashmiri recension is the nineteenth of the eastern recension, the eleventh is the twenty-first, the twelfth is the twenty-fourth, etc.

[33] Raghunath Temple Library of His Highness The Maharaja of Jammu and Kashmir, Ms. nos. 3266-3267 (J1), 2309 (J2), and 3330-3331 (J3).

[34] Rajasthan Oriental Research Institute, Udaipur, Ms. no. 1474.

[35] Rajasthan Oriental Research Institute, Alwar, Ms. no. 2498.

[36] According to its variant readings, C7 has the closest relation to the Alwar (A) manuscript. This manuscript (C7) most probably has been the copy used for Jīvānanda's edition (CS 1877).

[37] Asiatic Society of Bengal, Kolkata, Āyurveda handlist, Ms. no. G 2503/1.

In comparison to the western, Kashmiri recension, the eastern recension, which probably is based on the 12th-century manuscript from Nepal or a related manuscript, displays two branches: one that is represented mostly by Bengali manuscripts,[38] of which the oldest is a manuscript from Varanasi dated 1698 (V1)[39], and a second branch represented by a group of Devanagari manuscripts from manuscript libraries in Baroda (B),[40] Kota (K),[41] London (L2, L3),[42] Nepal (N1),[43] Pune (P4),[44] Tübingen (T1, T2)[45] and Varanasi (V5).[46]

Nevertheless, direct dependencies of the manuscripts of either group can be shown only in very few instances, but here is not the place to go into details. On the other hand, it may also be that most of the manuscripts will not allow a clear distinction of their interdependencies, but only a rough classification of their affiliations.

The problem of the recensions is not significant for the following proof passage, since all manuscripts of the different branches correspond to a certain extent. It rather is the problem of the editions that are influenced by the corrections and interpretations of Gaṅgādhara's *Jalpakalpataru*.

It seems clear that, in the list of topics concerning debate in the manuscripts,[47] the positioning of "example" (*dṛṣṭānta*), following

---

[38] National Library, Kolkata, Ms. no. RDS 101 (C4); Asiatic Society of Bengal, Kolkata, Āyurveda handlist, Ms. no. G 4474/3 (C5); Trinity College Library, Cambridge, Ms. no. R. 15. 85 (Ca); Sarasvati Bhavan Library, no. 108685 (V3); Sarasvati Bhavan Library, Varanasi, Ms. no. 108824 (V4, scribe Gaṅgādhara), and some other minor manuscripts which will not be specified here.

[39] Sarasvati Bhavan Library, Varanasi, Ms. no. 44842.

[40] Central Library, Baroda, Ms. no. 12489.

[41] Rajasthan Oriental Research Institute, Kota, Ms. no. 1563.

[42] India Office Library, London, Sanskrit Ms. no. 881 (L2) and 1445a & b (L3).

[43] Nepal-German Manuscript Preservation Project, Kathmandu-Berlin, Ms. no. E-40553 – Reel no. E 2211/10.

[44] Ānandāśrama, Pune, Ms. no. 1546.

[45] Universitätsbibliothek Tübingen, Ms. M. a. I. 458 (T1) and M. a. I. 459 (T2).

[46] Benares Hindu University, Varanasi, Ms. C 3688.

[47] *... hetur upanayo nigamanam uttaraṃ dṛṣṭāntaḥ siddhāntaḥ ...*

"reply" (*uttara*) and before "accomplished doctrine" (*siddhānta*) is the genuine sequence in both recensions. The other position of *dṛṣṭānta* between "reason" (*hetu*) and "application" (*upanaya*) as in Trikamji's edition,[48] which is not supported by any of the manuscripts, must be attributed to Gaṅgādhara's edition of his commentary *Jalpakalpataru* in which he tries to standardize the reading of the *Carakasaṃhitā* with the sequence in the *Nyāyasūtra* by stating directly following his commentary on *hetu*: "Now, according to the correct sequence [of members of proof], the example is defined."[49] Also the manuscript of the *Āyurvedadīpikā*, in its sequence of definitions, supports the manuscripts of the *Carakasaṃhitā* in the positioning of *dṛṣṭānta* after *uttara* and before *siddhānta*,[50] although Cakrapāṇidatta does not quote the list. The topic "*dṛṣṭānta*" in the *Carakasaṃhitā* is meant to define the general example (*dṛṣṭānta*), not the member of proof *udāharaṇa* (exemplification)[51] of the *Nyāyasūtra* as Gaṅgādhara suggests. Moreover, the sequence of the *Nyāyasūtra* does – to some extant – support Caraka's sequence. The general example (*dṛṣṭānta*) in the *Nyāyasūtra* is also placed directly before the *siddhānta* in the list of topics in NSū 1.1.1[52] and in the definition part of its Book 1 as well,[53] in which the definition of the example corresponds for the most part to that of the *Carakasaṃhitā*.[54]

---

[48] Cf. CS Vimānasthāna 8.27: ... *hetuḥ, dṛṣṭāntaḥ, upanayaḥ, nigamanam, uttaraṃ, siddhāntaḥ, ...*

[49] JKT 1580,23: *atha kramikatvād dṛṣṭāntaṃ lakṣayati.*

[50] Cf. CĀ fol. 70r,7–70v,2: ... *hetusāmyam uttaraṃ kriyate tadā viparyyayo bhavati evam evodāharaṇa dvayaṃ saviparyyayaṃ saṃpūr..m uttaraṃ bhavatīty arthaḥ. mūrkhaviduṣāṃ buddhisāmyam ity anena laukikānāṃ paṇḍitānāñ ca yo 'rthe. vivādasiddhaḥ sa dṛṣṭānto bhavati ...*

[51] NSū 1.1.36f.; cf. Prets 2004.

[52] NSū 1.1.1: *pramāṇaprameyasaṃśayaprayojanadṛṣṭāntasiddhāntāvayavatarkanirṇayavādajalpavitaṇḍāhetvābhāsacchalajātinigrahasthānānāṃ tattvajñānān niḥśreyasādhigamaḥ.*

[53] Cf. NSū 1.1.25f.

[54] Cf. CS Vimānasthāna 8.34: *dṛṣṭānto nama yatra mūrkhaviduṣāṃ buddhisāmyaṃ yo varṇyaṃ varṇayati*; and NSū 1.1.25: *laukikaparīkṣakānāṃ yasminn arthe buddhisāmyaṃ sa dṛṣṭāntaḥ.*

Even Gaṅgādhara, in his *Mṛtyuñjayasaṃhitā*,[55] does not support the reading of his own edition,[56] but reads in accordance with the manuscripts.[57]

With regard to the text of the establishment or proof (*sthāpanā*)[58] of the proposition (*pratijñā*), it is clear that all thirty-six manuscripts that have been consulted so far do not support Gaṅgādhara's reading and, accordingly, Trikamji's edition that depends on Gaṅgādhara's edition.[59] Again it seems that Trikamji believed in the correct reading of his antecessors when editing the *Carakasaṃhitā*, who for their part apparently believed more in the authenticity of the *Jalpakalpataru*'s reading[60] than in the evidence from the manuscripts. Gaṅgādhara comments on the example of the *sthāpanā* passage in his *Jalpakalpataru* firstly: *kaḥ punar iha dṛṣṭānta ity āha dṛṣṭānta ityādi. yathākāśam iti.* He then proceeds to explain why the ether is able to serve as an example for the case in question. Obviously it was Gaṅgādhara who placed the sequence *yathākāśam iti* as a Pratīka in his *Jalpakalpataru* and added it accordingly in his edition of the *Carakasaṃhitā*. And again, Gaṅgādhara

---

[55] To my knowledge this work of Gaṅgādhara exists in only a single copy in Gaṅgādhara's own hand at the Calcutta Sanskrit College (Sanskrit College, Kolkata, Āyurveda handlist, Ms. no. 153). It is a rearrangement of the *Carakasaṃhitā*, in which he has taken the text apart and arranged it anew according to a didactical point of view. (cf. various colophons of the Mṛtyuñjayasaṃhitā: ... *iti carakakṛtasaṃhitāyāṃ gaṅgādhareṇa pravibhaktamiśritāyāṃ mṛtyuñjayasaṃhitāyāṃ* ...).

[56] CS 1878/79 (1st edition 1868).

[57] This fact points to the assumption that he wrote his *Jalpakalpataru* later than the *Mṛtyuñjayasaṃhitā*.

[58] CS Vimānasthāna 8.31.

[59] Cf. CS Vimānasthāna 8.30f.: *atha pratijñā – pratijñā nāma sādhyavacanaṃ; yathā – nityaḥ puruṣa iti. atha sthāpanā – sthāpanā nāma tasyā eva pratijñāyā hetudṛṣṭāntopanayanigamanaiḥ sthāpanā. pūrvaṃ hi pratijñā, paścāt sthāpanā, kiṃ hy apratijñātaṃ sthāpayiṣyati; yathā – nityaḥ puruṣa iti pratijñā; hetuḥ – akṛtakatvād iti; dṛṣṭāntaḥ – yathākāśam iti; upanayaḥ – yathā cākṛtakam ākāśaṃ, tac ca nityaṃ, tathā puruṣa iti; nigamanaṃ – tasmān nitya iti.*

[60] JKT 1577,22-24: *kaḥ punar iha dṛṣṭānta ity āha dṛṣṭānta ityādi. yathākāśam iti, ākāśasamānadharmavattvena puruṣasya nityatvasādhako akṛtakatvam iti hetuḥ.*

himself does not support this reading in his *Mṛtyuñjayasaṃhitā*, but for the most part reads in accordance with the other manuscripts.

With regard to the counter-establishment or counter-proof (*pratiṣṭhāpanā*),[61] the relation of the editions of Gaṅgādhara, and respectively Trikamji, and the manuscripts is, structurally seen, completely the same.

The formulation of example and application in the provisional critical edition (cf. appendix) still has to be understood with due care. At present, it is too early to draw conclusions from formulations that may be revised when new material appears. Nevertheless, if one compares Trikamji's edition to the formulation in the manuscripts, one may appreciate what critical work on manuscripts can bring to light: Instead of the mere representation of an instance (*yathākāśam*) in which both properties are known to coexist in a kind of relationship that implicitly allows one to deduce one property from the other, as can only be seen by the formulation of the application, the manuscript's reading explicitly mentions both properties as coexisting in this instance. The function of the application is also clearly expressed, namely that the proving property subsists in the subject of proof and therefore allows, on condition of the concomitance of the proving property and the property to be proved in the example, the conclusion that also the subject of proof exemplifies the property to be proved.

To conclude, let me finally point out that the formulation of the *sthāpanā* in this form is very close in structure to the formulation of the proof in the *Nyāyabhāṣya*.[62] However, it will be possible to draw a conclusion from this statement only when the project has made further progress.

---

[61] CS Vimānasthāna 8.32.

[62] NBh 34,12-15: *tatra sādharmyokte tāvad dhetau vākyam, anityaḥ śabda iti pratijñā, utpattidharmakatvād iti hetuḥ, utpattidharmakaṃ sthālyādi dravyam anityam ity udāharaṇam, tathā cotpattidharmakaḥ śabda ity upanayaḥ, tasmād utpattidharmakatvād anityaḥ śabda iti nigamanam.*

APPENDIX:

Preliminary critical edition of *Carakasaṃhitā*, Vimānasthāna 8.30f. on *pratijñā* and *sthāpanā*

The preliminary critical edition is based on sixteen selected manuscripts. Six manuscripts (A, C6, C7, Ch, P1, U) represent the Kashmiri recension, of which the Sharada manuscript P1 is the oldest (1688). Ten manuscripts represent the two branches of the eastern recension: the branch which consists mainly of Bengali manuscripts (C4, C5, Ca, Vi, V4) of which V1 is the oldest (1698), and the branch which comprises only Devanagari manuscripts (B, K, L3, T1, T2), mainly from the 18th century. Additionally, Gaṅgādhara's *Mṛtyuñjayasaṃhitā* is listed at relevant passages in the critical apparatus to provide a comparison to the reading in his later *Jalpakalpataru*.

The critical edition contains only substantial variants. However, some non-substantial variants may be recorded in cases of relevance for establishing the stemmatological affiliation, etc., or in cases of special interest.

Punctuation and regular sandhi of the critical edition are editorial. The variants of the different manuscripts and independent sources are separated by semicolons.

<u>Sigla (of mentioned manuscripts)</u>:

Superscript letters indicate the script of the manuscript:

^{d} Devanagari
^{b} Bengali
^{ś} Sharada

A^{d} Alwar, Rajasthan Oriental Research Institute 2498
B^{d} Baroda, Central Library 12489
C1^{b} Calcutta, Sanskrit College 153, Mṛtyuñjayasaṃhitā (Gaṅgādhara)
C4^{b} Calcutta, National Library RDS 101
C5^{b} Calcutta, Asiatic Society G 4474/3

C6^{b}	Calcutta, Asiatic Society G 2503/1
C7^{d}	Calcutta, Asiatic Society G 4391
Ca^{b}	Cambridge, Trinity College Ms.R.15.85
Ch^{d}	Chandigarh, DAV College 2315
K^{d}	Kota, Rajasthan Oriental Research Institute 1563
L3^{d}	London, India Office Library Ms IO. 1445b
P1^{ś}	Pune, Bhandarkar Oriental Research Institute 555 of 1875-76
T1^{d}	Tübingen, Universitätsbibliothek 458
T2^{d}	Tübingen, Universitätsbibliothek 459
U^{d}	Udaipur, Rajasthan Oriental Research Institute 6294
V1^{b}	Varanasi, Sarasvati Bhavan 44842
V4^{b}	Varanasi, Sarasvati Bhavan 108824

Symbols used:

I	*daṇḍa*
*	*virāma*
’	*avagraha*
..	illegible *akṣara*, due to blurring, etc.
.	illegible part of an *akṣara*, due to blurring, etc.
[ ]	contain *akṣara* or part of text deleted by scribe; deleted text in grey
[ ]^{2}	contain *akṣara* or part of text unambiguously deleted by second hand; deleted text in grey
〈 〉	contain emendation or corrective insertion (interlinear / inter-*akṣara* / in margin); emended text in grey
〈 〉^{2}	contain emendation or corrective insertion (interlinear / inter-*akṣara* / in margin) unambiguously by second hand; emended text in grey
om.	omitted by manuscript
S:	secondary, additional testimonies / other sources / commentaries

Preliminary critical edition:

> *atha pratijñā*[1]*. pratijñā nāma sādhyavacanam; yathā nityaḥ puruṣa*[2] *iti.*

atha sthāpanā.[3] *sthāpanā nāma tasyā*[4] *eva pratijñāyā hetubhir dṛṣṭāntopanayanigamanaiś ca*[5] *sthāpanā. pūrvaṃ hi pratijñā*[6] *paścāt sthāpanā;*[7] *kiṃ hy apratijñātaṃ*[8] *sthāpayiṣyati?*[9] *yathā:*[10] *nityaḥ puruṣa*[11] *iti pratijñā;*[12] *hetur akṛtakatvād*[13] *iti;*[14] *dṛṣṭāntaḥ – akṛtakam ākāśaṃ tac ca nityam;*[15] *upanayaḥ – yathā cākṛtakam*[16] *ākāśaṃ tathā puruṣaḥ;*[17] *nigamanam – tasmān nitya*[18] *iti.*

---

[1] *atha pratijñā* : B^{d}, C4^{b}, C7^{d}, Ca^{b}, Ch^{d}, K^{d}, L3^{d}, P1^{ś}, T1^{d}, T2^{d}, U^{d}, V1^{b} pratijñā; A^{d} [pratijñā]^{2}⟨pratijñā kramaprāptā kathyate⟩^{2}; om. C5^{b}, C6^{b}

[2] *nityaḥ puruṣa* : C7^{d}, L3^{d} nityapuruṣa

[3] *atha sthāpanā* : A^{d}, C7^{d}, Ca^{b}, Ch^{d}, K^{d}, L3^{d}, P1^{ś}, T1^{d}, T2^{d}, U^{d} sthāpanā; om. B^{d}

[4] *nāma tasyā* : C4^{b}, C5^{b}, V1^{b} nāmaitasyā

[5] *hetubhir dṛṣṭāntopanayanigamanaiś ca* : T1^{d} hetu[bhir]^{2} dṛṣṭāṃtopanayabigaman[au]^{2}aiś ca; B, T2^{d} hetubhir dṛṣṭāṃtopāyanigamanaiś ca; L3^{d} hetubhi dṛṣṭāṃtopāyanigamanaiś ca; K^{d} hetubhir ṣṭāṃdṛtopanayanigamaiś ca; A^{d}, C4^{b}, C7^{d}, V1^{b} hetubhir dṛṣṭāntopanayanigamaiḥ; C5^{b} hetur dṛṣṭāntopanayanigaṃaineḥ; C6^{b} hetubhi .. .. nigamaiḥ; Ch^{d} hetubhiḥ dṛṣṭāntopanayaniga⟨ma⟩^{2}maiḥ; P1^{ś} hetubhiḥ dṛṣṭāntopanayanigamaiḥ; U^{d} hetubhir dṛṣṭāṃtopanayanigamai; Ca^{b}, V4^{b} hetudṛṣṭāntopanayanigamaiḥ

S: ĀD 276a,19: sa ca sādhyaṃ paraṃ prati hetvādibhiś caturbhiḥ sādhyati; C1^{b} hetudṛṣṭāntopanayanigamaiḥ

[6] *pratijñā* : V4 loke pratijñā; T1^{d} ⟨loke⟩^{2} pratijñā; Ca^{b} loko pratijñā

S: C1^{b} loke pratijñā

[7] *hi pratijñā paścāt sthāpanā* : U^{d} hi pratijñāpanā

[8] *kiṃ hi apratijñātaṃ* : B^{d}, L3^{d}, T1^{d}, T2^{d} kiṃcit pratijñātaṃ; K^{d} kiṃcit pratijñānaṃ

[9] *sthāpayiṣyati* : C4^{b}, C5^{b}, T1^{d}, V1^{b} sthāpayiṣyatīti |

[10] *yathā* : B^{d}, K^{d}, L3^{d} tathā; T1^{d} ta⟨ya⟩^{2}thā; T2^{d} sathā; om. Ch^{d}

[11] *nityaḥ puruṣa* : C7^{d}, K^{d} nityapuruṣa; T1^{d} nitya⟨ḥ⟩puruṣa

[12] *pratijñā* : T1^{d} [pratijñā]^{2}⟨prasiddhā⟩^{2}

[13] *akṛtakatvād* : B^{d}, C4^{b}, C5^{b}, K^{d}, L3^{d}, V1^{b} akṛtakatvaṃ; T1^{d} akṛtakatvaṃ⟨āt*⟩^{2}; T2^{d} akṛtakṛtvaṃ; P1^{ś} akṛtatvād

[14] *iti* : om. B^{d}, C4^{b}, C5^{b}, Ca^{b}, K^{d}, L3^{d}, T1^{d}, T2^{d}, V1^{b}

[15] *dṛṣṭāntaḥ – akṛtakam ākāśaṃ tac ca nityam* : B^{d}, T2^{d} dṛṣṭānto kṛtakam ākāśaṃ tac ca nityaṃ iti; L3^{d} dṛṣṭānto kṛtakam ākāśaṃ tac ca nityam; C6^{b}

REFERENCES

Texts and abbreviations

ĀD = [*Āyurvedadīpikā*]. See CS.

CU = [*Carakopaskāra*]. See CS 1920-22.

CS = [*Carakasaṃhitā*]. *The Charakasaṃhitā of Agniveśa. Revised by Charaka and Dṛidhabala. With the Āyurveda-Dīpikā Commentary of Chakrapāṇidatta.* Collated and edited by Vaidya Jādavji Trikamji Āchārya. 3rd edition. Bombay: Nirṇaya Sāgara Press, 1941 (1st edition 1933).

CS 1877 = *Carakasaṃhitā. Sūtra-nidāna-vimāna-śārīrendriya-cikitsita-kalpa-siddhisthānātmakā āyurvedīya bhagavatā ātreyeṇa upadiṣṭā agniveśa-nāmadheyena tat śiṣyeṇa viracitā carakābhidhānena ṛṣiṇā pratisaṃskṛtā.* Śrī jīvānanda vidyāsāgara bhaṭṭācāryyeṇa bahūni ādarśapustakāni samālocya saṃskṛtā prakāśitā ca. Kalikātā: Sarasvatī Yantra, 1877.

CS 1878/79 = *Charaka-sanhita. A System of Hindu Medicine with Notes Jalpa-kalpa-taru by Kaviraj Gangadhar Kaviratna.* Published by Dharanidhar Ray Kaviraj. *Ayurvvedīya carakasaṃhitā. vaidyagaṅgādhararayaka-viratnakavirājakṛta jalpakalpataru nāma vyākhyā sahitā.* Dharanidhar raya kavirāja karttṛka prakāśita. Baharampore-Saidābād: Pramāda-bhañjana-yantre mudrita 1878/1879 (saṃvat 1935). [New edition of the 1st edition. Kolkata: Saṃvādajñānaratnākarākhyayantra 1868 by Gaṅgādhara Kavirāj).

CS 1884/85 = *Carakasaṃhitā bhagavadatrinandana-punarvvasūpadiṣṭeṇa dhīmadagniveśena viracitā carakanāmadheyena vyādhipravareṇa pratisaṃskṛtā ca.* Śrīavināśacandra kaviratna kavirājena [vaṅga-bhāṣāyām] anūditā pariśodhitā ca. Kalikātā: Vidyāratna Yantra, 1884/85 (saṃvat 1941).

CS 1892-1919 = *Carakasaṃhitā, maharṣināgniveśena praṇītā maharṣicaraka-pratisaṃskṛtā bhiṣakkulatilakacarakacaturānanaśrīmaccakrapāṇidatta-kṛtaṭīkāsamvalitaṃ* (sic!) kavirāja śrīharinātha viśāradena saṃśodhitā sampāditā. Kalikātā: 1892-1919 (śakābdā 1814-41).

---

dṛṣṭāntaḥ ya akṛtakam ākāśaṃ tac ca nityaṃ; C4^{b}, V1^{b}, V4^{b} dṛṣṭānto yathā akṛtakam ākāśaṃ tac ca nityam iti; C5^{b} dṛṣṭānto yathā I akṛtakam ākāśaṃ tava nityam iti

S: C1^{b} dṛṣṭānto yathā cākṛtakam ākāśaṃ tac ca nityam

16 *cākṛtakam* : T1^{d} cākṛta⟨ka⟩^{2}m; C6^{b}, U^{d} cākṛtam; A^{d} cā[..]ta⟨ka⟩^{2}m; L3^{d} cākṣatakam

17 *ākāśaṃ tathā puruṣaḥ* : Ca^{b} ākāśa tathā puruṣa iti; T1^{d} ākāśaṃ tathā puruṣaḥ ⟨iti⟩^{2}; C6^{b}, Ch^{d} ākāśas tathā puruṣaḥ

18 *nitya* : C5^{b} nityam

CS 1894 = *Carakasaṃhitā.* Mūla o vaṅgānuvāda yaśodānandan sarkār. Calcutta 1894.

CS 1896 = *Carakasaṃhitā, sūtra-nidāna-vimāna-śārīrendriya-cikitsita-kalpa-siddhisthānātmakā āyurvedīya bhagavatā ātreyeṇa upadiṣṭā agniveśa-nāmadheyena tat śiṣyeṇa viracitā carakābhidhānena ṛṣiṇā pratisaṃs-kṛtā.* Śrī jīvānanda vidyāsāgara bhaṭṭācāryyeṇa bahūni ādarśapustakāni samālocya saṃskṛtā prakāśitā ca. Dvitīyasaṃskaraṇam [2nd edition]. Kalikātā: Nārāyaṇayantra, 1896.

CS 1897-98 = *Sārtha śrīcarakasaṃhitā.* Saṃpādaka āyurvedamahopādhyāya śaṃkara dājī śāstrī pade cikitsaka. Prakāśaka yajñeśvara gopāla dīkṣita bukselar. (Shree Charaka Sanhita. With translation & copious notes in Marāṭhī. A quarterly journal). 14 Vols.. Muṃbaī 1897-98.

CS 1920-22 = *The Caraka-samhita.* Edited with an original commentary in Sanskrit by Vaidyaratna Kaviraj Pandit Jogindra Nath Sen. Vol. I, containing the Sloka-sthana (Sutra-sthana), Published by Y. N. Sen, Calcutta 1920. Vol. II, containing the Nidana, Vimana, Sarira and Indriya Sthanas. Calcutta 1922.

CS 1922 = *The Carakasaṃhita by Agnivesha. With the Āyurveda-Dīpikā Commentary of Chakrapāni Dutta.* Ed. by Vaidya Bhūshan Vāman Kesheo Dātār of Nāsik. Bombay: Nirnaya Sagara Press, 1922.

CS 1927-33 = *Caraka-saṃhitā mahāmuninā bhagavadāgniveśena praṇītā maharṣicarakeṇa pratisaṃskṛtā. carakacaturānana-śrīmaccakrapāṇidatta-praṇītayā āyurvedadīpikākhyaṭīkayā mahāmahopādhyāya-śrīgaṅgādharakaviratnakavirājaviracitayā jalpakalpatarusamākhyayā ṭīkayā ca samalaṅkṛtā.* Kavirājaśrīnarendranāthasenaguptena kavirāja śrībalāicandrasenaguptena ca sampāditā saṃśodhitā prakāśitā ca. Calcutta 1927, 1928, 1933.

CS 1970 = *Carakasaṃhitā maharṣiṇā bhagavadāgniveśena praṇītā mahāmuninā carakeṇa pratisaṃskṛtā, āyurvedācāryaśrījayadevavidyālaṅkāreṇa praṇītayā tattvārthadīpikākhyayā hindīvyākhyayā ṭippaṇyā ca samanvitā.* Pūrvo bhāgaḥ, madhyo bhāgaḥ, uttaro bhāgaḥ. 8th edition. Varanasi: Motilal Banarsidas, 1970. [1st edition: Lahore 1934-36.]

CS 1976-97 = *Agniveśa's Caraka Saṃhitā (Text with English Translation & Critical Exposition Based on Cakrapāṇidatta's Āyurveda Dipikā)* by Dr. Ram Karan Sharma and Vaidya Bhagwan Dash. 5 vols. (Chowkhamba Sanskrit Studies, 94.) Varanasi 1976-97.

CS 1981-94 = *Caraka-Saṃhitā. Agniveśa's Treatise Refined and Annotated by Caraka and Redacted by Dṛḍhabala. (Text with English translation).* Editor-Translator Prof. Priyavrat Sharma. (Jaikrishnadas Ayurveda Series, 36.) Vol. I (Sūtrasthāna to Indriyasthāna); vol. II (Cikitsāsthāna to Siddhisthāna); vol. III Critical Notes (incorporating the commentaries of Jejjaṭa, Cakrapāṇi, Gaṅgādhara and Yogīndranātha); vol. III (Sūtrasthāna to Indriyasthāna); vol. IV Critical Notes (Cikitsāsthāna to Siddhisthāna). Varanasi: Chaukhamba Orientalia, 1981, 1983, 1985, 1994.

CS 1983-88 = *The Caraka-Saṃhitā (As Precepted by the Great Sage Ātreya Punarvasu) of Agniveśa. Elaborated by Caraka & Dṛḍhabala. Edited with "Charaka-Chandrika" Hindi Commentary along with Special Deliberation etc.* by Brahmanand Tripathi. Foreword by Ganga Sahay Pandey (1st vol.), Forword by Prabhakar Janardan Deshpande (2nd vol.). (Chaukhamba Ayurvijnan Granthamala, 11.) 2 vols. Varanasi: Chaukhamba Surbharati Prakashan, 1983, 1988.

JKT = [*Jalpakalpataru*]. See CS 1927-33.

NBh = [*Nyāyabhāṣya*]. *Gautamīyanyāyadarśana with Bhāṣya of Vātsyāyana.* Ed. by Anantalal Thakur. (Nyāyacaturgranthikā Vol. I.) New Delhi 1997.

NSū = [*Nyāyasūtra*]. See Ruben 1928.

Secondary literature

CORDIER, Palmyr 1902. Récentes découvertes de Mss. médicaux sanskrits dans l'Inde (1898-1902). Mémoire présenté au Congrès des Orientalistes de Hanoi (1902). [Un sommaire de ce mémoire a été publie dans les Actes du Congrès, p. 69.] In: Roşu 1989: 539-570.

DASGUPTA, Surendranath Dasgupta 1922. *A History of Indian Philosophy*, II. Cambridge 1922. (Reprint: Delhi: Motilal Banarsidass, 1991).

FRAUWALLNER, Erich 1984. *Nachgelassene Werke*, I: *Aufsätze, Beiträge, Skizzen.* Hrsg. Ernst Steinkellner. (Österreichische Akademie der Wissenschaften, phil.-hist. Kl., Sitzungsberichte, 438 = Veröffentlichungen der Kommission für Sprachen und Kulturen Südasiens, 19.) Wien 1984.

KANG, Sung Yong 1998. *Zur altindischen Tradition der Debatte gemäß der medizinischen Überlieferung. Übersetzung und ideengeschichtliche Untersuchung von Carakasaṃhitā Vi.8.15-28.* Wissenschaftliche Hausarbeit zur Erlangung des akademischen Grades eines Magister Artium der Universität Hamburg. Hamburg 1998.

MEULENBELD, G. Jan 1999. *A History of Indian Medical Literature.* Vol. IA: Text. Vol. IB: Annotation. (Groningen Oriental Studies, 15.) Groningen 1999.

OETKE, Claus 1994. *Vier Studien zum Altindischen Syllogismus.* (Philosophia Indica, Einsichten – Ansichten, Bd. 2.) Reinbek 1994.

PRETS, Ernst 2000. Theories of debate, proof and counter-proof in the early Indian dialectical tradition. In: Piotr Balcerowicz & Marek Mejor (eds.), *On Understanding Other Cultures – Proceedings of the International*

Conference on Sanskrit and Related Studies to Commemorate the Centenary of the Birth of Stanislaw Schayer (1899-1941). Warsaw University, Poland, October 7-10, 1999 (Studia Indologiczne, 7): 369-382. Warsaw 2000.

—— 2004. Example and exemplification in early Nyāya and Vaiśeṣika. In: Shoryu Katsura & Ernst Steinkellner (eds.), *On the Role of the Example* (dṛṣṭānta) *in Classical Indian Logic.* (Wiener Studien zur Tibetologie und Buddhismuskunde, 58): 197-224. Wien 2004.

ROŞU, Arion 1989. *Un demi-siècle de recherches āyurvediques. Gustave Liétard et Palmyr Cordier. Travaux sur l'histoire de la médicine indienne. Documents réunis et présentés par Arion Roșu.* (Publications de l'Institut de Civilisation Indienne in-8, 56.) Paris 1989.

ROTH, Rudolf von 1872. Indische Medicin. *Zeitschrift der Deutschen Morgenländischen Gesellschaft* 26: 441-452.

RUBEN, Walter 1928. *Die Nyāyasūtra's. Text, Übersetzung, Erläuterung und Glossar*. (Abhandlungen für die Kunde des Morgenlandes 18.2.) Leipzig 1928.

SOLOMON, Esther A. 1976. *Indian Dialectics. Methods of Philosophical Discussion.* 2 Vols. (B.J. Institute of Learning and Research, Research Series 70 & 74.) Ahmedabad 1976, 1978.

TUCCI, Guiseppe 1929. *Pre-Diṅnāga Buddhist Texts on Logic from Chinese Sources.* (Gaekwad's Oriental Series, 49.) Baroda 1929.

UI, Hakuju 1925. The Sanskrit text of the Caraka-Samhita. *Indo Tetsugaku Kenkyū* [The Studies in Indian Philosophy] 2: 600-587. Tokyo 1925.

TPHSI 1, 2 = *Terminologie der frühen philosophischen Scholastik in Indien. Ein Begriffswörterbuch zur altindischen Dialektik, Erkenntnislehre und Methodologie.* Gerhard Oberhammer, Ernst Prets und Joachim Prandstetter. Herausgegeben von Gerhard Oberhammer. Band 1: A-I, Band 2: U-Pū. (Beiträge zur Kultur- und Geistesgeschichte Asiens, 9 & 17.) Wien: Österreichische Akademie der Wissenschaften, 1991, 1996.

VIDYABHUSANA, Satis Chandra 1920. *A History of Indian Logic (Ancient, Mediaeval and Modern Schools).* 3rd edition. Delhi: Motilal Banarsidass, 1978.

ADDENDUM (March 2008)

This article is based on a paper I presented at the Helsinki World Sanskrit Conference in 2003. The final version was completed about one year later.

At the time of my final version I was engaged in the preliminary work on a critical edition of Vimānasthāna 8 of the *Carakasaṃhitā* together with Karin Preisendanz, who acted as project director. In October 2004, Philipp Maas joined the project as a second collaborator. At that point in time, the project was extended to all eight chapters of the Vimānasthāna. A year later, Cristina Pecchia also joined the project. And I left the project in 2006 to work on a new project of my own.

During the last years, not only did the number of manuscripts increase and the stemma was defined more precisely – mainly by Philipp Maas – but also the methodology of compiling the manuscripts gradually changed as well as the critical edition's method and form. Therefore my preliminary critical edition of the passage on proof, which I still hold to be more or less adequate, deviates fundamentally in form and character from the work being currently done.

In this place I must acknowledge my indebtedness to the following institutions for permitting the use of *Carakasaṃhitā* manuscripts as well as these institutes' members and employees for their gracious assistance (listed according to their appearance in this paper): DAV College, Lalchand Research Library (Chandigarh), National Library (Kolkata), Nepal-German Manuscript Preservation Project (Hamburg), Bhandarkar Oriental Research Institute (Pune), Raghunath Temple Library of His Highness The Maharaja of Jammu and Kashmir (Jammu), Rajasthan Oriental Research Institute (Jodhpur, Udaipur, Kota, Alwar), Asiatic Society of Bengal (Kolkata), Sarasvati Bhavan Library (Varanasi), Central Library (Baroda), India Office Library (London), Ānandāśrama (Pune), Universitätsbibliothek Tübingen, Benares Hindu University (Varanasi), and the Trinity College (Cambridge).

The Logical Reason Called *virodhin* in Vaiśeṣika and Its Significance for Connection-based Theories of Reasoning

BIRGIT KELLNER

INTRODUCTION[1]

In Indian logic, inference gradually acquired a standard form where one infers from the instantiation of one state of affairs in a locus to that of another, and whose three main components are a logical subject (*pakṣa*), a reason (*hetu*) and an inferendum (*sādhya*). Certain divergences notwithstanding, Indian logicians generally came to agree that the soundness of an inference is guaranteed by a specific type of connection between reason and inferendum.

Up to and including Dignāga (ca. 480-540 CE), we can broadly distinguish two connection-based approaches to reasoning. In Vṛṣagaṇa's *Ṣaṣṭitantra*, according to E. Frauwallner completed around 300 CE, inference is defined as "on the basis of a connection [between two objects], the establishment of the remainder from the one", or "... from the one [object which is] perceived".[2] The text

[1] Throughout this paper, sandhi and punctuation in Sanskrit passages have been standardised and may differ from the conventions used in the respective editions or manuscripts.

[2] YD 5,12: *sambandhād ekasmāc cheṣasiddhir anumānam*, NV 53,6 and NĀA 240,11: ... *ekasmāt pratyakṣāc cheṣasiddhir anumānam*. NC 240,1, which is commented upon in NĀA, also presupposes the text with *pratyakṣāt*.

enumerates seven such connections.[3] Along similar lines, *Vaiśeṣikasūtras* 3.1.9 and 9.18[4] list entities that can function as reasons (*apadeśa*) or inferential signs (*liṅga*), using terms like "conjunct" (*saṃyogin*) or "effect" (*kārya*) that denote relata of a connection.[5] These early sources represent *intension-based* views of connections: it is the content of the connection, the fact that it is a "conjunction" or an "opposition", which is responsible for the adequacy of the inference from one connected item to the other. Dignāga's *trairūpya*-theory, on the other hand, represents an *extension-based* approach in that the distribution of the reason among certain instances decides about its adequacy in an inference.

One of the items listed in VS 3.1.9 and 9.18 is termed *virodhin*, "the/an opposed". VS 3.1.9 lists four varieties of it. None of the vastly divergent accounts offered in the rather late commentaries of Candrānanda (active after Uddyotakara and probably before Helarāja), Bhaṭṭa Vādīndra (13th century)[6] and Śaṅkaramiśra (16th century), which consist largely of example inferences, indicates a plausible rationale behind the emergence of this fourfold list. Modern treatments of the *virodhin* thus far are based on one commentary or another and simply present its interpretation;[7] no

[3] Cf. Frauwallner 1958: 117, and Motegi 1985: 139-140; 1989: 51, n. 10.

[4] The numbering of *Vaiśeṣikasūtras* follows Isaacson's reconstruction of the *sūtrapāṭha* manuscripts (Isaacson 1995: 220, 274). The numbers in the various editions differ slightly.

[5] For a survey of early *sambandha*-based theories of reasoning, see Katsura, "On the Origin and Development of the concept of *vyāpti* in Indian Logic", *Hiroshima-Tetsugaku-Kai* 38 (1986), 1-16, an English summary of the more extensive Japanese publication "Indo-ronrigaku ni okeru henjū-gainen no seisei to hatten (The origin and development of the concept of *vyāpti* in Indian Logic)", *Hiroshima-Daigaku-Bungakubu-Kiyō* 45, *Tokushō* 1; cf. also Oberhammer, Prets & Prandstetter 1991: 43-60.

[6] For the dates of Candrānanda and Bhaṭṭa Vādīndra cf. Isaacson 1995.

[7] See e.g. Faddegon 1918: 298; Gough 1872: 82ff.; Oberhammer, Prets & Prandstetter 1991: 46; Röer 1867: 367; Sinha 1956: 289f.; Schuster 1972; Thakur 2003: 58f., and Ui 1917: 157. Most of these are complete or partial translations of *sūtras* with more or less extensive annotation. Oberhammer, Prets & Prandstetter, Schuster and Thakur rely on Candrānanda's account, whereas

attempts have been made to investigate the significance of the *virodhin* or the thought process that resulted in the puzzling list of its four varieties.

A fragment from what must have been a pre-Candrānanda, and most probably even a pre-Dignāga, commentary on the *sūtras*, preserved in Jinendrabuddhi's *Pramāṇasamuccayaṭīkā*, presents us with a unique account of the four forms of the *virodhin.* Viewed in connection with other evidence, such as certain passages in Vātsyāyana's *Nyāyabhāṣya* and Dignāga's *Pramāṇasamuccaya-vṛtti*, it indicates that the fourfold list is the result of a gradual process. This fragment also clarifies the relationship between the two *sūtras* 3.1.9 and 9.18, to the effect that 3.1.9 was most probably extracted from a prose-commentary on 9.18. Finally, what must have been the earliest form of the *virodhin* betrays an interesting connection with the topic of explanation that may well be significant for future, more detailed assessments of the character of early connection-based reasoning at large.

VAIŚEṢIKASŪTRAS 3.1.9 AND 9.18: TEXT AND TRANSLATION

VS 3.1.9 is transmitted as part of the commentaries by Candrānanda (C 26,2ff.) and Śaṅkaramiśra (ŚM 88,14ff.), and of the abridged version of Bhaṭṭa Vādīndra's commentary (BhV 35,19ff.). It is absent from the manuscript of the extensive version of Bhaṭṭa Vādīndra's commentary, published by A. Thakur in 1985, which only extends up to the second *āhnika* of the second *adhyāya*. The *sūtra* is further contained in the Trivandrum (T) and Ahmedabad (A) *sūtrapāṭha* manuscripts edited in Harunaga Isaacson's 1995 PhD thesis which unfortunately remains unpublished, but must nevertheless be referenced here because it is the sole source of much philological information about the *sūtra* text. VS 3.1.9 is part

---

earlier interpretations are based on the 16th-century *Vaiśeṣikasūtropaskāra* by Śaṅkaramiśra.

of an *āhnika* dealing predominantly with the *ātman* whose flow of argument has been viewed diversely by traditional and modern interpreters alike,[8] but these larger issues can be set aside for our examination of the list of reasons that it contains.

VS 3.1.9:

[1] *saṃyogi samavāyy ekārthasamavāyi virodhi ca.*
[2] *kāryaṃ kāryāntarasya, kāraṇaṃ kāraṇāntarasya.*
[3] *virodhy abhūtaṃ bhūtasya, bhūtam abhūtasya, bhūtaṃ bhūtasya, abhūtam abhūtasya.*

[1] A conjunct, [an entity] qualified by inherence, [an entity] qualified by inherence of [two] things in/by the same,[9] and an opposed (*virodhin*) [entity are reasons].[10]
[2] An effect [is a reason] for another effect, a cause for another cause.
[3] An opposed [entity is a reason in one of the following ways:] an absent [opposed entity is a reason] for [its] present [counterpart], a present one for [its] absent [counterpart], a present one for [its] present [counterpart], an absent one for [its] absent [counterpart].

Segment [1] lists four items that can function as reasons, or inferential signs, and segments [2] and [3] add varieties of the two items *ekārthasamavāyin* and *virodhin*. These varieties are not mentioned in Candramati's *Daśapadārthaśāstra*, composed roughly between 450 and 550 CE, and preserved only in Chinese translation,

---

[8] See especially Hattori 1966 and, as a reaction to it, Oetke 1988.

[9] The compound analysis, with its two alternatives comprising the two varieties of *ekārthasamavāyin* listed in segment [2], is borrowed from the Jinendrabuddhi fragment, cf. further below. Alternatively, *ekārthasamavāya* could be analysed as "inherence [of two entities] in/by the same thing". C, BhV and ŚM do not reveal their analysis of the compound.

[10] In the context of 3.1.9, the implied predicate must be *apadeśa*, here meaning "reason" and not, as in other contexts, "statement of a reason". Cf. BhV 36,4: *apadeśa iti śeṣaḥ*. C and ŚM supply *liṅga*, which may be a remnant of the context of 9.18 from which 3.1.9 was derived. For our purposes, *liṅga* and *apadeśa* can in this context be treated as synonyms.

Nenninger (1992: 52) translates segment [1] as a mere list, without an implied predicate. But would not someone who had just listened to *sūtra*s 3.1.7 and 3.1.8 that deal with reasons and now hears the list "a conjunct, [an entity] qualified by inherence ..." automatically supply an implied predicate and therefore treat the list as an elliptical sentence?

which might mean that segments [2] and [3] entered the *sūtra* text comparably late.[11]

The translations of *bhūta* and *abhūta* as "present" and "absent" respectively are influenced by the earliest preserved accounts of the *virodhin* in the *Nyāyabhāṣya* and the Jinendrabuddhi fragment as presented further below, where *bhūta* is taken to indicate the actual presence of an empirical phenomenon like rainfall in a specific situational setting, and *abhūta* the corresponding absence. The repetition of the expression "*virodhin*" from segment [1] at the beginning of segment [3] suggests that it reminds the target audience which of the four reasons is differentiated in the following list. In the above translation, it is therefore taken as an elliptical sentence in its own right, with the expectation of a specification to follow. Since the implied predicate "... is a reason" from the preceding segments most likely continues in segment [3], the neuter nominatives *abhūtaṃ* and *bhūtaṃ* can hardly be predicates, which would yield sentences like "an opposed is *abhūta* / an *abhūta* for *bhūta* / a *bhūta*".[12] Rather, the general construction will be: "an opposed [is a reason in one of the following ways:] an absent [opposed is a reason] for [its] present [counterpart] ...".[13]

As will be demonstrated further below, the Jinendrabuddhi fragment indicates that the list in VS 3.1.9 was derived from VS 9.18 through the intermediary of a prose-commentary on 9.18. VS 9.18

---

[11] Cf. the Chinese text of the general definition of inference in Miyamoto 1996: 262 (no. 149), English translation p. 192, and the text of the definition of the two forms of inference, with or without perception of a generality, on p. 257 (no. 43), translation p. 173. The latter is translated into German in Frauwallner, 1955: 73f.; cf. p. 80 there for Candramati's date.

[12] This possibility was adopted in Nenninger's translation (1992: 59, n. 106): "Gegensätzliches ist Nicht-Vorhandenes für Vorhandenes, Vorhandenes für Nicht-Vorhandenes, Nicht-Vorhandenes für Nicht-Vorhandenes, Vorhandenes für Vorhandenes." There it is more plausible because Nenninger construes segment [1] as a mere list, and not as an elliptical sentence.

[13] The translation in Schuster 1972: 388, "the non-existence of the contrary ...", is based on an, in my opinion, unlikely reading of *virodhyabhūtam* as a compound.

is contained in A and T, in C, in ŚM, and in the anonymous *Sena Court commentary* (S), the 9th *adhyāya* of which Thakur printed in the appendix to his 1985 edition of Bhaṭṭa Vādīndra's extensive commentary. The manuscript of Bhaṭṭa Vādīndra's abridged commentary does not extend up to this point. A survey of all presently known editions as well as quotations suggests the following as the earliest form of this *sūtra*:

> *asyedaṃ kāryaṃ kāraṇaṃ sambandhy ekārthasamavāyi virodhi ceti laiṅgikam.*[14]
>
> This is an effect of that, this is a cause of that, this is connected with that, this is, in regards to that, [an entity] qualified by inherence of [two] things in/by the same, and this is an opposed [entity] with reference to that – [cognition] caused by a sign (*laiṅgika*) [is characterised by] such [connections].[15]

This *sūtra* characterises inferential cognition – *laiṅgika* is short for *laiṅgikaṃ jñānaṃ* – through phrases of the common structure "this is X / an X with regards to that" (*asyedaṃ* X). All items listed are connection-based expressions, like "an opposed" (*virodhin*) or

---

[14] This form of the *sūtra* is contained in A, C, T, and SVR 531,21. It is also presupposed in the Jinendrabuddhi fragment.

SVR reads *veti* for *ceti*, apparently a misreading of the manuscript caused by the close resemblance of the letters °*va*° and °*ca*° therein. PSV K(Q) 116a8 has **kāraṇaṃ kāryaṃ*, while PSV V(D) 33b4 and PSV V(Q) 35a2 read **kāryaṃ kāraṇaṃ*. The Jinendrabuddhi fragment follows the latter sequence. A quotation in Vyom II 157,18 reads *asyedaṃ kāryaṃ kāraṇaṃ saṃyogi samavāyi virodhi ceti laiṅgikam*, and a quotation in KĀ 202,1f. has *asyedaṃ kāraṇaṃ kāryaṃ saṃyogi virodhi samavāyi ceti laiṅgikam*, but Udayana immediately afterwards gives the sequence *asyedaṃ kāryam*, *asyedaṃ kāraṇam* as the first two items. Other minor variants include the omission of *laiṅgikam* in S, and the omission of *ekārthasamavāyi* in ŚM and in the quotations in KĀ and Vyom.

As mentioned further below, the Jinendrabuddhi fragment expresses the view that *sambandhin* has the two varieties *samavāyin* and *saṃyogin*. This interpretation can be held responsible for the replacement of *sambandhin* by the other two terms in the *sūtra* versions preserved in S, ŚM, and in the quotations in KĀ and Vyom.

[15] For alternative translations, cf. Ui 1917: 156; Randle 1930: 148f.; Schuster 1972: 388; Katsura 1981: 53; Oberhammer, Prets & Prantstetter 1991: 46: On Praśastapāda's treatment of the *sūtra* cf. Nenninger 1992: 58f.

"connected" (*sambandhin*), or connection-indicating terms, like "effect" (*kārya*) and "cause" (*kāraṇa*). The *sūtra* can safely be read as conveying the idea that an inference from one entity to another is adequate because there is a connection between the two, even if it remains unclear how precisely this "adequacy" would have been thought of by the *sūtra*'s author. The neuter gender of the expressions *sambandhi*, *ekārthasamavāyi* and *virodhi* can be explained in different ways. Either these are predicative adjectives, in which case they are in agreement with the subject *idam*, or they are nouns, in which case their neuter gender may secondarily derive from a still older use of them as adjectives together with *liṅga* or with nouns used in individual example inferences; a combination of both possibilities is also conceivable. The above translation thus remains liberal in this respect.

The neuter gender of the three terms is also of relevance for assessing the relationship between VS 3.1.9 and 9.18. For while the terms listed in 3.1.9 are also of neuter gender, the *sūtra*s before and after discuss reasons (*apadeśa*)[16] and there is no neuter noun in them which might have occasioned the formation of neuter terms for reasons. If the terms had been formed as names for types of *apadeśa*, they would have been masculine. The neuter terms in

---

[16] VS 3.1.7: *anya eva hetur ity anapadeśaḥ*, with ŚM *anyad* for *anya* in all other witnesses; VS 3.1.8: *arthāntaraṃ hy arthāntarasyānapadeśaḥ*; VS 3.1.10: *prasiddhipūrvakatvād apadeśasya* (with variants for *prasiddhipūrvakatvāt* that need not be discussed here).

The *sūtra* 3.1.8 is absent in both manuscripts for the commentary of C consulted by Jambūvijaya, but present in BhV and ŚM and in the *sūtrapāṭha* manuscripts A and T. In addition, the Jaina Devanāgarī manuscript of C contains a separate *sūtrapāṭha* in the beginning which also contains 3.1.8, as noted by Jambūvijaya in his Sanskrit notes to C (228f.). Candrānanda's commentary makes it very likely that he, too, knew VS 3.1.8 (C 25,19f.), and that it was omitted from his text due to a scribe's eyeskip from the final °*napadeśaḥ* in 3.1.7 to that of 3.1.8. Probably for this reason, Isaacson 1995: 308, n. 8, conjectures 3.1.8 for C, though "with some hesitation". In Hattori 1966 and Oetke 1988, both of which rely on Candrānanda's *sūtra* text, the problems surrounding 3.1.8 are not discussed; both Hattori and Oetke read the *sūtra* text without 3.1.8, which has, especially in Oetke's case, implications for the interpretation of the entire *āhnika*. These will be addressed on a different occasion.

3.19 must therefore have been derived from neuter terms already in use elsewhere, and this can only have been the context of VS 9.18.[17]

THE PATTERN *ABHŪTAṂ BHŪTASYA* IN THE *NYĀYABHĀṢYA* AND AMONG EARLY MĪMĀṂSAKAS

In the period up to and including Dignāga, our only sources for the understanding of the *virodhin* apart from the Jinendrabuddhi fragment are Vātsyāyana's *Nyāyabhāṣya* and Dignāga's *Pramāṇasamuccaya* and *-vṛtti*, the chronological relationship of which is still uncertain. Out of the four forms of the *virodhin*, only the pattern *abhūtaṃ bhūtasya* occurs in the *Nyāyabhāṣya*. Passages in the *Nyāyabhāṣya* and the *Pramāṇasamuccayavṛtti* further show that certain Mīmāṃsakas appropriated *abhūtaṃ bhūtasya*, some as part of their own theory of inference and others as the basis for stipulating a separate means of valid cognition called "absence".

In the *Nyāyabhāṣya* on NS 2.2.1-2, the pattern *abhūtaṃ bhūtasya* is reported as a case of "absence" (*abhāva*), one of four means of valid cognition which are propounded by other schools and become subsumed under the Nyāya's accepted *pramāṇa*s (cf. Kellner 1997: 47ff.):

---

[17] A comparable antiquity of VS 9.18 in relation to VS 3.1.9 is also assumed in Oberhammer, Prets & Prandstetter 1991, but without any reasons given. In Bronkhorst 1994: 674, it is suggested that 3.1.9 (3.1.8 in Bronkhorst's numbering), just like 9.18, introduced inferential knowledge, and not inferential signs. Somebody, who Bronkhorst believed changed the order of the *sūtra*s in *āhnika* 3.1, may have "adjusted *sūtra* 3.1.8 to his purposes by trimming it". The comparative advantages of this hypothesis, which is formulated in rather vague terms, over alternative candidates are not spelled out. I was unable to find any indicators of such large-scale manipulations in the *sūtra* text itself or in available traditional interpretations. Bronkhorst also remarks that commentators on 3.1.9 (our numbering) "seem to think that these adjectives (*saṃyogi* etc.) characterise the word *liṅga* 'inferential mark', which is not mentioned in the *sūtra*". However, the commentators in fact understand *saṃyogi* etc. as nouns and construe them as subject terms with *liṅga/apadeśa* as predicate.

NBh 99,12-15 on NS 2.2.1:

abhāvo virodhi, abhūtaṃ bhūtasya. avidyamānaṃ varṣakarma vidyamānasya vāyvabhrasaṃyogasya pratipādakam, vidhārake hi vāyvabhrasaṃyoge gurutvād apāṃ patanakarma na bhavatīti.

[Explanation of the means of valid cognition called "absence" assumed by an opponent:] Absence [has the form of] an opposed, [i.e.] [an] absent (*abhūta*) [opposed entity is a means of valid cognition] for [its] present [counterpart] (*bhūta*).[18] Non-existing (*avidyamāna*) rainfall makes existing contact of a rain cloud with wind understood, for if there is contact of a rain cloud with wind, as an obstructive [factor] (*vidhāraka*), there is no movement of falling on the part of water due to its heaviness.

The example, which is the only one given for *abhūtaṃ bhūtasya* in all known sources up to Śaṅkaramiśra,[19] is related to VS 5.2.3 *saṃyogābhāve 'pāṃ gurutvāt patanam*, "water falls due to [its] heaviness if contact [of a rain cloud with wind] is absent." Contact of a rain cloud with wind serves as an obstructive factor (*vidhāraka*) that prevents the heaviness of water from bringing about the motion of rainfall.[20] In accordance with NS 2.2.2, Vātsyāyana subsumes the opponent's "absence" under inference, clarifying its structure as follows: "When an opposition (*virodhitva*) is established [in the form] 'when this exists, that is not possible', a [factor] obstructing the cause (*pratibandhaka*) is inferred from the non-arising (*anutpatti*) of the effect".[21] The "opposition" is therefore a rather con-

[18] Taking into account that *virodhy abhūtaṃ bhūtasya* is word-material incorporated from a Vaiśeṣika text, the placement of *abhāvaḥ* before this phrase suggests that the syntax of the source text was changed in the process of appropriation, turning *virodhi* into a predicate. Alternative construals, e.g. with *abhāvaḥ* as an elliptical sentence in its own right, appear unnecessarily complicated.

[19] ŚM 88,14–89,6 adduces the additional example of an absent, i.e. non-arisen, tumor as a sign for present *mantra*-recitation, which is based on the same structure as the more common one.

[20] Cf. further PDhS section 297: *gurutvaṃ jalabhūmyoḥ patanakarmakāraṇam* and C 40,13 on VS 5.2.3: *vidhārakavāyvabhrasaṃyogābhāve 'pāṃ gurutvāt patanakarma bhavati.*

[21] Cf. NBh 100,3-11, where Vātsyāyana refutes each of the four spurious means of valid cognition *aitihya, arthāpatti, sambhava* and *abhāva* in exactly this sequence, which is taken from NS 2.2.1 and 2.2.2. Authoritative transmission (*aitihya*) is verbal knowledge (*śabda*), and the remaining three means of

crete relation between an effect, like rainfall, and a factor that prevents its instantiated cause from producing it, like the cloud's contact with wind.

In the commentary on the item *liṅga* in the list of 27 causes of recollection in NS 3.2.41, Vātsyāyana once more refers to the *virodhin*. Segment [1] from VS 3.1.9 is cited, and examples for each of the four reasons are added in nominative-genitive phrases, conforming in structure to segments [2] and [3]. While two examples are given for *ekārthasamavāyin* which respectively exemplify its two varieties given in segment [2] in reverse sequence, for the *virodhin* only *abhūtaṃ bhūtasya* is mentioned.[22] Either Vātsyāyana knew a *sūtra* transmission that lacked the other patterns, or he did not consider them as relevant, perhaps because his opponent on NS 2.2.1 had only appropriated *abhūtaṃ bhūtasya* and left aside the other varieties he might have known.

---

valid cognition are inference (*anumāna*). The text dealing with the latter three reads as follows (100,7-11): *pratyakṣeṇāpratyakṣasya sambaddhasya pratipattir anumānam. tathā cārthāpattisambhavābhāvāḥ.* [1] *vākyārthasampratyayenānabhihitasyārthasya pratyanīkabhāvād grahaṇam arthāpattir anumānam eva.* [2] *avinābhāvavṛttyā ca sambaddhayoḥ samudāyasamudāyinoḥ samudāyenetarasya grahaṇaṃ sambhavaḥ. tad apy anumānam eva.* [3] *asmin satīdaṃ nopapadyata iti virodhitve prasiddhe kāryānutpattyā kāraṇasya pratibandhakam anumīyate.*

Something seems to have gone missing between segment [2] on *sambhava* and segment [3] on *abhāva*. In segments [1] and [2], Vātsyāyana expressly mentions the *pramāṇa* at issue and identifies it with inference, but even though segment [3] must deal with *abhāva*, this is not stated. The Jaisalmer manuscript omits *sambhavas tad apy anumānam eva*, but this only aggravates the problem. Uddyotakara's commentary also suggests that something became omitted, see NV 263,2: *sambhavo 'numānam, abhāvo 'py evam eva.* The Calcutta edition here reads *abhāvo 'py anumānam eva* (NV_C 578,9). Uddyotakara must have taken *tat* in NBh *tad apy anumānam eva* as referring to *abhāva*, which is hardly possible in NBh due to the absence of *abhāva* as a preceding referent for *tat.* Some word-material may therefore have become lost on one side of *tad apy anumānam eva* in NBh.

[22] NBh 198,18–199,1: *liṅgaṃ punaḥ saṃyogi samavāyy ekārthasamavāyi virodhi ceti, yathā dhūmo 'gneḥ, gor viṣāṇam, pāṇiḥ pādasya, rūpaṃ sparśasya, abhūtaṃ bhūtasya.* Here the example for *kāraṇaṃ kāraṇāntarasya* (i.e. "a hand [is a reason] for a foot") precedes that for *kāryaṃ kāryāntarasya* (i.e. "colour [is a reason] for temperature").

Vātsyāyana's unnamed opponent clearly appropriates the beginning of segment [3] of VS 3.1.9 for his stipulation of "absence", though we do not know whether he knew it already as a *sūtra*. More likely than not he also took over the example inference from his Vaiśeṣika source. Since only Mīmāṃsakas are known to have propounded a means of valid cognition called "absence", this appropriation can be assumed to have taken place in Vaiśeṣika-friendly Mīmāṃsā circles. However, not all early Mīmāṃsakas turned the pattern *abhūtaṃ bhūtasya* into a separate means of valid cognition, for the Vṛttikāra criticised in Dignāga's *Pramāṇasamuccayavṛtti*, according to E. Frauwallner identical with Bhavadāsa (Frauwallner 1968), appears to have taken over the Vaiśeṣika classification of reasons without a modification in this respect. According to Dignāga,[23] this Vṛttikāra did not teach any inferential connections (*sambandha*) other than those taught by the Vaiśeṣika. Dignāga further implies that inherence (*samavāya*), inherence of two things by/in the same (*ekārthasamavāya*) and opposition (*virodha*) were among the connections adopted by the Vṛttikāra. In addition, the Vṛttikāra propounds a *pramāṇa* called "absence", exemplified with the realisation that Caitra must be outside from observing that he is not in the house, a pattern which comes to be classified under the heading of the *pramāṇa* "implication" (*arthāpatti*) from the *Śabarabhāṣya* onwards. If Bhavadāsa had also considered the Vaiśeṣika's *virodhin* in at least one of its potentially many forms known to him under the heading of "absence", Dignāga's argumentation would have taken a different course. He would have singled out this departure from the Vaiśeṣika theory, he would have made mention of this second paradigm while refuting

[23] The Tibetan text of the relevant section in the *Svārthānumāna*-chapter of PS and PSV is edited and translated into German in Frauwallner 1968: 86ff.; cf. also Frauwallner's analysis of its content on pp. 97f. More detailed textual remarks can be omitted here because Horst Lasic is currently preparing a reconstruction of Dignāga's Sanskrit text of this chapter. Bhavadāsa's view on absence and Dignāga's refutation are also given, in slightly expanded form, in YD 74,9-16, attributed to "others" (*anye*).

the Vṛttikāra's "absence", or he would have done both. There must therefore have been (at least) two distinct Mīmāṃsā appropriations of the pattern *abhūtaṃ bhūtasya*, one by Bhavadāsa within the fold of inference, and one by an unnamed Mīmāṃsaka within the fold of "absence". Their relationship remains uncertain.[24]

When examined more closely in connection with the account of rainfall as given in VS 5.2.3, the example inference for *abhūtaṃ bhūtasya* betrays an interesting relation to the topic of explanation. In VS 5.2.3, "water falls due to [its] heaviness if contact [of a rain cloud with wind] is absent (*saṃyogābhāve 'pāṃ gurutvāt patanam*)", the presence of the condition *saṃyogābhāve* is conspicuous. It can only have been intended as a limiting condition for the validity of the general principle: water falls due to heaviness *provided that* such contact is absent, and if such contact is present, water does not fall. As a limiting condition, *saṃyogābhāve* must have been introduced with the purpose of revising the earlier held general belief that rainfall is, like any other motion of falling, caused by heaviness pure and simple – a revision that served to explain away observed exceptions. Situations will have been observed where rain failed to fall even though rain clouds, holding heavy water, were present in the sky. One can well imagine that someone will then have noticed correlations between the lack of rainfall from existing clouds and the presence of wind, and concluded that these correlations are not coincidental. This conclusion is epitomised in the example inference for *abhūtaṃ bhūtasya*, where absent rainfall is an inferential sign for present contact of the cloud with wind. When it is assumed that normally in such situations rain *does* fall, the premise "rainfall is absent" in this inference represents a phenomenon that requires explanation. The conclusion "contact of a rain cloud with wind is present" represents the

[24] In Oberhammer, Prets & Prandstetter 1991: 82 it is remarked that Bhavadāsa developed the view of Vātsyāyana's opponent further. However, it remains unclear in what sense Bhavadāsa's approach should be a "further development", and there is no clear evidence that Bhavadāsa postdates Vātsyāyana's opponent.

explanation – in the view of a Vaiśeṣika, its best explanation.[25] The inference is therefore a so-called "inference to the best explanation" where one infers from the truth of an explanandum to that of its explanans.[26]

THE JINENDRABUDDHI FRAGMENT

Dignāga treats the Vaiśeṣika theory of inference in verses 30-36 in the chapter on inference for oneself (*svārthānumāna*) of his *Pramāṇasamuccaya* and *-vṛtti*. The section begins with a quotation of VS 9.18 (PSV K (Q) 116a8, V (D) 33b4 = V(Q) 35a2) as **asyedaṃ kāryaṃ kāraṇaṃ sambandhy ekārthasamavāyi virodhi ceti laiṅgikam*, followed immediately by a refutation of each inferential sign listed in this *sūtra*. Diverging from the thematic sequence in Dignāga's text, Jinendrabuddhi's *Pramāṇasamuccayaṭīkā*, composed in the 8th century, immediately after the quotation of VS 9.18 presents us with a prose passage that comments on all items in the *sūtra*. The Buddhist refutation is stated *en bloc* only afterwards. This structural difference between Dignāga's text and Jinendrabuddhi's commentary can only be explained on the ground that Jinendrabuddhi incorporated a whole passage from another text by way of *pūrvapakṣa*. The *pūrvapakṣa* passage commenting upon VS

---

[25] As a caveat, it should be added that even if the example inference for *abhūtaṃ bhūtasya* was involved in the formation of the principle expressed in VS 5.2.3 this does not entail that segment [3] of 3.1.9 was, as part of the *sūtra* text, composed prior to 5.2.3. After all, parameters other than relationships between principles may determine when a particular piece of wording is incorporated into an authoritative text.

[26] The *locus classicus* for the theory of inferences to the best explanation are three papers by Gilbert Harman (1965; 1967; 1968). Harman argued that inference to the best explanation is a foundational inference pattern underlying all inductive argument. Its foundational role has been questioned several times. In an interesting and very accessible article, Timothy Day and Harold Kincaid (1994) argue that such inferences are not foundational, but also not completely illegitimate.

Note that explanans and explanandum are often understood not as phenomena themselves, but as the statements, or propositions, describing them. For our purposes, however, these theoretical distinctions can be set aside.

9.18 must therefore be a genuine Vaiśeṣika fragment, most probably from an unknown *sūtra*-commentary that, again most probably, was composed prior to Dignāga, and may have become incorporated into the PSṬ with minor variations. This fragment will subsequently be referred to as "J". Based on the Tibetan translation, Jambūvijaya published a Sanskrit reconstruction of J in the 7th appendix to his edition of C (188f.), from where I also borrowed the numbering of Dignāga's verses. This reconstruction can now be confirmed, and partly corrected, on the basis of a recently discovered Sanskrit manuscript of the PSṬ that is currently being edited at the Institute for the Cultural and Intellectual History of Asia of the Austrian Academy of Sciences.[27] A parallel passage derived from the fragment can be found in the Jaina treatise *Syādvādaratnākara* by Vādidevasūri (SVR 531,21–532,9).

For the items *kārya* and *kāraṇa*, J rather curiously reverses the roles of sign and inferendum in that *idaṃ* in VS 9.18 is said to refer to the inferendum, and *asya* to the inferential sign. In other words, the terms *kārya* and *kāraṇa* come to denote the inferendum and not, as in other accounts of 9.18, the inferential sign. The item *kārya* is accordingly exemplified with certain inferences from cause to effect, namely from the perception of a sunrise to the manifestation of a jar (through sunlight), and from the perception of threads, being spread (individually?) and stretched out (collectively on the loom?), which are worked by a weaver, to the cloth that is being produced.[28] Reversing these inferences yields the examples for

---

[27] I would like to thank Helmut Krasser for generously providing me with a transliteration of the PSṬ manuscript. Note that in the passages from PSṬ cited in this paper, orthographical peculiarities of the manuscript such as gemination of consonants after °*r*° are not reported.

[28] PSṬ ms. 79a4-6: ... *asyedam ityādi. asyeti liṅgam āha, idam ity anumeyam. ... yathā dinakarodayadarśanād ghaṭābhivyaktau, tantūn ātānavitānāvasthitāṃs tantuvāyādhiṣṭhitān* {*em. tantu*° : *tanta*° ms.} *dṛṣṭvā bhāvini paṭe*. The semantics of *ātānavitāna*° are uncertain. PSṬt (Q124b7=D110a6) *bres śiṅ brkyaṅ bar gnas pa*, "being in the state of being spread out and spread/stretched out", does not offer much assistance. One of the two terms *ātāna* and *vitāna* could refer to single threads being individually spread, while the other could refer to the entire arrangement of threads being stretched out on the loom. However, the standard

kāraṇa. The parallel in SVR maintains the commonly more known syntax of VS 9.18 and exemplifies *kārya* with the inference from a swollen river to rain, i.e. from an effect to its cause, and *kāraṇa* with the inference from the ascent of clouds to (future) rain, i.e. from cause to effect.

With the item *sambandhin*, J tacitly switches to considering the connection-based item as the inferential sign, and not as inferendum. The *sambandhin* is said to be twofold, comprising both "conjunct" (*saṃyogin*), exemplified with the inference from smoke to fire, and "[an entity] qualified by inherence" (*samavāyin*), exemplified with the inference from a horn to a cow, that is, from part to whole. With minor syntactical variations, the same statement already occurs in Dignāga's *Pramāṇasamuccayavṛtti*, prior to the refutation of *sambandhin*.[29] This suggests that Jinendrabuddhi may have incorporated, possibly with variations, Dignāga's authentic source that he could have known through the *Vaiśeṣikaparīkṣā*, a lost polemical treatise of Dignāga.[30]

The two varieties of *ekārthasamavāyin* are said to involve different analyses of the compound *ekārthasamavāya*: when a cause is an inferential sign for another cause, like a hand for a foot, both these things (*artha*) are inhered by the same (*eka*), namely the whole of the human body. The reason is then an entity qualified by inherence of two things *by* the same, or, more literally, by "inherence of the same in [two] things" (*ekasyārtheṣu samavāyaḥ*). When on the other hand an effect is an inferential sign for another effect, like colour for temperature, both these things inhere *in* the

---

Sanskrit dictionaries (Apte, Monier-Williams, Böthlingk-Roth) do not attest to such a subtle terminological difference between *ā-√tan* and *vi-√tan* in general.

[29] PSV V(D) 33b5 = V(Q) 35a4: *'brel pa* (**sambandhi*) *ni rnam pa gñis te ldan pa* (**saṃyogi*) *dang 'du ba'o* (**samavāyi*) *|| de yang me dang du ba dang ba lang dang rva lta bu 'o zhes so* | PSV K(Q) 116b2= *'brel pa ni rnam pa gñis te ldan pa daṅ 'du ba ste || dper na du ba me la | rva ba laṅ la'o* || In PSṬ, the individual examples are placed immediately after the corresponding item, cf. the text in footnote 31.

[30] Cf. Hattori 1968: 9 for the passage in PSV where the *Vaiśeṣikaparīkṣā* is mentioned.

same, so that the reason is an entity qualified by "inherence of [two] things *in* the same" (*ekasminn arthānāṃ samavāyaḥ*).[31] These compound analyses are absent from the parallel in SVR which only lists the two examples.

Finally there follows the account of the *virodhin*, consisting in a complete example set for all four patterns from segment [3] of VS 3.1.9.

> PSṬ ms. 79b3f. [PSṬ D110b2-4 = Q125a3-7]:
> *virodhi caturvidham.*
> *abhūtaṃ bhūtasya. tad yathā 'vidyamānaṃ varṣakarma sato vāyvabhrasaṃyogasya, tasmin sati varṣakarmābhāvāt.*
> *bhūtam abhūtasya. tad eva varṣakarma vidyamānaṃ tasyaiva vāyvabhrasaṃyogasyātivṛttatāṃ pravṛttyabhāvaṃ gamayati.*
> *bhūtaṃ bhūtasya dravatvaṃ setubandhasya. dravatvakāryeṇa syandanena virodhāt, dravatvena virodho darśitaḥ.*[32]
> *abhūtam abhūtasyātivṛttā śyāmatā ghaṭe pākajarūpotpattāv ativṛttasya ghaṭāgnisaṃyogasya.*[33]
>
> The opposed is fourfold.
> [Something] absent (*abhūta*) [is a reason] for [something] present, as for instance non-existing (*avidyamāna*) rainfall for existing (*sataḥ*) contact of a rain cloud with wind, for if this [contact] exists, rainfall is absent.

---

[31] PSṬ ms. 79a7-b2: *sambandhi dvividham. saṃyogi ca, yathā dhūmo 'gneḥ, samavāyi* {*em. samavāyi* : *samāvāyi* ms.} *ca, yathā viṣāṇaṃ goḥ. ekārthasamavāyy api dvividham, kāryaṃ kāryāntarasya* {*em. kāryāntarasya* (*gźan gyi 'bras bu* PSṬt) : *kāryasya* ms.}, *kāraṇaṃ kāraṇāntarasya. tatra kāraṇasyaikārthasamavāyaḥ ekasyārtheṣu samavāyaḥ, kāryasya punar ekasminn arthānāṃ samavāya iti, vigrahabhedāt. tatra kāryāt kāryāntare 'numānam, tad yathā rūpāt sparśe, kāraṇāt kāraṇāntare, tad yathā pādād pāṇau.*

[32] In all cases, ms. reads *dravyatva* for *dravatva.* The emendation to *dravatva* is supported by the context and by the Tibetan translation: *byuṅ ba byuṅ ba'i ni gśer ba ñid* {*ñid om.* Q} (**dravatva*) *chu lon* {*lon* D : *len* Q} *'chiṅ ba'i* (**setubandhasya*) *ste* | *gśer ba ñid kyi 'bras bu rlan pa* (**syandana*) *daṅ 'gal ba'i phyir gśer ba ñid daṅ 'gal bar bstan to* |

[33] The Tibetan translation presupposes *abhivṛtta°* for *ativṛtta°* in both places in this sentence, which can be explained through the close resemblance of the syllables °*ta*° and °*bha*° in certain Indic scripts: *ma byuṅ ba ma byuṅ ba'i ni mṅon par grub pa* (**abhivṛttā*) *ljaṅ gu ñid kyi bum pa tshos pa las skyes pa'i ṅo bor byuṅ ba la* | *mṅon par grub pa'i* (**abhivṛttasya*) *bum pa me daṅ yaṅ dag par sbyor ba'o* | Jambūvijaya also reconstructs *abhivrtta°*.

> [Something] present [is a reason] for [something] absent. Same rainfall, if it exists, makes understood that same contact of a rain cloud with wind is past, [i.e.] that its activity is [now] absent.[34]
> [Something] present [is a reason] for [something] present. Liquidity [of water in a river is a reason] for a dam. Because [a dam] is in [direct] opposition to the flow [of water], which is the effect of liquidity, [it] is shown to be in opposition [also] to liquidity.
> [Something] absent [is a reason] for [something] absent. When [red] colour resulting from burning (*pākajarūpa*) arises in a jar, past black colour [is a reason] for past contact of the jar with fire.

The initial part "*virodhi caturvidham. abhūtaṃ bhūtasya*" also occurs at the appropriate place in Dignāgas *Pramāṇasamuccayavṛtti* (see below p. 109), which further strengthens the assumption that Jinendrabuddhi here incorporates Dignāga's authentic source.

The example for *abhūtaṃ bhūtasya* is the same as in all other known sources. The example for *bhūtam abhūtasya* is a temporal extension of it: when rain falls from a rain cloud after not having fallen before, one infers that the contact of the cloud with wind which before obstructed rain is past, i.e. that its activity is now absent.[35] This temporal connection between the two example inferences, which is not indicated in any other known example set, turns the second one also into an inference to the best explanation: when it is assumed that lack of rainfall is due to wind, the sudden onset of rain emerges as an explanandum and is, on this background, best explained through the cessation of wind. In the other known example sets, absent rainfall is in a general fashion presented as a sign for present contact, and present rainfall as one for absent contact. The atemporal version is most likely derived from the temporal version in J through a perhaps even merely coincidental omission of temporal qualification.

---

[34] The Tibetan translation construes *ativṛttatāṃ* and *pravṛttyabhāvaṃ* as conjuncts, as does Jambūvijaya's reconstruction: ... *śin tu 'jug pa ñid daṅ rab tu 'jug pa med pa ñid rtogs par byed do* | In either case, it is clear that the current absence of activity of the contact is believed to result from its being past.

[35] The conceptual implications of *pravṛtti* in this context remain unclear.

The example for *bhūtaṃ bhūtasya* in J is altogether unknown from any other text except, with certain reservations, the parallel in SVR: present liquidity of water is a reason for a present dam. This example is connected with VS 5.2.4 *dravatvāt syandanam*, "water flows because of liquidity", the *sūtra* which directly follows 5.2.3 and also addresses a form of movement on the part of water.[36] The situation envisaged here must be the same as in the first example: the cause (= liquidity) is present, the obstructive factor (= the dam) is present, and the effect (= flow of water) is absent. The text adds that the dam is opposed to liquidity because it is opposed to the flow of water, which is the effect of liquidity. This added explanation indicates a deliberate attempt to make further use of the already known structure of cause, effect, and obstructive factor in order to devise an additional form of the *virodhin*, by extending the concept of the "opposition" involved, and by simply moving on from 5.2.3 to the next *sūtra* for construing an example inference. Unlike the examples for the first two patterns, this inference can hardly be considered as one to the best explanation. One would hardly have wanted to explain why water in a river that does not flow is liquid, and even if someone had posited such a rather bizarre explanandum, they would hardly have resorted to the presence of a dam for its explanation.

Lastly, the example for *abhūtam abhūtasya* is taken from the account of the causation of qualities through chemical processes, i.e. the discussion of the so-called *pākajaguṇa*s, but presents certain difficulties. When an earthen jar, qualified by dark colour, comes into contact with fire, dark colour vanishes and red colour is produced. As Jinendrabuddhi's refutation of this inference (cf. below) makes clear, in his view the opposition obtains between dark colour and contact of the jar with fire. This is consistent with, e.g., the *Praśastapādabhāṣya*, where colour in earth atoms is said to be in

[36] Cf. further PDhS, section 298: *dravatvaṃ syandanakarmakāraṇam.* C adds the absence of an obstructive factor as a limiting condition also to this principle, cf. C 41,1: *vidhārakābhāvād apāṃ syandanakarma dravatvād bhavati.*

opposition to contact with fire (*agnisaṃyogavirodhin*).[37] In J's example, past dark colour is an inferential sign for past contact with fire. The inference must consequently relate to a point in time when red colour has already been produced and dark colour destroyed. It is not clear why, at this time, contact with fire can be inferred as in the past, i.e. as no longer existing. Perhaps it was assumed that once red colour exists, contact with fire has done its duty and ceases to be, but available accounts of *pākajaguṇa*s in classical Vaiśeṣika literature do not seem to hold further clues. Still, the opposition involved here is clearly one between an entity and a cause for its destruction, in contrast to the opposition involved in the other examples which obtains between an entity and a factor which prevents its production. Furthermore, even if our (tentative) understanding of the example may seem artificial, this need not be disturbing, for if the first three patterns were understood as they are exemplified in J, someone might at a later stage have added a fourth pattern mainly in order to complete a systematic list of formulas, without much concern about whether or not the final example inference was intuitive.

The parallel in SVR[38] likewise begins with *virodhi caturvidham*. But it continues with a list of the four patterns pure and simple, in different sequence: *abhūtaṃ bhūtasya*, *abhūtam abhūtasya*, *bhūtaṃ bhūtasya*, *bhūtam abhūtasya*. In other words, the four patterns are arranged according to whether the reason is some-

---

[37] Cf. PDhS, sections 117 and 118: *tatra rūpaṃ cakṣurgrāhyam. pṛthivyudakajvalanavṛtti dravyādyupalambhakaṃ nayanasahakāri śuklādyanekaprakāraṃ salilādiparamāṇuṣu nityaṃ pārthivaparamāṇuṣv agnisaṃyogavirodhi sarvakāryadravyeṣu kāraṇaguṇapūrvakam āśrayavināśād eva vinaśyatīti*. According to PDhS p. 20, n. 8, the *Kiraṇāvalī*, the *Nyāyakandalī* and one edition of the text read *sarvakāryeṣu* for *sarvakāryadravyeṣu*.

[38] SVR 532,4-9: *virodhi caturvidham. abhūtaṃ bhūtasya, abhūtam abhūtasya, bhūtam abhūtasya, bhūtaṃ bhūtasya. tatrābhūtaṃ bhūtasya yathā, abhūtaṃ varṣakarma bhūtasya vāyvabhrasaṃyogasya liṅgam. abhūtam abhūtasya yathā, abhūtā śyāmatā abhūtasya ghaṭāgnisaṃyogasya liṅgam. bhūtam abhūtasya yathā, bhūtaṃ varṣakarma abhūtasya vāyvabhrasaṃyogasya liṅgam. bhūtaṃ bhūtasya yathā, bhūtaṃ syandanakarma* {*em. syandanakarma* : *syandanaṃ karma* SVR} *bhūtasya setubandhasya liṅgam iti.*

thing absent or something present. Because this breaks up the unity of *abhūtaṃ bhūtasya* and *bhūtam abhūtasya*, both of which are exemplified from the same semantic field, it must be a secondary rearrangement. Next follow example inferences for all four patterns. The ones for *bhūtam abhūtasya* and *abhūtam abhūtasya* lack the temporal dimension expressed in J. The example for *bhūtaṃ bhūtasya* differs slightly in that in the SVR parallel, present flow of water is said to be an inferential sign for a present dam. But if a dam is actually supposed to *prevent* the flow of water, like contact with wind prevents rainfall, this can only be a mistake.[39] Because of the structural rearrangement, the omission of a temporal dimension in two examples, and a misunderstanding of a third, the SVR parallel can therefore only be a secondary derivation of the account preserved in J, possibly through further, presently unknown intermediaries.

There is sufficient evidence to support that, taken as a whole, J represents the missing link between VS 9.18 and 3.1.9. The list of inferential signs in VS 9.18 in its earliest form lists the items *kārya*, *kāraṇa*, *sambandhin*, *ekārthasamavāyin*, and *virodhin*. J, a commentary on this *sūtra*, explains *sambandhin* as comprising *saṃyogin* and *samavāyin*, and adduces two varieties of *ekārthasamavāyin* and four of *virodhin* respectively. VS 3.1.9 for its part lists the four items *saṃyogin*, *samavāyin*, *ekārthasamavāyin* and *virodhin*, with two and four varieties given respectively for the last two. To extract VS 3.1.9 out of J, one only has to set aside *kārya* and *kāraṇa*, adopt the differentiation of *sambandhin* into *saṃyogin* and *samavāyin* and pick up the varieties for *ekārthasamavāyin* and *virodhin*.[40] Motivations for setting aside *kārya* and *kāraṇa* are not

---

[39] Some sense could be made of it if one introduces a temporal sequence: a present dam is a sign that flow of water once existed (but does not exist any longer), but this seems far-fetched.

[40] Candrānanda, by contrast, connects both "effect" and "cause" in 9.18 with *samavāyin* in 3.1.9 and declares *saṃyogin* and *sambandhin* to be identical (C 69,15f.). In comparison to the account in J, his account is therefore more likely a secondary attempt to explain away the differences between the two *sūtra*s.

difficult to find: the rather puzzling inversion of the roles of sign and inferendum for *kārya* and *kāraṇa* in J could have driven someone to drop these items altogether. The heterogenous character of the entire list, in that both the example for *saṃyogin* and the one for *kāraṇa* in J are inferences from effect to cause, might have called for some systematisation that led to the omission of *kāraṇa*, and qualms about the acceptability of predictive inferences might additionally have supported the omission of *kārya*.

What is for our purposes more important in J is that it provides us with a rationale for the emergence of the fourfold list. In this respect it is superior to all other example sets preserved in commentaries on the *Vaiśeṣikasūtra*s and in other texts.[41] In J, the example for *bhūtam abhūtasya* is formulated as a temporal extension of the one for *bhūṭam abhūtasya*; both are inferences to the best explanation and exemplified from the same semantic field of the account of rainfall as given in VS 5.2.3. The third pattern

---

[41] A detailed examination of all these sets cannot be given here, due to lack of space. The pertinent passages are C 26,6ff., ŚM 88,14–89,6, and BhV 36,5-11. A further, still different example set is given in NVTṬ 134,21–133,3, cf. also KĀ 202,6f.

The text of BhV requires emendation; Harunaga Isaacson kindly provided the readings of the Malayalam manuscript. *jātasya pavanasaṃyogasya* in this manuscript and in Thakur's edition is to be emended to *bhūtasya jātasya pavanasaṃyogasya*, as was already suggested by Thakur. Before *abhūtam abhūtasya*, the following sentence is to be inserted on the basis of the manuscript: *bhūtaṃ bhūtasya, yathā nadīpūro vṛṣṭeḥ*. On the whole, the sets in BhV and ŚM leave the impression of almost desparate attempts to make sense of something that these authors, or their sources, could not understand any longer.

The set in C can be explained as derived from J, through omission of temporal qualification in the examples for *bhūtam abhūtasya* and *abhūtam abhūtasya*, in combination with a reversal of the sequence of the two last patterns *bhūṭaṃ bhūtasya* and *abhūtam abhūtasya* that may result from a scribal error – eyeskip – in a manuscript together with subsequent correction. C's example for his last item *bhūṭaṃ bhūtasya* is formed on the basis of the one for *abhūtam abhūtasya*. The differences between C and J are therefore considerable, and the example set in J must be older than the one contained in C. Nancy Schuster's claim that Candrānanda's examples are "repeated with minor variations" in Jinendrabuddhi's text (Schuster 1972: 388, n. 15) is misleading, not the least because the chronological relationship between these two authors – though not between the example sets in their texts – is far from certain.

bhūtaṃ bhūtasya also relies upon the same reference frame of present cause, absent effect, and present obstructive factor, moves ahead to VS 5.2.4 for construing an example, and alters the focus: the "opposition" shifts from one between an effect and an obstructive factor to one between a cause and an obstructive factor. The resulting relative proximity of the first two patterns and the third in terms of their reference frame is the decisive advantage of the example set in J over all other sets, for there, the two "uneven" patterns *abhūtaṃ bhūtasya* and *bhūtam abhūtasya* are separated from the "even" pattern(s) *bhūtaṃ bhūtasya* and/or *abhūtam abhūtasya* by a huge gap both in terms of the semantic field relied upon for example inferences and in terms of the "opposition" and its involvement in the inference. If someone aimed to expand an existing set of two patterns by adding a third, it is more likely that they would have stayed closer to what was already there, rather than creating something entirely different. Though J's example inference for the fourth pattern *abhūtam abhūtasya* remains unclear in certain respects, it is most likely a further extension motivated through an attempt to formally complete and "close" the list, even if this involves the creation of a rather artificial example inference. The entire process may well have involved different personalities; it first led to the account of four patterns and example inferences in an old *sūtra*-commentary on VS 9.18, from which VS 3.1.9 in its present form must have been extracted, at once or, if Candramati's ignorance of segments [2] and [3] of 3.1.9 and/or Vātsyāyana's mention of only *abhūtaṃ bhūtasya* indeed point towards a *sūtra* transmission that contained shorter versions of 3.1.9, gradually.

DIGNĀGA'S AND JINENDRABUDDHI'S CRITICISM OF THE *VIRODHIN*

Dignāga's and Jinendrabuddhi's criticism of the *virodhin* does not pass judgment on the acceptability of the example inferences given in J; rather, it is their analysis by means of an opposition as an inferential connection that is rejected.[42] The Sanskrit of the pertinent passage in Dignāga's text can be reconstructed on the basis of Jinendrabuddhi's commentary. Again, an earlier reconstruction, based entirely on the Tibetan translation at PSV V(D) 35a3-5 = V(Q) 36b5-7 and K(Q) 118a3-5, was published by Jambūvijaya in the 7th appendix to C, 187,8-11. Text in italics is attested in the manuscript of PSṬ, while non-italic text is purely reconstructed.

> PSV: *virodhi caturvidham abhūtaṃ bhūtasy*etyādi. eṣu sarvatrāpi[43]
>
> PS II 35a: *yad virodhi na tal liṅgam* I
>
> PSV: *vāyvabhrasaṃyogo hi varṣakarmaṇā virodhī.*[44] *na cātra varṣakarma liṅgam, kiṃ tarhi tadabhāvaḥ. na ca varṣakarmābhāvavāyvabhrasaṃyogayor virodhaḥ. evam anyatrāpi vācyam.*

> [Vaiśeṣika view:] The opposed is fourfold: [something] absent [is a sign] for [something] present, and so forth.
>
> [Dignāga's refutation:] In all these [cases] –
> PS II 35a: That which is [an] opposed [entity] is not a sign.
>
> For contact of a rain cloud with wind is opposed to rainfall. But in this [inference], the sign is not rainfall, but its absence, and there is no opposition between the absence of rainfall and contact of a rain cloud with wind. In the same way it is also to be stated for the other [three cases].[45]

---

[42] Probably misled by the terminological resemblance of *virodhin* and *viruddha*(*hetvābhāsa*), Sh. Katsura claims that Dignāga views the *virodhin* as a fallacious reason, cf. Katsura 1981: 64, n. 13.

[43] For *eṣu sarvatrāpi*, reconstructed also by Jambūvijaya, cf. PSV K *'di dag thams cad la yaṅ*, PSV V *'di la* {*la om.* D} *yaṅ*.

[44] Jambūvijaya reconstructs *vāyvabhrasaṃyogasya varṣakarmaṇā virodhaḥ*, and suggests as a possible alternative *vāyvabhrasaṃyogavarṣakarmaṇor virodhaḥ*. Jinendrabuddhi's *pratīka* is closer to PSV(K).

[45] Cf. Katsura 1981: 58 for a Japanese translation of this passage.

Jinendrabuddhi's commentary in PSṬ ms.83b2-7 [PSṬ$_t$ D115a2-b1 = Q130b5-131a6] was also reconstructed from the Tibetan by Jambūvijaya in C 193,21–194,6. Bold print indicates *pratīkas*.

yad virodhī*tyādi.* ***vāyvabhrasaṃyogo***[46] ***hi varṣakarmaṇā virodhī****ti tayoḥ sahānavasthānāt.*[47] ***na cātra varṣakarma liṅgam*** *iti, tadviruddhadharmasādhanāt,* ***kiṃ tarhi tadabhāva*** *iti, vāyvabhrasaṃyoge sati varṣakarmābhāvāt.* ***na ca varṣakarmābhāvavāyvabhrasaṃyogayor virodha*** *iti, sahāvasthānāt ...* ***evam anyatrāpi vācyam*** *iti. yatrābhūtasya liṅgam, tatrāpi. vāyvabhrasaṃyogābhāvo hi {..}*[48] *varṣakarmābhāvena virodhī.*[49] *na cātra varṣakarmābhāvo liṅgam, kiṃ tarhi varṣakarma.*[50] *na ca varṣakarmavāyvabhrasaṃyogābhāvayor virodhaḥ. evaṃ bhūtaṃ bhūtasyety*[51] *atrāpi. dravatvakarmasyandanaṃ*[52] *setubandhena virodhi. na ca syandanaṃ liṅgam, kiṃ tarhi tadabhāvaḥ. tathā 'bhūtam abhūtasyety atrā~~pi~~. śyāmatāgnisaṃyogayor virodhaḥ. na cātra tayor liṅgaliṅgibhāvaḥ, kiṃ tarhi tannivṛttyoḥ.*

"That which is [an] opposed [entity]" etc. "For contact of a rain cloud with wind is opposed to rainfall" because these two do not occur together. "But in this [inference], the sign is not rainfall" because it establishes a property incompatible with this [contact with wind], but its absence, for rainfall is absent when contact of a rain cloud with wind exists. "And there is no opposition between the absence of rainfall and the contact of a rain cloud with wind" because [these two] occur together ... "In the same way it is also to be

---

[46] em. *vāyvabhra°* (*rluṅ daṅ sbrin* PSṬ$_t$) : *nānyatra° ms.*

[47] em. *sahānavasthānāt* (so also Jambūvijaya on the basis of *lhan cig mi gnas pa'i phyir* PSṬt) : *sahānasthānāt ms.*

[48] Here, at the end of the line, a syllable resembling °*na*° has been deleted.

[49] em. *virodhī* : *virodhāt* ms. Cf. *rluṅ daṅ sprin yaṅ dag par ldan pa med pa ni char pa'i las med pa daṅ 'gal ba'i phyir* for the entire sentence in PSṬt. While *'gal ba'i phyir* may translate *virodhāt*, it might also be a rather strong translation of *hi ... virodhī*.

The emendation is necessary because the manuscript reads a nominative °*saṃyogābhāvaḥ*; the sentence must therefore be an adaptation of PSV *vāyvabhrasaṃyogo hi varṣakarmaṇā virodhī* to the second example. Jambūvijaya reconstructs *virodhāt*, which in his case is syntactically justified because he reconstructs a genitive subject *vāyvabhrasaṃyogābhāvasya*.

[50] em. *varṣakarma* : *varṣakarmā* ms.

[51] em. *bhūtasyety* : *bhūtasyaity* ms.

[52] em. *dravatva°* : *dravyatva°* ms. Without a change in meaning, what I have considered a compound could also be construed as two separate words *dravatvakarma* and *syandanaṃ*.

> stated for the other [three cases]." In the case of a sign [namely present rainfall] for absent [contact it is] also [to be stated in this way]. For absence of contact of a rain cloud with wind is opposed to the absence of rainfall. But in this [inference], not the absence of rainfall is the sign, but rainfall. And there is no opposition between rainfall and the absence of contact of a rain cloud with wind. In the same way [it is to be stated] also in this [case of] "[something] present for [something] present". Flow of water, a motion [resulting from] liquidity, is opposed by a dam; and not the flow of water is a sign, but its absence. Likewise, it is also [to be stated] in this [case of] "[something] absent for [something] absent". There is an opposition between dark colour and contact with fire, and here there is no relation of sign and indicated between these two, but between their [respective] absences.

In all four cases, Dignāga argues, the entities assumed to share a *virodha*-connection are not the ones which are posited as reason and inferendum: rainfall is opposed to contact of a rain cloud with wind, but in the envisaged inference for *abhūtaṃ bhūtasya* the *absence* of rainfall is the sign. The opposition does therefore not connect reason and inferendum as such, but only a component of the one with the other. By extension, the same applies to the example for *bhūtam abhūtasya.* This incongruence is also raised in Vācaspatimiśra's rejection of *abhūtaṃ bhūtasya* and *bhūtam abhūtasya*: present rainfall is not a *virodhin* with respect to absent contact because it is in fact favourable to it (*anukūla*); the same applies to absent rainfall, which is after all not unfavourable (*nāpratikūlam*) towards present contact (NVTṬ 134,21ff.)

For the remaining two patterns, Jinendrabuddhi provides the following explanations. In case of *bhūtaṃ bhūtasya*, the dam and flow of water are in opposition to each other, but it is the absence of that flow which serves as inferential sign for the existing dam, and not its existence. As we have seen, the *pūrvapakṣa* passage J clearly envisages not this inference, but an inference from present liquidity to a present dam, derived through a shift of the opposition involved in the first two examples. But Jinendrabuddhi does not follow this shift; his criticism amounts to saying that based on the opposition between effect and obstructive factor, the inference should have been formulated otherwise, and in that case would conform to the pattern *abhūtaṃ bhūtasya* (to which the already stated criticism of that pattern would then apply). It is worth noting that Jinendrabuddhi's intuitive understanding of the third inference turns this example, too, into an inference to the best explanation. Conceivably, Jinendrabuddhi at least implicitly understood that the first two example inferences were inferences to the best explanation and expected the third pattern to be of the same kind. As for *abhūtam abhūtasya*, Jinendrabuddhi claims that while fire and dark colour are in opposition, the respective absences are related to each other as sign and inferendum.

Dignāga's criticism[53] assumes that the Vaiśeṣika is committed to a specific understanding of inferential connections and their role, namely that an inferential connection connects reason and inferendum in precisely the form in which they are involved in the inference, and not in any other form. He must therefore have understood the phrase *abhūtaṃ bhūtasya*, which in a general fashion can be construed as "an absent [opposed is a reason/sign] for its present [counterpart]", to assign the role of a reason to the *absence of* the opposed entity. However, one could also propose an alternative understanding, with narrower scoping, and assign the role of reason or inferential sign to an opposed entity as such. At least one passage in Vaiśeṣika literature indeed evidences such an interpretation. In the discussion of the quality of number (*saṅkhyā*) in the *Praśastapādabhāṣya*, an opponent proposes how the cognition of the quality "two" may arise even though the quality itself has already ceased to exist, invoking the pattern *abhūtaṃ bhūtasya* as a model: a quality may be cognised merely on the basis of cognition in general (*jñānamātra*), just as in the inference *abhūtaṃ bhūtasya*

[53] As a chronological aside, if a Dignāga-style criticism – after all, we do not know whether Dignāga was the first to attack the *virodhin* in this way – had targeted first and foremost *abhūtaṃ bhūtasya*, one possible reaction might have been to take this paradigm out of the fold of inference and accord it the status of a separate *pramāṇa*. In that case, Dignāga's Vṛttikāra who includes *abhūtaṃ bhūtasya* in the fold of inference might be adhering to an older Mīmāṃsā view than Vātsyāyana's anonymous opponent, regardless of the chronological relationship between the *Pramāṇasamuccayavṛtti* and the *Nyāyabhāṣya* as texts.

an inference takes place merely on the basis of cognition in general, even though the inferential sign is absent, i.e. not instantiated (*liṅgābhāve 'pi*).[54] Here it is not the *absence of* an entity which serves as a sign; rather, an entity is a sign, *and this entity is absent*. This narrow-scoped reading of *abhūtaṃ bhūtasya* may well have been an *ad hoc* interpretation occasioned by the specific discussion about the quality "two". However, that Praśastapāda does not deny it in his refutation of the objection indicates that the understanding presupposed for the Vaiśeṣika in Dignāga's rejection of the *virodhin* was in turn not something that every Vaiśeṣika consciously and proactively embraced.

CONCLUSION

A survey of various sources dealing with the *virodhin* indicates that the inference from absent rainfall to present contact of a rain cloud with wind, adduced unanimously as an example for the pattern *abhūtaṃ bhūtasya*, was the earliest important inference associated with this type of inferential sign. This is the paradigmatic example inference for the *virodhin* in the *Nyāyabhāṣya*, and was appropriated by some early Mīmāṃsakas for their stipulation of a separate means of valid cognition called "absence". Moreover, a Vaiśeṣika prose fragment preserved in Jinendrabuddhi's *Pramāṇasamuccayaṭīkā* suggests that this example inference set the formation of the fourfold pattern *abhūtaṃ bhūtasya bhūtam abhūtasya bhūtaṃ bhūtasyābhūtam abhūtasya* that is now preserved in VS 3.1.9 into motion.[55] The second pattern *bhūtam abhūtasya*, whose example is

---

[54] PDhS section 141: *laiṅgikavaj jñānamātrād iti cet. syān matam: yathā 'bhūtaṃ bhūtasyety atra liṅgābhāve 'pi jñānamātrād anumānam tathā guṇavināśe 'pi guṇabuddhimātrād dravyapratyayaḥ syād iti.* According to PDhS p. 25, n. 1, two editions and the *Vyomavatī* read *dve dravye iti pratyayaḥ* for *dravyapratyayaḥ*.

[55] Nancy Schuster claims that the *virodhin* is part of an "archaic" stratum of the *Vaiśeṣikasūtra*s characterised by intense speculations about knowledge related to time, and suggests that the "notion of contraries" is inscrutable "due to its being really an 'old-fashioned' idea". For this assessment, she relies on the

according to same fragment temporally connected with the one for the first, may have been taken into consideration simultaneously with the first or at a later point in time. The third and fourth patterns, *bhūtaṃ bhūtasya* and *abhūtam abhūtasya*, were most likely added out of a desire to further expand and formally complete the list.

For the incorporation of the *virodhin* into VS 9.18 prior to the formation of the four patterns, the following scenario then seems the most likely: the idea that connections guarantee the adequacy of inferences was to some extent current. At the same time, the inference from absent rainfall to present contact of a rain cloud with wind had become involved in revising the general account of rainfall to its specific form now stated in VS 5.2.3. Some Vaiśeṣika philosopher now pondered over what sort of connection underlies this inference, decided to focus on a connection between rainfall and contact with wind, and referred to it as an "opposition" (*virodha*). The emergence of the phrase *abhūtaṃ bhūtasya* might then be explained as follows: example inferences for some other items known to function as reasons had already been contracted into brief nominative-genitive phrases that were easy to remember, such as

account of knowledge of non-existence in VS 9.6-7 (cf. Kellner 1997: 50ff.), which, rather boldly, she takes as "yet another definition of inferential knowledge". There are several problems with this claim. First, the unquestioned equation of *virodha* with the notion of logical "contrariety" at this stage is not supported by any evidence. Second, while the claim in VS 9.6 that the perception of a *virodhin* is involved in the knowledge that a past entity no longer exists may well have been intended, and understood, as adducing an inference, it hardly amounts to a "definition" of inferential knowledge unless all inferential knowledge were to yield the conclusion that what once existed is no longer. Lastly, even on the level of the envisaged processes of knowledge the contexts of VS 9.6 and of the example inference for *abhūtaṃ bhūtasya* are very different: in 9.6, one knows from the perception of one "opposed" entity that its previously existing counterpart is now absent, whereas in the example inference, one infers from one *absent* "opposed" entity the *presence* of its counterpart. All in all, it appears that Schuster's claim is supported solely by the fact that the expression *virodhi* occurs in 9.6, but in view of these problems, this linguistic observation is hardly sufficient ground to consider 9.6 as the source of the conception of *virodhin* in 9.18 and 3.1.9.

dhūmo 'gneḥ, "smoke [is an inferential sign] for fire". But how to contract the *virodhin*-inference into such a formula? A phrase like *varṣakarma vāyvabhrasaṃyogasya* would have been misleading because it did not convey the important information that rainfall is an inferential sign *when it is absent*. This peculiarity of the inference, namely the involvement of an absent entity, placed the focus on whether or not sign and inferendum are involved in a *virodhin*-inferences as absent or present and led to the formulation of the phrase *abhūtaṃ bhūtasya*; this may also originally have been a more extensive phrase like *abhūtaṃ varṣakarma bhūtasya vāyvabhrasaṃyogasya* that was further shortened for economic reasons. If the first two example inferences were taken into consideration simultaneously, then the choice of the abstract formulations *abhūtaṃ bhūtasya bhūtam abhūtasya* could additionally have been intended as emphasising their differentiating characteristics.

Viewed in a broader context, the fact that the earliest important *virodhin*-based inferences are inferences to the best explanation and thus betray a close relationship to the topic of explanation may be significant for assessing the character of intension-based connections in early Indian logic at large. If inferences based on a certain form of connection are inferences to the best explanation, the connection in question might have been thought of as an "explanatory connection" which accounts for the plausibility of an explanation, rather than an "inferential connection" in a narrower sense, a connection that guarantees the adequacy of a reason in more strictly formal terms. More specifically, such a connection might have served to ensure that the state of affairs which is posited as an explanans is altogether relevant for explaining the explanandum – in other words, to account for why among certain propositions that are all logically connected with a proposition expressing the explanandum, only some are considered as potentially explaining it. A question that remains to be worked out in future studies is whether considerations of explanatory relevance were significant only for some specific forms of connection-based inferences in the early period, or whether they were responsible for introducing the very notion of connection-based reasoning as such. C. Nenninger once suggested the latter, but in view of the fluctuation among early Vaiśeṣika classifications and exemplifications of reasons that is attested in the Jinendrabuddhi fragment, it seems advisable to defer judgment until the remaining types of reasons listed in VS 9.18 and 3.1.9 have been subjected to similar inquiries as the one above.[56]

For the *virodhin*, lastly, considerations of relevance may well help us to determine the theoretical foundation of the disagreement between early Vaiśeṣika approaches and Dignāga's criticism of them. If someone were to seek a relevance-ensuring "explanatory connection" in the paradigmatic example inference for the *virodhin*, they might well satisfy themselves with pointing out an opposition between rainfall and contact of a rain cloud with wind, based on the belief that the opposition between rainfall and contact ensures that *some* facts about such contact are relevant to explain *some* facts about rainfall, and that *which* facts about contact explain *which* facts about rainfall is understood from the content of the concept "opposition". On such a background it would not have been necessary to insist, as Dignāga did, that the "opposition" must connect reason and inferendum in precisely the form in which they are involved in an inference – arguably, this requirement emerges only when the demand is placed upon an inferential connection that it guarantees the instantiation of one connected item whenever the other one is instantiated. Dignāga's criticism of the *virodhin* may therefore well have been driven by a changed perspective on inferential connections at large.

---

[56] Cf. Nenninger 1994: 831. He suggests that considerations of relevance, which he discussed as one important criterion for the plausibility of inductive arguments, might have "urged early Indian logicians to formulating [sic] the concept that logical entailment is based on some special relations between *liṅga* and *sādhyadharma*".

REFERENCES

Sanskrit texts and general abbreviations

A = Ahmedabad ms. of the *sūtrapāṭha* of the *Vaiśeṣikasūtra*s. The text is printed in Isaacson 1995.

BhV = [Bhaṭṭa Vādīndra's abridged commentary on the *Vaiśeṣikasūtra*s.] *Vaiśeṣikadarśana of Kaṇāda with an anonymous commentary*. Ed. by A. Thakur. Darbhanga 1957.

D = sDe dge Tibetan Tripiṭaka, Bstan ḥgyur. Preserved at the Faculty of Letters, University of Tokyo. Ed. by J. Takasaki, Z. Yamaguchi, Y. Ejima. Tokyo 1977ff.

em. = emendation.

KĀ = *Praśastapādabhāṣyam with the Commentary Kiraṇāvalī of Udayanācārya*. Ed. by J. S. Jetly. Vadodara 1991.

C = [*Vaiśeṣikasūtravṛtti* by Candrānanda]. *Vaiśeṣikasūtra of Kaṇāda with the Commentary of Candrānanda*. Ed. by Muni Śrī Jambuvijayaji. (Gaekwad 's Oriental Series, 136.) Baroda 1961.

J = "Jinendrabuddhi fragment". The fragment of an unknown commentary on VS 9.18 preserved in Jinendrabuddhi's PSṬ and discussed in the present article.

T = Trivandrum ms. of the *sūtrapāṭha* of the *Vaiśeṣikasūtra*s. ,The text is printed in Isaacson 1995.

NĀA see NC.

NC = *Dvādaśāraṃ Nayacakram of Ācārya Śrī Mallavādi Kṣamāśramaṇa. With the Commentary Nyāyāgamānusāriṇī of Śrī Siṃhasūri Gaṇi Vādi Kṣamāśramaṇa*, I. Edited with critical notes by Muni Jambūvijayajī. Bhavnagar 1966.

NBh = *Gautamīyanyāyadarśana* with *Bhāṣya* of Vātsyāyana. Ed. by A. Thakur. *Nyāyacaturgranthikā*, I. New Delhi 1997.

NV = *Nyāyabhāṣyavārttika* of Bhāradvāja Uddyotakara. Ed. by A. Thakur. *Nyāyacaturgranthikā*, II. New Delhi 1997.

NV$_{C}$ = [*Nyāyavārttika*, Calcutta edition]. *Nyāyadarśanam with Vātsyāyana's Bhāṣya, Uddyotakara's Vārttika, Vācaspatimiśra's Tātparyaṭīkā & Viśvanātha's Vṛtti*. Ed. by Taranatha Nyaya-Tarkatirtha (Chapter I, section I) and Amarendramohan Tarkatirtha (Chapters I, section II-IV). 2nd edition. Calcutta 1986.

NVTṬ = *Nyāyavārttikatātparyaṭīkā* of Vācaspatimiśra. Ed. by A. Thakur. *Nyāyacaturgranthikā*, III. New Delhi 1996.

om. = omitted in.

PSV V = [*Pramāṇasamuccayavṛtti* by Dignāga]. *Tshad ma kun las btus pa'i 'grel pa*, D 4204, Tshad ma vol. 1, Ce 14b1-85b7, Q 5701, Ce 13a6-93b4. Translated by Vasudhararakṣita and Źa ma Seṅ (ge) rgyal (mtshan) (D), i.e. Seṅ rgyal (Q).

PSV K = [Pramāṇasamuccayavṛtti by Dignāga]. *Tshad ma kun las btus pa'i 'grel pa*, Q 5702, vol. 130, Ce 93b4-177a7, translated by gSer gyi go cha (Kanakavarman) and Dad pa śes rab.

PDhS = J. Bronkhorst & Y. Ramseier, *Word Index to the Praśastapādabhāṣya. A Complete Word Index to the Printed Editions of the Praśastapādabhāṣya*. Delhi 1994.
(N.B.: This "Index", which in fact contains the complete Sanskrit text, is here used as reference point because it provides easy access to all printed editions, and not because it is a critical edition of the text.)

PSṬt = [*Viśālāmalavatīnāmapramāṇasamuccayaṭīkā* Jinendrabuddhi]. *Yaṅs pa daṅ dri ma med pa daṅ* {*daṅ om. D*} *ldan pa źes bya ba tshad ma kun las btus pa'i 'grel bśad*, D 4268, Ye 1b1-314a7, Tshad ma vol. 20, Q 5766, vol, 139, Re 1b1-355a8. Translated by (dPaṅ lo) Blo gros brtan pa (D), i.e. dPal ldan Blo gros brtan pa (Q).

Q = The Tibetan Tripitaka. Peking Edition. Reprinted under the Supervision of the Otani University, Kyoto. Ed. by D. T. Suzuki. 168 vols. Tokyo – Kyoto 1955-1961.

YD = *Yuktidīpikā. The Most Significant Commentary on the Sāṅkhyakārikā*, I. Critically ed. by A. Wezler & Sh. Motegi. Stuttgart 1998.

ŚM = [*Vaiśeṣikasūtropaskāra* by Śaṅkaramiśra]. *Vaiśeṣikadarśane maharṣipravarapraśastadevācārcaviracitaṃ praśastapādabhāṣyam, vidvaccūḍāmaṇiśrīśaṅkaramiśravinirmitaḥ upaskāraś ca*. Ed. by Duṇḍirāja Śāstri. (Kashi Sanskrit Series, 3.) Varanasi 1923.

S = ["Sena Court commentary" on the *Vaiśeṣikasūtras*]. The 9th *adhyāya* is given on pp. 317-380 of *Bhaṭṭavādīndraracitavaiśeṣikavārtikakṛṣṇabhūpālaracitatrisūtrīprakāśājñātakarttṛkavṛttibhir vilasitam maharṣikaṇādapraṇītaṃ vaiśeṣikadarśanam*. Ed. by A. Thakur. Darbhanga 1985.

SVR = [*Syādvādaratnākara* by Vādidevasūri]. *Pramāṇanayatattvālokālaṅkāraḥ tadvyākhyā ca syādvādaratnākaraḥ*. Ed. by Motīlāl, Puṇyapattana 1927- (Reprint: Delhi 1988.)

Secondary literature

BRONKHORST, J. 1994. Once again Vaiśeṣikasūtra 3.1.13. *Asiatische Studien/ Études Asiatiques* 48(2): 665-681.

DAY, T. & H. KINCAID 1994. Putting inference to the best explanation in its place. *Synthese* 98: 271-295.

FADDEGON, B. 1918. *The Vaiśeṣika-System. Described with the Help of the Oldest Texts*. Amsterdam.

FRAUWALLNER, E. 1955. Candramati und sein Daśapadārthaāstram. In: O. Spies (ed.), *Studia Indologica. Festschrift für Willibald Kirfel zur Vollendung seines 70. Lebensjahres*: 65-85. Bonn 1955.

—— 1958. Die Erkenntnislehre des klassischen Sāṃkhyasystems, *Wiener Zeitschrift für die Kunde Süd- und Ostasiens* 2: 84-139.

—— 1968. *Materialien zur ältesten Erkenntnislehre der Karmamīmāṃsā*. Wien.

GOUGH, A. 1872. *The Vaiśeshika Aphorisms of Kaṇāda. With Comments from the Upaskāra of Śaṅkara Misra and the Vivritti of Jaya-Nārāyaṇa Tarkapañchānana*. Benares. (2nd edition: Delhi 1975.)

HARMAN, G. 1965. The inference to the best explanation. *Philosophical Review* 74: 88-95.

—— 1967. Detachment, probability, and maximum likelihood. *Nous* 1: 401-411

—— 1968. Knowledge, inference, and explanation. *American Philosophical Quarterly* 5: 164-173.

HATTORI, M. 1966. Studies of the Vaiśeṣikadarśana (I), On the Vaiśeṣikasūtra III,i,13. *Indogaku-Bukkyōgaku-Kenkyū* 14: 902-890.

—— 1968. *Dignāga – on Perception. Being the Pratyakṣapariccheda of Dignāga's Pramāṇasamuccaya from the Sanskrit Fragments and the Tibetan Versions.* Cambridge, Mass.

ISAACSON, H. 1995. Materials for the study of the Vaiśeṣika system. PhD thesis submitted to the University of Leiden.

KATSURA, Sh. 1981. Waisheeshika-gakuha no suiriron ni tai suru Digunāga no hihan. (Dignāga's criticism of the Vaiśeṣika Theory of Inference.) *Tetsugaku* 33: 51-65.

—— 1986. On the Origin and Development of the concept of *vyāpti* in Indian Logic. *Hiroshima-Tetsugaku-Kai* 38: 1-16.
(An English summary of the more extensive Japanese publication *Indo-ronrigaku ni okeru henjū-gainen no seisei to hatten.* (The origin and development of the concept of *vyāpti* in Indian Logic.) *Hiroshima-Daigaku-Bungakubu-Kiyō* 45, *Tokushō* 1.)

KELLNER, B. 1997. *Nichts bleibt nichts*. Wien.

MIYAMOTO, K. 1996. *The Metaphysics and Epistemology of the Early Vaiśeṣikas.* With an appendix *Daśapadārthī* of Candramati (a translation with a reconstructed Sanskrit text, notes and a critical edition of the Chinese version). (Bhandarkar Oriental Series, 28.) Pune.

MOTEGI, Sh. 1985. Saṃbandha no mondaiten (The problem of saṃbandha). *Shūkyō no Kenkyū* 58.4: 139-140.

MOTEGI, Sh. 1989. Sānkya-gakuha no suirisetsu (The theory of inference according to the Sāṅkhya school). *Indo-Shisōshi-Kenkyū* 6: 41-52.

NENNINGER, C. 1992. *Aus gutem Grund. Praśastapādas anumāna-Lehre und die drei Bedingungen des logischen Grundes*. Reinbek.

—— 1994. *sāmānyato dṛṣṭam anumānam* – analogical reasoning in early Nyāya-Vaiśeṣika. In: J. Bronkhorst (ed.), *Proceedings of the Panel on Early Vaiśeṣika, Hong Kong, August 1993* (= *Asiatische Studien/ Études Asiatiques* 48(2)): 819-832.

OBERHAMMER, G., E. PRETS & J. PRANDSTETTER 1991. *Terminologie der frühen philosophischen Scholastik in Indien*, I: A-I. Wien.

OETKE, C. 1988. *Ich und das Ich*. Stuttgart.

RANDLE, H. N. 1930. *Indian Logic in the Early Schools. A Study of the Nyāyadarśana in Its Relation to the Early Logic of Other Schools*. Oxford.

RÖER, E. 1867. Die Lehrsprüche der Vaiçeshika-Philosophie von Kaṇāda. *Zeitschrift der Deutschen Morgenländischen Gesellschaft* 21: 309-420.

SCHUSTER, N. 1972. Inference in the Vaiśeṣikasūtras. *Journal of Indian Philosophy* 1: 341-395.

SINHA, J. 1956. *History of Indian Philosophy*, I. Calcutta.

THAKUR, A. 2003. *Origin and Development of the Vaiśeṣika System*. (History of Science, Philosophy and Culture in Indian Civilization, II, Part 4. Ed. by D. P. Chattopadhyaya.) New Delhi.

UI, H. 1917. *The Vaiśeshika Philosophy According to the Daśapadārtha-Śāstra*. Chinese text with introduction, translation and notes. London.

The Discussion of *pramāṇas* in the Spitzer Manuscript

ELI FRANCO

It is remarkable that the topic of *pramāṇa* appears at least twice in the Spitzer Manuscript[1]; once on folio 133-134 and once towards the end of the manuscript ca. folio 395.[2] No apparent connection between the two discussions could be established so far and the two seemingly independent discussions indicate perhaps that the manuscript is a compilation, or a Sammelhandschrift. In spite of its fragmentary nature, the discussion of the *pramāṇas* in the Spitzer Manuscript is of crucial importance. As far as I know, this manuscript is the only Sanskrit source that testifies to the fact that certain Buddhists, probably affiliated to the Sarvāstivāda school, accepted a theory of four *pramāṇas*. It confirms thereby the testimony of **Upāyahṛdaya/*Prayogasāra* which is available only in Chinese translation (cf. Tucci's Sanskrit translation quoted in fn. 13 below).

Of the first discussion four fragments remain, three of folio 133 and one of 134. Although large portions are missing, I have argued elsewhere[3] that these folios are the remnants of a discussion of four *pramāṇas*: perception (which must have been discussed in folios ca

[1] Shortly after writing this paper I published a complete edition of the Spitzer fragments: *The Spitzer Manuscript. The Oldest Philosophical Manuscript in Sanskrit*. Austrian Academy of Sciences Press 2004. I am indebted to Karin Preisendanz for her useful comments on a previous draft of this paper.

[2] This folio is discussed in Franco 2004.

[3] Cf. Franco 2001.

131-132 – nothing seems to remain of this discussion), inference, comparison and verbal testimony (which must have been discussed ca folios 135-136). The available fragments come from the middle part of this discussion, that is, they contain the end of the portion on inference and the beginning of that on comparison. I have already dealt with these fragments on a different occasion and, therefore, a word of explanation is due here as to why I take the trouble to deal with them again. Three reasons: First, our convener and friend, Brendan Gillon, wanted the Spitzer Manuscript to be represented in this panel on Indian logic before Vātsyāyana and I believe he is right because, given that the *Upāyahṛdaya* and *Tarkaśāstra* survive only in Chinese translation, these fragments represent the earliest discussion of *pramāṇa*s in a Buddhist text that survived in the original Sanskrit. Second, the fragments were not published in a scholarly journal, but in the newsletter of the Bukkyō Dendō Kyōkai and thus remain widely unknown and not easily accessible. Thirdly, and most importantly, I would like to take this opportunity to correct, revise and expand on certain points in my earlier interpretation. For those parts about which I still agree with my previous *skandha*s, I will simply repeat portions from the above-mentioned publication.

When I first put together the three fragments from frames 85 and 132 that belong, so I claimed, to fol. 133, I was unaware of Miyasaka's paper "Fragments of materials of Indian logic found in Kizil",[4] and I would like to thank warmly Professor Akira Yuyama for drawing my attention to it. Miyasaka has used hand-copies by Shōkō Watanabe that were made in the thirties and it is clear from those transcriptions that the three fragments were together at that time and in the order in which I placed them. So we can now be certain about their arrangement as presented below. Note that the distance between the three fragments is distorted in the reproduction. The original size of the leaf must have been ca. 40 cm and the fragments were certainly more widely apart.

---

[4] Cf. Miyasaka 1963.

fol. 133r

[frames 85 (left fragment) and 132 (middle and right fragment);
size from left to right: 4.2 x 5.2; 4.3 x 6.4; 4.4 x 12.7]

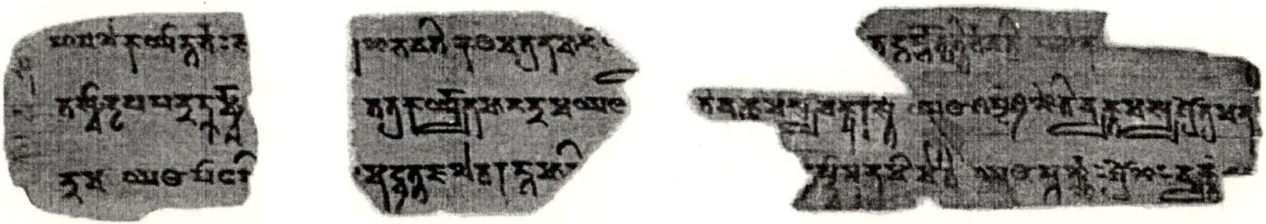

1) habalākāyāṅ garbhaḥ s./// ///r(e)ṇa bhavati ◊ katham atrānumānaṃ .. .[y]./// ///+ + + + + + + + tād garbbhotpattir bhavati ◊ [balākā] + + + + + + .t.///

2) tasmād upapannaṅ karmmā(numāna?)/// ///◊ tatra kāryyānumānan nāma yath(ā)/// ///ti[5] v[ya]k[t]am asya cakṣur asti ◊ yathā śabdaṃ śṛṇoti vyaktam asya śrotram anu///

3) n nāma ◊ yathā pāṭa[l]i(putra?)/// ///.. m udvṛttajalataraṅgamā .i + +/// ///+ + + + .. [dṛ?]ṣṭvā anumimīte ◊ yathā pūrṇṇaḥ śroṇaḥ vyaktaṃ [me](gha?)///

---

[5] I expect here something like *yathā rūpaṃ paśyati*.

fol. 133v

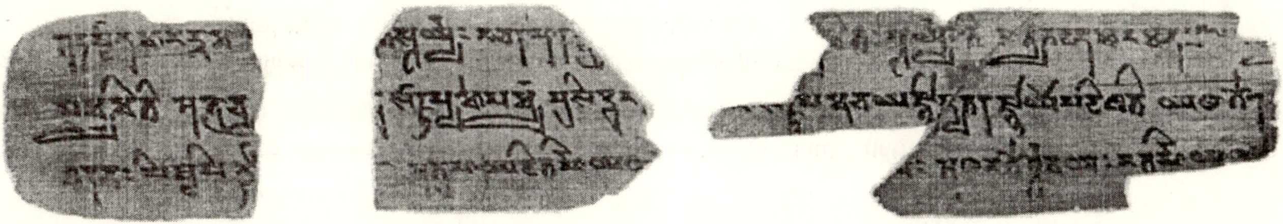

1) adṛṣṭānumānan nāma /// ///.[y]. [t]. sūryyaḥ na ca rāhur ā. .r. .[ṛ] + +/// ///+ + + .. mitaḥ sūryya iti ◊ ity [e]tad anumānam a[numā] .. .. .y.///

2) (au?)pamyam iti ◊ atrocya(te)/// ///.[dh]. sārūpyam aupamyaṃ ◊ prasiddhena ../// ///.. ..[6] rūpam ubhayajño (')[n]yatarajñāyopadiśati ◊ yathā gaur e[va?]///[7]

3) śarabhaḥ piṣṭapiṇḍī/// /// | atrāha yadi tarhi yath[ā] ../// /// + + + + + + .. ḥ ◊ atha na gaur ggavayaḥ na tarhi ya[thā gau]///

[6] The remnants of the *akṣaras* are compatible with *ṇābh.* or *ṇās.*; one should probably read *sarūpam.*

[7] Perhaps: *yathā gaur evaṃ gavayaḥ.*

The fourth fragment presented below we no longer have in the original. It was either destroyed or misplaced during World War II. In any case it no longer appears among the fragments of SHT 810 and we only know of it thanks to a transcription effected by Moritz Spitzer in 1927 or 1928. This fragment had no folio number on it, but I think it must belong to folio 134.

folio 134[8]

a.[9]

[1] /// j[i]jñ[ā]te cārtthe prasiddhaṃ saṃpratipattiḥ [sa]ṃ[j]ñ[ā]vyavasāyo nāma ajijñāte cāpra . ///

[2] /// t [v]yavasāye sati bhavaty etad astīdan na ca jānīmaḥ kim apīdan na hīdaṃ vyaktam upalabhāmahe ///

[3] /// smān na puras[t]ād darśanāt saṃjñāvyavasāyo bhavati tasmiṃ punar ārtthe vyapadeśābuddhiḥ [p] ///

b.

[1] /// (a)tredān[īṃ] dvitīyatṛtīyagrahaṇamātra[ṃ] bhavati sarvv(aṃ) tatpūrvvavad anumāna[ṃ][10] yatretad vya[p](adiś)[y](a) . . ///

[2] /// . . . vān yair gguṇair gguṇīyair gguṇaguṇaguṇair gguṇaguṇīyair gguṇaguṇāvayavair gguṇag. ///

[3] /// . . gavayo gaur api sāddhyo tatra yadaca[11] kīrt[t]ir bhavān na ca sārdhyena sādhanam tasmān na [gav](ayo gaur) [api sāddhyo] ///

---

[8] The transcription is copied from Spitzer's Nachlass page 44. There is a reference there to a certain, not further specified location: "2 oben".

[9] The designation "a" and "b" nowadays usually refers to the sides of the glass frame, which are not necessarily identical to the recto and verso of the fragment. However, Spitzer used "a" and "b" also in cases where there is no doubt about the recto and the verso. In the case of the present fragment it is not possible to determine with certainty which side is the recto.

[10] So in Spitzer's transcription. I would prefer to read *tat pūrvavadanumānaṃ* or even *tat pūrvavad anumānaṃ*.

[11] Perhaps: *yadā ca*.

Folio 133 takes us right into the middle of the discussion on inference (*anumāna*). This discussion must have been preceded by a discussion on perception (*pratyakṣa*), but unfortunately no fragments from that part of the manuscript seem to have survived. The discussion on inference continues up to folio 133v1 and is immediately followed (on the same line) by a discussion on comparison or analogy (*aupamya*). The discussion on comparison continued beyond folio 134 and was most probably followed by a discussion on verbal testimony (*aitihya?*), of which also no fragments remain.[12] The sequence of the discussion is significant because it shows that the exposition followed the same tradition as that of the *Nyāyasūtra* and the **Upāyahṛdaya*[13] as opposed to the one followed in the *Carakasaṃhitā*, where comparison and verbal testimony are discussed in reverse order. However, in terminology the discussion follows the same tradition as that of the *Carakasaṃhitā*, and uses the terms *aupamya* and, possibly, *aitihya*[14] rather than *upamāna* and *śabda*.

The discussion of inference must have begun with a general definition and an enumeration of various types of inferences. Both sections are now lost, but we can recover some of the types of inference from the preserved fragments. In folio 133r2 I tentatively suggest the reading *karmmānumāna* (inference of or, better, from[15] an action); in the same line we can clearly read *kāryyānumāna* (inference [of a cause] from an effect). In folio 133v1 an inference

---

[12] Theoretically, therefore, it is possible that only three *pramāṇa*s were discussed. It is, however, less probable that comparison was discussed and verbal communication was not.

[13] Cf. NS 1.1.3ff., and UP, p. 6,11-12: *atha katividhaṃ pramāṇam. caturvidhaṃ pramāṃam. pratyakṣam anumānam upamānam āgamaś ceti.*

[14] The word *aitihya* appears in the discussion on ca. folio 395. We cannot be certain that the same terminology was used here too, but there is at least no evidence to the contrary.

[15] Among the types of inference in the *hetuvidyā* section of the *Yogācārabhūmi* (cf. YBhū, p. 12*), we find *karmato'numāna*. It is interesting to note that among the examples for an inference from action one finds the inference of the senses, which appears in the fragments above (folio 133r2) as an example for an inference from effect. Cf. below.

of something invisible (*adṛṣṭānumāna*) is mentioned. In the discussion on comparison (folio 134b1), yet another type of inference may be mentioned: *pūrvavadanumāna*, i.e., presumably an inference that is based on the observation that a present state of affairs which is only partly visible, is similar to a state of affairs that was seen in its entirety before, justifying that the invisible is inferred from the presently visible aspects of the present state of affairs. This interpretation, however, is not certain because one can also read *tat pūrvavad anumāna*, i.e., this [so called comparison] is [not an independent means of cognition, but] an inference as above.

The stock-examples for inferences that are mentioned and shortly discussed in our fragments are highly interesting because they are uncommon; some of them seem to be unique. The first example (in 133r1) was misinterpreted by me because I could not make sense of the word *balākā* in its usual sense of "crane".[16] So I decided to follow the second meaning of *balākā*, namely, a mistress, a beloved woman, and I made up an inference somewhat similar to that in CS, Sūtrasthāna 11.21: *maithunaṃ garbhadarśanāt.* "[One infers] sexual intercourse from seeing the foetus."

Dieter Schlingloff, however, has rightly chastised me. *Balākā*, he said, simply does not mean a mistress, no matter what the dictionaries say, and he is probably right. I assume that this meaning is merely due to context. In other words, it is not because one may call one's lover "my dove" that the word "dove" can mean a mistress or a beautiful woman. Schlingloff has also pointed out the following passage in *Meghadhūta* 1.10 (in some editions 1.9).[17]

---

[16] By seeing the "crane" and "foetus" together one is immediately reminded, of course, of the fable about the stork dropping babies down the chimney. However, such an interpretation of the example seems improbable for several reasons. First, the word *garbha* does not mean a baby, at least not a born one. Second, the word *balākā* does not mean a "stork"; in fact, as Professor André Couture kindly informed me, it does not even mean a "crane", but an egret (Mesophoyx intermedia or Egretta garzetta) (cf. Dave 1985: 130). Besides, to my knowledge, only Europeans believe that babies are brought by storks. I am not aware that this belief was prevalent in India as well.

mandaṃ mandaṃ nudati pavanaś cānukūlo yathā tvāṃ
vāmaś cāyaṃ nadati madhuraṃ cātakas te sagandhaḥ |
garbhādhānakṣamaparicayān nūnam ābaddhamālāḥ
seviṣyante nayanasubhagam khe bhavantaṃ balākāḥ ||

As a favouring breeze drives thee very slowly forward,
And thy companion the Chataka warbles sweetly[18] here on the left,
Surely the hen-cranes, for the intimacy that can make them fertile,
Will attend, forming a garland in the air; in thee their eyes rejoice.

The Edgertons, as well as all the Sanskrit commentaries available to me (of Vallabhadeva, Dakṣiṇāvartanātha, Mallinātha and Sumativijaya), point out that egrets are supposed to get fertilized by clouds. Dakṣiṇāvartanātha also refers to a passage in the *Rāmāyaṇa* 4.28.23 to the same effect.[19] Furthermore, the commentaries also mention a certain inference in this connection. However, it is not entirely clear what inference is involved here. Do the egrets infer what is the right moment to be united with the clouds? Or do we infer that the egrets are impregnated by the clouds from their apparent happiness when they fly around them? Sumativijaya classifies the entire verse as *anumānālaṅkāra*[20] and Maurer explains (SA,

[17] Cf. Edgerton & Edgerton 1964. Note that other editions and commentaries read *kṣaṇa* or *sthira* instead of *kṣama* and *paricayā* instead of *paricayān*. I am not sure whether the Edgertons are right in their interpretation of *paricaya* as intimacy. For precisely this verse Apte (s.v. 4) glosses it with "recognition". Thus, one should understand that the egrets recognize their capacity of impregnation, or have firm (*sthira*) recognition (i.e. firm knowledge – due to an inference?) of their impregnation.

[18] It seems unlikely that the *cātaka*s (or Cuckoos) "warble sweetly". They rather call with monotonous persistency. According to Dave (1985: 130), a few species of Cuckoos "go under the common name of *cātaka* in Sanskrit, as their notes are plaintive in character. The breeding time for these often runs into the rainy season and the males are then very vocal. This, coupled with the fact that they derive all the moisture they need from their soft food consisting of caterpillars and various kinds of figs etc. and are therefore not seen to visit the water, has given rise to the popular fiction that they drink only rain-drops and that ground water is harmful to them... Hence also the conceit that their persistent calls are an appeal to the rain-cloud for a few drops to cool their parched throats. This interesting belief has given us some very beautiful *anyokti* type of poetry." I owe this reference to the kindness of André Couture.

[19] Cf. MSP, p. 54,17.

vol. 2, p. 40) that "[a]ccording to this *alaṅkāra* inference is drawn and set forth in an elegant fashion". The *Kāvyaprakāśa* defines this *alaṅkāra* as the statement of the reason and the property to be proved: *anumānam tad uktam yat sādhyasādhanayor vacas.*[21] And Maurer suggests that the fact that the egrets (or "cranes") will attend the cloud is inferred from the blowing of the favourable wind and the sweet singing of the *cātaka.* He even formulates the inference according to the five members scheme of the Nyāya syllogism (SA, vol. 2, p. 41):

1. The female-cranes will attend you (*pratijñā*),
2. because there is a gentle wind blowing and the *cātaka* is singing sweetly (*sādhana, hetu* or *liṅga*);
3. cranes always attend clouds when there is a gentle wind blowing and the *cātaka* is singing sweetly;
4. there is a gentle breeze blowing and the *cātaka* is singing sweetly (*upanayana*);
5. therefore the female cranes will attend you (*nigamana*).

If this is indeed the inference intended by Kālidāsa,[22] it is clear that it cannot be the same as the one in the Spitzer Manuscript. Dakṣiṇāvartanātha, however, seems to have another inference in mind when he says:

> *meghasaṅgatyā balākā garbhaṃ dhārayantīti prasiddham. meghābhikāmā parisampatantī saṃmoditā bhāti balākapaṅktiḥ* (*Rāmāyaṇa* 4.28.23) *iti liṅgadarśanaṃ cāsti* (MSP 54,16-17).
>
> It is well-known that egrets become pregnant by a union with clouds. And one observes a sign [for this fact, as it is said in the Rāmāyaṇa] "a row of egrets, desirous of clouds,[23] flying around [them] together, delighted, appears [like a garland of white lotuses]".[24]

---

[20] Cf. SA, p. 102,13.

[21] Cf. KP, p. 696.

[22] In support of Maurer's opinion note that *seviṣyante* is used in the future, unlike *nudati* and *nadati.*

[23] The AM thereon (vol. 5, p. 255) also explains this desire as a desire for children: *megheṣv abhikāmaḥ garbhārthaḥ yasyāḥ sā tathā.*

Here too it is not stated explicitly what exactly is the inferential sign. Perhaps it is the fact that egrets fly in a garland formation around clouds and seem to be delighted while doing that. The property to be inferred from this sign is, presumably, that egrets are impregnated by clouds. This suggestion is at least compatible with the wording of the fragment 133r1 (cf. *balākāyaṃ garbhaḥ ... garbhotpattir bhavati*). If we are to connect the example of the arising of the foetus to the beginning of next line, we may classify very tentatively this inference as *karmānumāna*[25] (the reading, however, is not certain).

The use of examples from the mythical realm is rather unusual for the early manuals of debate (and for that matter for the later ones as well). However, later on the author refers to the myth of the demon Rāhu swallowing the sun, and towards the end of the discussion, possibly in the context of comparison, the author seems to refer to the mythical animal *śarabha.* I shall return to that in a moment. It is also noteworthy that none of these examples refers to a Buddhist myth or legend. It seems probable that the author has just integrated a discussion of *pramāṇa*s from a Brahminical source. In other words, it seems that in this early period the Buddhists did not compose their own manuals of debate, as was the case at least ever since Vasubandhu, but were content to use the Brahminical ones.

Next in the discussion (133v2) comes the inference (of the cause) from the effect. Here the example is entirely clear: One infers the senses from the respective sense perceptions. For instance, it is clear that someone has a sense of vision because he sees a

---

[24] The addition in brackets is based on the second half of the verse which reads: *vātāvadhūtā varapauṇḍarikī lambeva mālā racitāmbarasya.* Dutt's translation (Dutt 1892: 771): "And rows of egrets, fond of clouds, rising up in the sky, delighted and moved by the wind, are appearing like a garland of white lotuses, spread along the welkin."

[25] Such compound is, of course, ambiguous, as it can refer to an inference of action or from action. It seems to me that the latter alternative is more probable, i.e., the action would not be the arising of the foetus, but the activities of the egrets.

shape and/or colour; it is clear that someone has a sense of hearing because he hears a sound, etc.[26] The senses themselves, it may be reminded, are invisible.[27]

The next example seems to involve the city of Pāṭaliputra which, as is well known, lies on the bank of the Ganges, and swollen waves of water (*udvṛttajalataraṅgama*). This example can be interpreted easily as yet another illustration for an inference from the effect to its cause. One can infer rain or the melting of snow upstream from the excessive amount of water downstream. However, the words *nāma yathā* in folio 133r3 probably indicate that a new type of inference has just been introduced (cf. the formulation in the previous line: *tatra kāryānumānaṃ nāma yathā* ...). Therefore, perhaps the inference here was meant to be from cause to effect, for instance, from swollen waves upstream to floods downstream.

The next example of a reason of an inference (*pūrṇṇaḥ śroṇṇaḥ*) is problematic in more than one respect. We know neither what type of inference it illustrates, nor what can be inferred from it, and even the meaning of the words themselves is uncertain. Dieter Schlingloff has kindly suggested that this example must refer to the two famous travellers Pūrṇa[28] and Śroṇa,[29] and he may be right, but I have my difficulties with this interpretation. It seems that *yathā pūrṇṇaḥ śroṇṇaḥ* is a full sentence because *vyaktam* most probably begins a new sentence just as in the previous line, *vyaktam asya*

---

[26] Cf. the *hetuvidyā* section of the *Yogācārabhūmi* (in Yaita 1992: 12*): *darśanena cakṣuḥ* [*anuminoti*], *śravaṇena śrotram, jighritena ghrāṇam, svāditena jihvām, sparśitena kāyam, vijñātena manaḥ*. Cf. also NBh on 3.1.56 (*indriyārthapañcatvāt*): *rūpagrahaṇaprayojanaṃ cakṣur anumīyate ... gandhagrahaṇaprayojanaṃ ghrāṇam anumīyate ...*

[27] One should not confuse, as often happens in discussions of Indian and Buddhist epistemology, the sense faculties with the sense-organs. The word *indriya* (and the words *cakṣus*, *śrotra*, etc.) always refers to the faculty or capacity (of seeing, hearing, etc.) and never to the organ, such as the material eyeball, the ear, etc. The latter are visible and need not be inferred.

[28] Cf. e.g. Tatelman 2001.

[29] Cf. Waldschmidt 1989.

cakṣur asti ... vyaktam asya śrotram ... . But if this is the case, then *pūrṇṇaḥ* must be a predicate to *śroṇṇaḥ*, i.e., *śroṇa* is *pūrṇa* ("*śroṇa* is full"?), whatever the two words may mean in this context.

Yet another type of inference is presented in folio 133v1, namely, an inference of an invisible object (*adṛṣṭānumāna*). The example for this inference seems clear. As is well known, Rāhu is a head-only Daitya demon who swallows the sun and the moon, thereby causing eclipses. In the present example one infers perhaps the invisible sun[30] while it stays in Rāhu's mouth (or in any case in Rāhu's head).[31]

The discussion of inference is concluded towards the end of folio 133v1 and is followed by that of comparison in the same line. Comparison is defined as similarity (folio 133v2: *sārūpyam aupamyam*). This definition may seem surprising at first sight because usually a comparison is not a similarity; rather it is based on a similarity. Indeed, this is how *Nyāyasūtra* 1.1.6 defines comparison: *prasiddhasādharmyāt sādhyasādhanam upamānam.* "Comparison is a means to prove what is to be proved on the basis of a similarity with a well-known [object]." It is clear, however, that our fragment defines *aupamya* as a means of cognition, not as the resulting cognition. This usage of the word *upamāna* is also well-known from other sources, for instance, from the *Śābara-bhāṣya*[32]: *upamānam api sādṛśyam asaṃnikṛṣṭe 'rthe buddhim ut-pādayati.* "Comparison, in its turn, [understood as] similarity, produces a cognition in respect to an object which is not in contact [with the senses]."

Our fragment explains further: When (an unknown object) is similar to a well-known one (*prasiddha*), the person who knows both instructs the person who knows only one of the two (i.e. only

---

[30] Read in 133v1 *(anu)mitaḥ sūryya iti*?

[31] As the sun leaves Rāhu's head on the opposite side from where it enters at the beginning of the eclipse, it presumably has to travel also through other parts of Rāhu's head. Or does Rāhu turn around before its reemergence?

[32] Cf. Frauwallner 1968: 32,4.

the well-known object). For instance, a gayal is similar to a cow (*prasiddhena ... rūpam ubhayajño '[n]yatarajñāyopadiśati yathā gaur ...*)

The example of the cow and the gayal is ubiquitous in the context of comparison. The next example (133v3), however, is unusual and I fail to understand it. Assuming that *piṣṭapiṇḍī* is the remaining first part of a *cvi*-formation (i.e., that the text read *piṣṭapiṇḍībhavati/bhūta-*; *piṣṭapiṇḍīkaroti/-kṛta-* or similar), it would mean that a *śarabha* turns or has turned (or, similarly, should be turned) into a flour cake or causes something (or someone?) to turn into a flour cake. Perhaps a similarity between a *śarabha* and a flour cake in a certain form is meant here, but this would be a mere guess. It s also possible that *piṣṭapiṇḍī* stands for *piṣṭapiṇḍin*. Further, who is the *śarabha* referred to here? The *Purāṇic Encyclopedia* mentions no less than seven Śarabhas, two *nāgas*, a Dānava, a Mahārṣi, various figures who play minor roles in the *Mahābhārata* and one in the *Śivapurāṇa*.[33] The *Rāmāyaṇa* knows a monkey-chief of this name. Hopkins points out that *śarabha* is one of the names of Viṣṇu, as of honoured apes, demons and *nāgas*. Apparently it is also used as title of the Buddha.[34] It seems more probable, however, is that we are not dealing with a proper name, for one expects a general state of affairs to be used in the illustrations of the *pramāṇas*. I suggest that *śarabha* here is the demonic animal with eight feet, who kills lions and eats raw flesh, that is mentioned several times in the *Mahābhārata*.[35] In Śāntiparvan 117.38 there is a story about a vegetarian dog who is turned successively into a tiger, an elephant, a lion and finally into a *śarabha*. In the process he turns into a meat eater and loses his morals too. At the end he plots to eat up the *ṛṣi* who turned him into all these animals for his own protection. But the *ṛṣi* who figures out the plot turns him back into a miserable dog. In this context the word *piśitāśana* (a flesh-

[33] Cf. Mani 1975, s.v.

[34] Cf. Hopkins 1915: 19.

[35] Cf. Hopkins 1915: 18.

eater) occurs several times. Should one conjecture *piśita* for *piṣṭa*? This would be perhaps more becoming of a *śarabha*, but in either case I fail to recover the analogy or the similarity that was intended here.

The rest of the line seems to discuss the basic notion of similarity. The difficulty of this notion is sometimes expressed in the form of a dilemma: If two things are identical they are not similar precisely because they are identical,[36] and if two things are different they cannot be similar precisely because they are different. The remnants of the line seem to mention the second horn of this dilemma: "If the gayal is not a cow, then [it cannot be said that a gayal is] like a cow" (*atha na gaur gavayaḥ na tarhi ya*[*thā gau*] ...).

The details of the next lines (folio 134a1-3) are obscure, but the subject matter can be identified with relative certainty: the object of cognition resulting from comparison. Indeed, it is not obvious what exactly is newly apprehended by means of comparison when one sees a gayal for the first time after being told that a gayal is like a cow. It is not the animal as such because it is apprehended by sense perception. It is also not the fact that there is a similarity between the cow and the gayal because this is already known at the time of the corresponding communication by the knowledgeable person; thus, comparison would be indistinguishable from verbal communication. The resulting cognition can also not be the mere understanding or the conclusion that the particular animal that is being observed for the first time is a gayal because in that case comparison would not be different from inference. Some Mīmāṃsakas of the Bhāṭṭa school claimed the result of comparison to be the cognition that the remembered cow is similar to the gayal and were criticised by the Naiyāyikas for reducing comparison to inference.[37] Our text, however, professes a different opinion: The result of comparison is the cognition of the designation (*vyapadeśabuddhi*), i.e.,

[36] In this case to say that a gayal is like a cow does not convey anything new; it is like saying that a cow is like a cow.

[37] Cf. Bhatt 1962: 290ff.

the cognition that the animal in front is called "gayal". Cf. folio 134a3: *(ta?)smān na puras*[*t*]*ād darśanāt saṃjñāvyavasāyo bhavati tasmiṃ punar ārthe vyapadeśabuddhiḥ* [*p*] ... . "Therefore, the determination of the term is not due to the observation in front; in respect to this object [in front], however, the cognition of the term [arises due to comparison only]."

This statement is remarkable because it is virtually identical with the Nyāya doctrine as expressed in Vātsyāyana's *Nyāyabhāṣya*[38]:

> *samākhyasambandhapratipattir upamānārtha iti ... asya gavayaśabdaḥ saṃjñeti saṃjñāsaṃjñisambandhaṃ pratipadyate* (NBh 1.1.6).
>
> The purpose of comparison is the cognition of the relation of the term [and what is designated by it]. ... One apprehends the relation between the designation and designated [in the form] "the word *gavaya* is the designation of this [animal]".

The rest of the fragment is difficult to interpret. In folio 134b1 an opponent may attempt to reduce comparison to inference in general or to a special type of inference such as *pūrvavadanumāna*. The formulation *dvitīyatṛtīyagrahaṇamātra*[*ṃ*] could thus indicate that he argues that the so-called comparison is in fact an inference inasmuch as it brings about its result only after the second and subsequent apprehensions of the cow and the gayal, just as an inference can bring about its result only upon the second and subsequent apprehensions of the *liṅga*.

The next line is extremely obscure. My guess is that it enumerates various objects that can be responsible for the arising of the notion of similarity. The similarity can obtain between qualities, qualifiables, qualities and qualities of qualities, qualities and qualifiables, qualities and parts of qualities, etc. (... *guṇair guṇīyair guṇaguṇaguṇair guṇaguṇīyair guṇaguṇāvayavair* ...).[39] There are

---

[38] Cf. NBh, p. 13,14-16.

[39] For a detailed discussion of the notion of similarity cf. *Ślokavārttika*, *Upamāna* 18ff.

two remarkable things about this statement. First, the word *guṇīya* which is not recorded by the dictionaries is probably irregularly derived from the denominative *guṇayati.*[40] Second, the compounds *guṇaguṇa* and *guṇāvayava* indicate that our text was written before the establishment of the classical Vaiśeṣika doctrine that qualities may not be qualified by further qualities and not have parts.[41]

These remarks conclude my short investigation. The endeavour, I believe, has been worthwhile. Even though many details remain obscure and the interpretation is at places only tentative, I hope I was able to convey a convincing image of what is certainly one of the earliest discussions of the means of knowledge that has survived, albeit in a fragmentary form. So little is known about Indian and Buddhist philosophy in the Kuṣāṇa period that almost every meaningful fragment, regardless of its size, imparts something new to us and enriches our understanding of this period. Further, even when a certain doctrine or theory is not new to us because it is available from later sources, it is pertinent to know that it was current at such an early stage. A clear example of this is presented by the discussion of comparison. Although the theory of comparison as resulting in the apprehension of the relation between designation and designated is not new to us in the sense that a similar idea is expressed in later Nyāya texts, its appearance here is of a considerable importance. So far our earliest source for this theory has been the *Nyāyabhāṣya* and accordingly it has been generally assumed that it is a product, if not of Vātsyāyana himself, then at least of his time (second half of 5th century) because it appears neither in the *sūtra*, nor in other early sources on comparison, viz., *Śābarabhāṣya*,

---

[40] Another irregular formation in this fragment is the word *jijñāta* (also in a negated form *ajijñāta*) in 134a1 which is probably a BHS-form of *jijñāsita*.

[41] Professor Bronkhorst's objection (in a personal communication) that this is improbable because we deal with a Buddhist text is not entirely convincing. As pointed out above, this discussion of the *pramāṇa*s in the Spitzer manuscript, although of course accepted by the group of Buddhists probably from the Sarvāstivāda school, seems to have originated in a Brahminical milieu. However, it goes without saying that my suggestion is made only tentatively as the context of these compounds is missing.

**Upāyahṛdaya*, *Carakasaṃhitā* and **Tarkaśāstra*. Thanks to the precious fragment of the "Spitzer Manuscript" we can now establish that this doctrine of comparison was current at least two centuries before Vātsyāyana.

As is obvious from the above, there are still many obscure points in the Spitzer fragments. My hope in presenting them here is that someone else will be able to understand more and better than I did.

REFERENCES

Texts and abbreviations

AM = [*Amṛtamataka*]. *Śrīmadvālmīkirāmāyaṇa with Amṛtamataka of Madhavayogi*. Ed. by K. S. Varadacharya. Mysore 1960.

CS = [*Carakasaṃhitā*]. *The Cāraka Saṃhitā of Agniveśa Revised by Caraka and Dṛḍhabala.* With the Āyurveda-Dīpikā Commentary of Cakrapāṇidatta and with "Vidyotinī" Hindī Commentary by Kāśinātha Śāstrī. Ed. by Gaṅgāsahāya Pandeya. 2 vols. (Kashi Sanskrit Series, 194.) 2nd edition. Varanasi 1983.

KP = [*Kāvyaprakāśa*]. *Kāvyaprakāśa of Mammaṭa*. Ed. by V. M. Jhalakikar. Poona 1983.

MSP = [*Meghasandeśapradīpa*]. In: N. P. Unni, *Meghasandeśa of Kālidāsa with the Commentary Pradīpa of Dakṣiṇāvartanātha.* Delhi 1984.

NBh = [*Nyāyabhāṣya*]. *Gautamīyanyāyadarśana with Bhāṣya of Vātsyāyana.* Ed. by A. Thakur. New Delhi 1997.

NS = [*Nyāyasūtra*]. W. Ruben, *Die Nyāyasūtra's*. Leipzig 1928.

SA = [*Sugamānvayā Vṛtti*]. Sumativijaya, *Sugamānvayā Vṛtti*. Ed. by W. H. Maurer. Poona 1965.

UP = [*Upāyahṛdaya*]. In: G. Tucci, *Pre-Diṅnāga Buddhist Texts on Logic from Chinese Sources*. Baroda 1929. (Reprint: Madras 1981.)

YBhū = [*Yogācārabhūmi*]. In Yaita 1992.

Secondary literature

BHATT, G. P. 1962. *Epistemology of the Bhāṭṭa School of Pūrva Mīmāṃsā.* Varanasi.

DAVE, K. N. 1985. *Birds in Sanskrit Literature*. Delhi.

DUTT, M. N. (trans.) 1892. *The Rāmāyaṇa*. Calcutta.

EDGERTON, E. & F. EDGERTON (trans.) 1964. *Kalidasa, The Cloud Messenger*. Michigan.

FRANCO, E. 2001. Fragments of a Buddhist pramāṇa-theory from the Kuṣāṇa period. *Bukyō Dendō Kyōkai Fellowship Newsletter* 4: 2-12.

—— 2004. A Note on Nāgārjuna and the Naiyāyikas. In: S. Hino & T. Wada (eds.), *Three Mountains and Seven Rivers: Prof. Musashi Tachikawa's Felicitation Volume*: 203-208. Delhi.

FRAUWALLNER, E. 1968: *Materialien zur ältesten Erkenntnislehre der Karmamīmāṃsā*. Wien.

HOPKINS, E. W. 1915. *Epic Mythology*. (Grundriss der Indo-Arischen Philologie und Altertumskunde, 3.1.B.) Strassburg.

MANI, V. 1975. *Purāṇic Encyclopedia*. Delhi.

MIYASAKA, Y. 1963. Fragments of materials of Indian logic found in Kizil. *Syūkyō Kenkyū* 36.3 (Serial Nr. 174, January 1963): 115-116. (Reprinted in *Indo-Koten-Ron*, II [= Bhāratīyasaṃskṛtagranthanirūpaṇam, 2] (February 1984): 309-311.

TATELMAN, J. 2001. *The Glorious Deeds of Pūrṇa. A Translation and Study of the Pūrṇāvadāna*. Delhi.

WALDSCHMIDT, E. 1989. Ein Beitrag zur Überlieferung vom Sthavira Śroṇakoṭikarṇa. In: H. Bechert & P. Kieffer-Pülz (eds), *Ausgewählte Kleine Schriften*: 210-216. Stuttgart.

YAITA, H. 1992. Yugaron no inmyō: Bonbun tekisuto to wayaku. *Naritasan Bukkyō Kenkyūjo Kiyō* 15: 505-576.

The Logic of the *Saṃdhinirmocanasūtra*: Establishing Right Reasoning Based on Similarity (*sārūpya*) and Dissimilarity (*vairūpya*)

CHIZUKO YOSHIMIZU

1. INTRODUCTION

The logic of the *Saṃdhinirmocanasūtra* (hereafter SNSū)[1] is represented by *upapattisādhanayukti* ("the reason [consisting in] the establishment by argument") taught in the tenth chapter, through

[1] The text of the SNSū cited in the present paper is its Tibetan version edited by E. Lamotte based on the sNar thang Kanjur (Bibliothèque Nationale no. 410). The sDe dge, Peking and Them spangs ma editions, as well as the old translation edited by N. Hakamaya based on Stein no. 194, are also to be consulted. The Chinese translations by Bodhiruci (菩提流支, Taishō no. 675, vol. 16), Hsuan-tsang (玄奘, Taishō no. 676, vol. 16) and Guṇabhadra (求那跋陀羅, Taishō no. 679, vol. 16) are referred to as well. As for the old and new Tibetan translations of the SNSū, cf. Hakamaya 1984 and 1987. The Them spangs ma edition available in the form of a handwritten manuscript is reported to have been copied between 1858 and 1878 and brought to Japan by Ekai Kawaguchi (cf. Saitō 1977). According to Eimer (1983, I: 120f.; 1992: xviii), and Harrison (1992: 89), this edition belongs to the tradition descended from the old sNar thang manuscript of the 14th century. Katō (2003) has recently launched the comparative study of the Them spangs ma edition of the SNSū with its younger editions. Insofar as the passages treated in this paper are concerned, the Them spangs ma edition offers several different translations. With regard to the date of the establishment of the SNSū as well as that of the Chinese translations, cf., e.g., Schmithausen 1969: 822f.; Suguro 1976; Hakamaya 1982: 51f.; Powers 1993: 4ff. With regard to the numerous studies of the SNSū, cf. Powers 1993: 167-179 (Bibliography).

which the *Sūtra* provides a method for establishing important Buddhist tenets such as impermanence (*anityatā*), painfulness (*duḥkhatā*) and non-self (*anātman*).[2] There is a great difference between the reasoning presented by the SNSū and the reasoning in the form of *anumāna* by later Buddhist logicians, as I have closely investigated in my previous papers.[3] Neither the idea of *dharma-dharmin* relation nor that of the logical reason (*hetu*) with three characteristics (*trairūpya*) is introduced.[4] Inference (*anumāna*) is

---

[2] Regarding the terms *yukti* and *upapattisādhanayukti*, cf. Yoshimizu 1996a: 114, n. 85; 1996b: 123-130, 160ff. (English summary), and the references cited therein. The Tibetan versions give the translation *'thad pa* (DP, Lamotte) or *gtan tshigs* (Them spangs ma) to the Sanskrit word *upapatti*. I am of the opinion that the term *yukti* common to the four kinds of *yukti* (viz., *apekṣā-*, *kāryakaraṇa-*, *upapattisādhana-* and *dharmatāyukti*) is to be rendered by "reason" in the sense of principle or fundamental truth as the bases of investigation or action, which well corresponds to Hsuan-tsang's Chinese translation *tao-li* (道理). I do not accept Powers' interpretation of the four *yukti*s as "analysis of dependence, analysis of performance of functions, analysis of logical correctness, and analysis of reality" (Powers 1995: 285), since the first member of each compound does not refer to the object of analysis. The term *upapattisādhana* in *upapattisādhana-yukti* is supposed to mean the establishment of the existence of an object, a fact or the truth of a statement by means of an argument that it is directly cognized, inferred and ascertained by scriptural authority. Hence, I interpret *upapatti-sādhanayukti* as the reason for understanding something, which consists in the idea that whatever is established by a solid argument based on the three kinds of valid means of cognition (*pramāṇa*) is true. These *yukti*s are the means of investigation of existents and tenets for early Yogācāra thinkers. Refer to the definitions of the four kinds of *yukti* and *upapattisādhanayukti* in other Yogācāra literature such as in the SNSū, the ŚrBh, the AS, MSA XIX 45, BBh IV, and MAV III 12 cited in Yoshimizu 1996a: 114, n. 85 and 1996b: 130-143, 160ff. (English summary). The citation from ŚrBh 143, 14ff. describing *dharmatāyukti* in Yoshimizu 1996a: 117, n. 85 and 1996b: 134, n. 27 should be corrected as follows: (ŚrBh, cf. Shōmonji 120*,11ff.) *sarvatraiva ca dharmataiva pratisaraṇaṃ dharmataiva yuktiḥ cittanidhyāpanāya cittasaṃjñāpanāya. iyam ucyate dharmatāyuktiḥ.* Besides the ŚrBh, the AS and the MSA, the RGV should also be referred to for its mentioning of *dharmatāyukti* in the first chapter (RGV 73: 12-16: *yaiva cāsau dharmatā saivātra yuktir yoga upāyaḥ paryāyaḥ. evam eva tat syāt. anyathā naiva tat syād iti. sarvatra dharmataiva pratiśaraṇam. dharmataiva yuktiś cittanidhyāpanāya cittasaṃjñāpanāya. sā na cintayitavyā na vikalpayitavyādhimoktavyeti.*).

[3] Yoshimizu 1996a: 120, n. 92; 1996b: 143ff.

[4] It is known that the three characteristics (*trairūpya*) of a proper logical reason (*hetu*) appear in some earlier texts on logic than Dignāga such as the

considered to be the conjecture of the existence of an imperceptible object from related perceptible evidence. An example (*dṛṣṭānta*) serves as a parallel instance of the evidence. The theory of pervasion (*vyāpti*) has not yet been formulated.[5] Instead, the *Sūtra* suggests, in my view, the idea that the concomitance (*anvaya*) of the proof (*sādhana*) with the object to be proven (*sādhya*) is confirmed by the cognition of similarity (*sārūpya*) and dissimilarity (*vairūpya*). This idea appears in the *Sūtra*'s description of the seven "impure" (*yongs su ma dag pa, *apariśuddha*) or faulty characteristics of reason, which contrast with the five "pure" (*yongs su dag pa, *pariśuddha*) or right characteristics. Since I have not discussed these faulty characteristics in my previous studies, I should like to focus on them in the present paper. I am thereby aiming at the full clarification of the logic of the SNSū. The analysis of the seven faulty characteristics is expected to serve to specify more clearly the conditions that the *Sūtra* requires for establishing right reasoning. This should also greatly help to trace out the early development of Indian epistemology and logic within the Buddhist tradition. In the following, I shall first give my translation of the entire passage including both "pure" and "impure" characteristics, and proceed to a critical discussion thereof.

Ru-shi-lun (如実論,**Tarkaśāstra*, Taishō no. 1633, vol. 32) attributed to Vasubandhu and the *Shun-zhong-lun* (順中論, Taishō no. 1565, vol. 30) attributed to Asaṅga, which are preserved in their Chinese translations. Cf., e.g., the studies by Ui 1929; Tucci 1929a; 1929b; Kajiyama 1984; Katsura 1986a.

[5] According to Katsura (1986b: 63), it is safe to regard Dignāga as the first logician to have introduced the idea of *vyāpti*.

2. TRANSLATION

2.1. Definition of *upapattisādhanayukti* and five pure characteristics[6]

[*Definition of upapattisādhanayukti*] "Whatever is the cause and condition of the verifying and correct understanding of the objects that are known, explained and stated, that is the reason [consisting in] the establishment by argument."

---

[6] SNSū 155,23–157,2, 157,19ff. (D51a5-52a1, 52a4f., P56a2-56b6, 57a1ff., Taishō 675: 686b, 676: 709bc, 679: 719a, Them spangs ma 65a5-66a2, 66a5f., cf. Stein 194 edited in Hakamaya 1987: 25,5-18, 27,4-7, mDo btus pa P70b7f. cited in Yoshimizu 1996a: 115, n. 85; 1996b: 129, n. 21): **so so'i shes pa dang | bshad pa dang | smras pa'i don sgrub pa dang | legs par khong du chud par bya ba'i* rgyu gang dag yin pa dang | rkyen gang dag yin pa de ni 'thad pas grub pa'i rigs pa** yin no || de'ang*(0) *mdor sdu na rnam pa gnyis te | yongs su dag pa dang | yongs su ma dag pa'o || de la yongs su dag pa'i mtshan nyid ni lnga'o | yongs su ma dag pa'i mtshan nyid ni bdun no || de la yongs su dag pa'i mtshan nyid lnga po dag gang zhe na |* ***a.*** *de mngon sum du dmigs pa'i mtshan nyid dang |* ***b.*** *de la gnas pa mngon sum du dmigs pa'i mtshan nyid dang |* ***c.*** *rang gi rigs kyi dpe nye bar sbyar ba'i mtshan nyid dang |* ***d.*** *yons su grub pa'i mtshan nyid dang |* ***e.*** *lung shin tu rnam par dag pa gtan la phab par*(1) *bstan pa'i mtshan nyid do ||* ***a.*** *de la 'du byed thams cad mi rtag pa nyid dang | 'du byed thams cad sdug sngal ba nyid dang | chos thams cad bdag med pa nyid 'jig rten na mngon sum du dmigs pa dang |***de lta bu dang mthun pa*(2) *gang yin pa de ni de*(3)**** mngon sum du dmigs pa'i mtshan nyid yin no ||* ***b.*** *'du byed thams cad skad cig pa nyid dang | 'jig rten pha rol yod pa nyid dang | las dge ba dang | mi dge ba chud mi za ba de la gnas pa'i mi rtag pa rags pa nyid*(4) *mngon sum du dmigs pa gang yin pa dang | sems can sna tshogs las sna tshogs la gnas pa mngon sum du dmigs pa gang yin pa dang | sems can bde ba dang sdug sngal ba las dge ba dang mi dge ba la gnas pa mngon sum du dmigs pa gang yin pa dang | gang gis ****mngon sum du ma gyur pa la**** rjes su dpag par bya ba dang | ***de lta bu dang mthun pa*(2) *gang yin pa de*** ni de la gnas pa mngon sum du dmigs pa'i mtshan nyid yin no ||* ***c.*** ******nang dang phyi rol gyi 'du byed rnams la 'jig rten thams cad la grags pa'i 'chi 'pho dang skye ba dmigs pa'i***** nye bar sbyar ba dang | skye ba la sogs pa'i sdug sngal dmigs pa nye bar sbyar ba dang | rang dbang med pa'i dmigs pa nye bar sbyar ba dang | ******phyi rol*(5) *dag na'ang*(6) *'jig rten thams cad la grags pa'i 'byor pa dang | rgud pa*(7) *dmigs pa****** nye bar sbyar ba dang |*** de lta bu dang mthun pa(2) gang yin pa*** de ni rang gi rigs kyi dpe nye bar sbyar ba'i mtshan nyid yin par rig par bya'o ||* ***d.*** *de ltar de mngon sum du dmigs pa'i mtshan nyid dang | de la gnas pa mngon sum du dmigs pa'i mtshan nyid dang | rang gi rigs kyi dpe nye bar sbyar ba'i mtshan nyid gang yin pa de ni grub par bya ba la gcig du nges pa'i phyir yongs su grub pa'i mtshan nyid yin par rig par bya'o ||* ***e.*** *'jam dpal gtan la*

[*Division of upapattisādhanayukti*] "This is further [divided] into two kinds: the pure and the impure. Between these [two], the

---

dbab par(8) *bstan pa thams cad mkhyen pas gsungs pa 'di lta ste* | *mya ngan las 'das pa ni zhi ba'o zhes bya ba dang* ****de lta bu dang mthun pa*(2) *gang yin pa**** *de ni lung shin tu*(9) *rnam par dag pa gtan la phab par*(8) *bstan pa'i mtshan nyid yin par rig par bya'o* || *de lta bas na mtshan nyid rnam pa lnga po de dag gis rigs pa brtag pa*(10)******* *yongs su dag pa ste* | *yongs su dag pa'i phyir bstan par bya'o*(11) || ... *de ltar 'thad pas(12) grub pa'i rigs pa de ni mngon sum gyi tshad ma dang* | *rjes su dpag pa'i tshad ma dang* | *yid ches pa'i lung gi tshad mas mtshan nyid lnga po dag gyis yongs su dag pa yin no* ||

(0) Cf. DP: *yang*.
(1) Cf. P: *gtan la bab par*.
(2) Cf. DP: *'thun pa*.
(3) Missing in D and P.
(4) Corrected according to Them spangs ma and SNSūV P172a8: *mi rtag par rags pa nyid* (SNSū); cf. DP and Powers 1995: 286: *mi rtag par rigs pa nyid*.
(5) Corrected according to SNSūV P174a5; cf. Stein: *phyi rol gyi 'jig rten thams cad la*.
(6) Cf. DP: *yang*.
(7) Corrected according to DP and Them spangs ma: *rgyud pa* (SNSū).
(8) Cf. DP: *bab par*.
(9) Corrected according to DP: *cin tu* (SNSū).
(10) Cf. SNSū 158,24: *rigs pas brtag pa*; Them spangs ma: *rigs par brtags pa*; Stein: *rigs pas rtog pa ste*!.
(11) Cf. DP, Stein: *bsten par bya'o*.
(12) corrected according to P: *'thad pa'i* (SNSū).
* Them spangs ma: *dam bcas shing bstan te* | *smras pa'i don sgrub pa dang* | *yang dag par shes par bya ba'i phyir* |
** Them spangs ma: *gtan tshigs sgrub pa'i rigs pa*.
*** Them spangs ma: *rnam pa 'di lta bu dag*.
**** Them spangs ma: *mngon sum du gyur pa* (to be corrected).
***** Them spangs ma: *gang yang nang dang phyi'i 'du byed rnams kyi 'jig pa dang* | *skye bar dmigs pa 'jig rten thams cad la grags pa*.
****** Stein: *phyi rol gyi 'jig rten thams cad du* | *grags pa 'byor pa dang* | *myi 'byor pa dmyigs pa*; Them spangs ma: *pha rol gyi phyun sum tshogs dang* | *rgud par dmigs pa 'jig rten thams cad la grags pa*.

In my translation, the numbers 1), 2) and 3) are inserted to indicate the correspondence to the three main objects to be established through perception (viz., impermanence, painfulness and non-self). Here I have slightly revised my previous German and Japanese translations of the same passage in Yoshimizu 1996a: 114, 115, n. 85, 119f., 120-124, n. 92 and 1996b: 128, 143, 145f. For the detailed interpretation of the five characteristics as well as the comparison with the reasonings formulated by the SNSūV according to later Buddhist logicians' system, see Yoshimizu 1996a: 119, n. 92 and 1996b: 143ff.

characteristics of the pure [reason] are fivefold. The characteristics of the impure [reason] are sevenfold."

[*Five pure characteristics*] "What are the five pure characteristics among them?

a. the characteristic of the direct cognition of the [object itself] (*tatpratyakṣopalabdhilakṣaṇa*, Mvy 4405 [N 4391]);
b. the characteristic of the direct cognition [of something] depending on the [imperceptible object to be inferred] (*tadāśrityapratyakṣopalabdhilakṣaṇa*, Mvy 4406 [N 4492]);[7]
c. the characteristic of the adduction of an example of the same kind (*svajātīyadṛṣṭāntopasaṃhāralakṣaṇa*, Mvy 4407 [N 4493]);
d. the characteristic of being complete (*pariniṣpannalakṣaṇa*, Mvy 4408 [N 4494]);
e. the characteristic of the instruction of a very pure scripture (*suviśuddhāgamopadeśalakṣaṇa*, Mvy 4409 [N 4495]).

a. Among them, the characteristic of the direct cognition of the [object itself consists in] such kinds of worldly direct cognition as [the direct cognitions] of 1) the impermanence of all conditioning factors; 2) the painfulness of all conditioning factors; and 3) the non-self of all things.

b. The characteristic of the direct cognition [of something] depending on the [imperceptible object to be inferred consists in] such kinds of direct cognition, through which something directly not [cognizable] is inferred, as 1') [the direct cognition of] coarse impermanence depending on the momentariness of all conditioning factors; 2') the cognition of various living beings [coming into this world] owing to various deeds [in the previous world] depending on the existence of another world[8]; and

[7] In my previous studies (Yoshimizu 1996a; 1996b), I have interpreted this second characteristic in accordance with its Tibetan version (*de la gnas pa mngon sum du dmigs pa*) to mean "the direct cognition of that which depends on the [imperceptible object to be inferred]".

3') the cognition of happy and suffering living beings [existing in this world] owing to good and bad deeds [in the previous world] depending on the imperishability [of the influence] of good and bad deeds [in the previous world].

c. The characteristic of the adduction of an example of the same kind is to be known [to consist in] such kinds of adduction of cognitions as [the adduction of cognitions] of 1*) death and birth, which are known to all worlds, with regard to internal and external conditioning factors; 2*) painfulness of birth and the like; and 3*) the lack of independence as well as wealth and poverty, which are known to all worlds, with regard even to external [conditioning factors].

d. The characteristic of being complete is to be known [to consist in a reasoning], insofar as thus (**a**) the characteristic of the direct cognition of the [object itself], (**b**) the characteristic of the direct cognition [of something] depending on the [imperceptible object to be inferred] and (**c**) the characteristic of the adduction of an example of the same kind are conclusive (**ekāntika*) with regard to the object to be proven (**sādhya*).

e. Mañjuśrī, the characteristic of the instruction of a very pure scripture is to be known [to consist in] such kinds of words taught by the omniscient [Buddha] as [the words] '*nirvāṇa* is calm'.

In this manner, a reasoning to be investigated is pure through these five characteristics, and, since it is pure, it is to be relied on. ... The reason [consisting in] the establishment by argument is thus pure through the five characteristics based on the valid means of perception, the valid means of inference and the valid means of scriptural authority."

---

[8] "Another world" refers to the previous world rather than the future world that Powers has proposed (1995: 287).

2.2. Seven impure characteristics[9]

"What are the seven kinds of characteristic of an impure [reason]?

a. the characteristic of the cognition of similarity in what is other than the [object to be proven] (*tadanyasārūpyopalabdhilakṣaṇa*, Mvy 4410 [N 4396]);

---

[9] SNSū 158,1-28 (D52a5-52b3, P57a2-57b1, Taishō 675: 686c, 676: 710a, 679: 719b, Them spangs ma 66a6-66b7, cf. Stein 194 edited in Hakamaya 1987: 27,7-29,5): *yongs su ma dag pa'i mtshan nyid rnam pa bdun gang zhe na* | ***a.*** *de las gzhan dang mthun par*(1) *dmigs pa'i mtshan nyid dang* | ***b.*** *de la gzhan dang mi mthun par*(2) *dmigs pa'i mtshan nyid dang* | ***c.*** *thams cad mthun par*(1) *dmigs pa'i mtshan nyid dang* | ***d.*** *thams cad mi mthun par*(2) *dmigs pa'i mthan nyid dang* | ***e.*** *gzhan gyi rigs kyi dpe nye bar sbyar ba'i mtshan nyid dang* | ***f.*** *yongs su ma grub pa'i mtshan nyid dang* | ***g.*** *lung shin tu rnam par ma dag pa bstan pa'i mtshan nyid do* | *de la chos thams cad yid kyi rnam par shes pas rnam par shes par bya ba nyid gang yin pa de ni thams cad mthun par(1) dmigs pa'i mtshan nyid yin no* || *rtags dang ngo bo nyid dang* | *las dang chos dang rgyu dang 'bras bu *mtshan nyid mi mthun pa*(2) *rnams kyi mtshan nyid mi mthun pa*(2) *gang yang rung bas phan mtshun mtshan nyid mi mthun par*(2) *nges pa nyid gang yin pa* de ni thams cad mi mthun par*(2) *dmigs pa'i mtshan nyid yin no* || *'jam dpal de la de las gzhan dang mthun par*(1) *dmigs pa'i mtshan nyid dpe dang bcas pa la thams cad mi mthun par*(2) *dmigs pa'i mtshan nyid yod pas** des na de ***grub par bya ba la gcig tu ma nges pa'i phyir*** de ni yongs su ma grub pa'i mtshan nyid ces bya'o* || *de las gzhan dang mi mthun par*(2) *dmigs pa'i mtshan nyid dpe dang bcas pa la'ang*(3) *thams cad mthun par*(1) *dmigs pa'i mtsan nyid yod pas** des na de grub par bya ba la gcig tu ma nges pa'i phyir de'ang*(3) *yongs su ma grub pa'i mtshan nyid ces bya'o* || *yongs su ma grub pa'i phyir rigs pas brtag pa yongs su ma dag pa yin te* | *yongs su ma dag pa'i phyir bstan par mi bya'o* || *de*(4) *lung shin tu rnam par ma dag pa bstan pa'i mtshan nyid ni rang bzhin nyid kyis yongs su ma dag pa*(5) *yin par rig par bya'o* ||

(1) Cf. DP and Them spangs ma: *'thun par*.

(2) Cf. D: *mi 'thun par*, *mi 'thun pa*.

(3) Cf. DP: *yang*.

(4) *la* and the phrase [*gzhan gyi rigs kyi dpe nye bar sbyar ba'i mtshan nyid dang*] is here added by Lamotte according to Taishō.

(5) Corrected according to D: *yongs su dag pa* (SNSū); cf. Them spangs ma: *rang bzhin gyis ma dag pa yin par shes par bya'o*.

* Them spangs ma: *mi mthun pa gang yang rung ba gcig gi mi thun pas phan tshun nges par mi mthun pa zhes bya ba*.

** Them spangs ma: *yod pa'i phyir*.

*** Them spangs ma: *'grub par bya ba la gcig tu nges pas na* (to be corrected).

In my translation, the letters in parentheses **(a)-(g)** are inserted to indicate the correspondence to the seven characteristics.

b. the characteristic of the cognition of dissimilarity in what is other than the [object to be proven] (*tadanyavairūpyopalabdhilakṣaṇa*, Mvy 4411 [N 4397]);

c. the characteristic of the cognition of similarity in all [things] (*sarvasārūpyopalabdhilakṣaṇa*, Mvy 4412 [N 4398]);

d. the characteristic of the cognition of dissimilarity in all [things] (*sarvavairūpyopalabdhilakṣaṇa*, Mvy 4413 [N 4399]);

e. the characteristic of the adduction of an example of a different kind (*anyajātīyadṛṣṭāntopasaṃhāralakṣaṇa*, Mvy 4414 [N 4400]);

f. the characteristic of being incomplete (*apariniṣpannalakṣaṇa*, Mvy 4415 [N 4401]);

g. the characteristic of the instruction of an impure scripture (*aviśuddhāgamopadeśalakṣaṇa*, Mvy 4416 [N 4402])

(**c**) Among them, the characteristic of the cognition of similarity in all [things is exemplified by the cognition of the similarity that] all things are known by mental consciousness (**manovijñāna*).

(**d**) The characteristic of the cognition of dissimilarity in all [things] [consists in] the ascertainment that [all things] are of a mutually dissimilar characteristic for the reason that [they have] one dissimilar characteristic of the dissimilar characteristics with regard to sign (**liṅga*), nature (**svabhāva*), action (**karman*), quality (**dharma*), and cause and effect (**hetuphala*).

(**a**) Mañjuśrī, among them, the characteristic of the cognition of similarity in all [things] exists in the characteristic of the cognition of similarity in what is other than the [object to be proven] endowed with an example. Therefore, this [characteristic (**a**)] is inconclusive (**anaikāntika*) with regard to the object to be proven. Accordingly, (**f**) this is called the characteristic of being incomplete.

(**b**) Likewise, the characteristic of the cognition of similarity in all [things] exists in the characteristic of the cognition of dissimilarity in what is other than the [object to be proven] endowed with an example. Therefore, this [characteristic] is inconclusive (**an-

aikāntika) with regard to the object to be proven. Accordingly, (**f**) this is also called the characteristic of being incomplete.

(**f**) Since it is incomplete, the investigation by [such] reasoning is impure. Since it is impure, it is not to be taught.

(**g**) Among them, the characteristic of an instruction of an impure scripture should be known to be impure by its own nature."

3. CRITICAL DISCUSSION

3.1. Five pure characteristics

Let us first review the five "pure" characteristics of *upapattisādhanayukti*. According to the *Sūtra*, a right reason bears the five characteristics based on three kinds of *pramāṇa*, viz., perception (*prayakṣa*), inference (*anumāna*) and scriptural authority (*āgama*).[10] These characteristics are respectively called[11] a) the characteristic of the direct cognition of the [object itself] (*tatpratyakṣopalabdhilakṣaṇa*); b) the characteristic of the direct cognition [of something] depending on the [imperceptible object to be inferred] (*tadāśrityapratyakṣopalabdhilakṣaṇa*); c) the characteristic of the adduction of an example of the same kind (*svajātīyadṛṣṭāntopasaṃhāralakṣaṇa*); d) the characteristic of being complete (*pariniṣpannalakṣaṇa*); e) the characteristic of the instruction of a very pure scripture (*suviśuddhāgamopadeśalakṣaṇa*). The object is to be proven by means of the three *pramāṇa*s in conformity with its state of being either perceptible, imperceptible or transcendental. Such objects as the imperpanence (*mi rtag pa nyid, *anityatā*) and the painfulness (*sdug sngal ba nyid, *duḥkhatā*) of all conditioning factors (*'du byed, *saṃskāra*) as well as the non-self (*bdag med pa nyid, *an-*

---

[10] *Upapattisādhanayukti* thus includes these three kinds of *pramāṇa*. Apart from *upapattisādhanayukti*, the *Hetuvidyā* accepts these three as *pramāṇa*, as will be seen below, in the same way as AKBh II (76,25) and *Vyākhyāyukti* III (D87b3), the latter of which has been discussed by P. Verhagen (2008: 244-247; cf. also the text cited on pp. 253-258).

[11] The Sanskrit is recorded in Mvy 4405-4409 (N 4391-4395) and used by Lamotte too (SNSū 156).

ātmatva) of all things (*chos thams cad, *sarvadharma*)[12] are, according to the SNSū, directly cognizable, and therefore established by means of perception (*pratyakṣa*).[13] For a transcendental object such as the calmness of *nirvāṇa*, one needs a scriptural authority to know it. For an imperceptible object, the *Sūtra* proposes the following inferential reasoning endowed with examples: 1) The momentariness (*skad cig ma nyid, *kṣaṇikatva*) of all conditioning factors (*'du byed, *saṃskāra*) is proven by the direct cognition of coarse impermanence such as death and birth; 2) the existence of another world (*'jig rten pha rol, *paraloka*) is proven by the direct cognition of various living beings [which are the effects of various deeds performed in the previous world] in the same manner as it is proven by the direct cognition of the pain of birth [which is likewise the effect of deeds performed in the previous world]; 3) the imperishability of [the influence of] good and bad deeds [performed in the previous world] is proven by the direct cognition of happy and unhappy living beings [which are the effects of the deeds] in the same manner as it is proven by the direct cognitions of the lack of independency as well as wealth and poverty [in the present world, which are likewise the effects of deeds performed in the previous world].

Similar and dissimilar examples (*sapakṣa*, *vipakṣa*) do not appear here. Regarding the relation between *sādhya* and *sādhana*, the *Sūtra* simply describes it by the expression *tadāśritya*, which means that the direct cognition of *sādhana* occurs in dependence on the imperceptible *sādhya*. This relation could be subsumed under

---

[12] This teaching is known by early Pāli literatures such as *Dhammapada* (20) 277-279, which says: *sabbe saṃkhārā anicca, sabbe saṃkhārā dukhā, sabbe dhammā anattā*. Cf. also HV 14*,22f. (3.283): *anityāḥ sarvasaṃskārāḥ, duḥkhāḥ sarvasāsravāḥ, sarvadharmā anātmānaḥ*.

[13] Although the impermanence etc. are the qualities of conditioning factors and hence universals, the SNSū seems to consider them neither to be merely conceptualized nor to be the object of conceptual cognition alone. Since the SNSū clearly states that such coarse impermanence as death and birth is well known in the world and directly cognized, there is no need either to confine the impermanence etc. to the objects of yogic perception.

causal relation (*tadutpatti*) and essential identity (*tādātmya*), for the second and the third inferences are apparently to conjecture a cause from its effect(s), whereas the first one is based on the essential identity of imperceptible momentariness and perceptible impermanence. Thus considered, the association with Dharmakīrti's concepts of *kāryahetu* and *svabhāvahetu* may well follow, but the SNSū does not give any more explanation. The character of the logical reason (*hetu*) is not really the chief concern of the SNSū. It seems that the *Sūtra* just makes use of causality and identity, which are well known in the world and accepted by Buddhists too. However, this does not mean that the SNSū is not interested in the inevitable connection between *sādhya* and *sādhana*. The *Sūtra*'s commitment to this issue is, I think, implied in the following teaching of the seven "impure" characteristics.

3.2. Seven impure characteristics

Although there might have occurred a textual corruption in the last sentences, for the elucidation of the fifth characteristic (**e**) concerning an example is lacking, the last three characteristics are understandable as the opposites of the last three of the "pure" characteristics. In contrast, the meaning of the first four characteristics is very obscure.[14] What sorts of fault are indicated by the characteristics of *tadanyasārūpyopalabdhi*, *tadanyavairūpyopalabdhi*, *sarvasārūpyopalabdhi*, and *sarvavairūpyopalabdhi*? What are *sārūpya* and *vairūpya* actually? The later commentary ascribed to Byang chub rdzu 'phrul (i.e., the SNSūV) has elucidated them, identifying *sārūpya* and *vairūpya* with *sapakṣa* and *vipakṣa* in terms of the later tradition.[15] The SNSūV, however, as I have

[14] It is hardly acceptable that Powers (1995: 291f.) interprets the first four impure characteristics as the "characteristic of having objects of observation" in contradiction with his own interpretation of the same word *dmigs pa* (*upalabdhi*) as "cognition" in the case of the five pure characteristics. A fallacy is caused by the cognition on which the reasoning relies, not by the "types of objects of observation" as Powers notes (1995: 368, n. 19).

[15] Kajiyama's interpretation (1984) follows this commentary.

discussed in my previous studies, offers the interpretation that deviates to a large extent from the original intention of the *Sūtra*. The fact is that one cannot find any ground in the SNSū for this identification. Apart from such a later interpretation, one should pay more attention to the SNSū's contemporary Yogācāra literature. In particular, the *Hetuvidyā* (hereafter HV) of the *Yogācārabhūmi* promises a great help for our purpose to clarify the logic of the SNSū,[16] because these two texts, in my view, not only share the concepts of *sārūpya* and *vairūpya* but also present a similar framework of logical reasoning. According to the HV, a means of proof (*sādhana*) is of eight members: 1) proposition (*pratijñā*), 2) logical reason (*hetu*), 3) example (*udāharaṇa*), 4) similarity (*sārūpya*), 5) dissimilarity (*vairūpya*), 6) perception (*pratyakṣa*), 7) inference (*anumāna*), and 8) reliable authority (*āptāgama*).[17] Although the SNSū does not mention the terms *pratijñā* and *hetu*, it has the other

---

[16] As for the chronology of the SNSū and the *Yogācārabhūmi*, cf., e.g., Schmithausen 1969: 822f. and Powers 1993: 4. The *hetuvidyā* is thought to be one of the five worldly sciences (*pañcavidyāsthāna*). The *Yogācārabhūmi* provides the detailed explanation thereof in its *Śrutamayībhūmi* chapter, which I call the *Hetuvidyā* here. The text has been studied by Tucci (1929a; 1929b), Ui (1929; 1933, on the basis of the Chinese translation), and Kajiyama (1984). Based on the Sanskrit manuscript photographed by Rāhula Sāṅkṛtyāyana, Pandey (1986) has published its half Hindi text. The facsimile edition of another manuscript is now available in ŚrBh (Ms) and Yaita has published its critical edition together with Japanese translation (1992). In this paper, I refer to Yaita's edition as well as his latest studies (2003a; 2003b), which deal with the idea of *sārūpya* and *vairūpya* of the HV, although I partly propose a different reading from that of Yaita.

[17] HV 4*,15f. (3.2): *sādhanam aṣṭavidhaṃ katamat. pratijñā hetur udāharaṇaṃ sārūpyaṃ vairūpyaṃ pratyakṣam anumānam āptāgamaś ca.* These eight means of proof are taught in the AS (105,2f.) too, where, however, *upanaya* and *nigamana* are counted instead of *sārūpya* and *vairūpya*. Cf. Kajiyama 1984: 73ff. and Yaita 2003a: 134, 138. For the time being, I would tentatively say that the SNSū shares few ideas on logical method with such early texts as the *Carakasaṃhitā*, the **Upāyahṛdaya* (or **Prayogasāra*), and the **Tarkaśāstra*, although I am far from being in a position to draw any conclusion. It is a matter of course that one needs further comprehensive and thorough investigation of these materials including the dialectical portion of the Spitzer Manuscript that has been newly reconstructed and reported to have some lines similar to the **Tarkaśāstra* by Franco 2002.

members in common.[18] In this respect, it is certainly worth consulting the HV in order to clarify the meaning of *sārūpya* and *vairūpya*.

3.2.1. *sārūpya and vairūpya in the HV*

The HV gives *sārūpya* and *vairūpya* the following definitions:

> What is similarity?[19] Insofar as any thing (*kasyacid dharmasya*) has any particular similarity (*kenacid eva*[20]*sādṛśyena*[21]), the very [thing is said to] have a similarity. This [similarity] is to be known to [divide into] five kinds: similarity by sign (*liṅgasādṛśya*), similarity by nature (*svabhāvasādṛśya*), similarity by action (*karmasādṛśya*), similarity by quality (*dharmasādṛśya*), and similarity by cause and effect (*hetuphalasādṛśya*).
>
> What is dissimilarity? Insofar as any [thing] has any particular dissimilarity, the very [thing is said to] have a dissimilarity. This [dissimilarity] is also to be known to [divide into] the same five kinds, for it is the opposite of that [i.e., similarity].[22]

---

[18] The HV, in turn, uses the word *yukti* too, by identifying the "statement of reason" (*yuktivāda*) with "logical reason" (*hetu*). Cf. HV 5*,3ff. (3.22, trans. Yaita 1992: 551): *yas tasyaiva pratijñātasyārthasya siddhaya udāharaṇāśritaḥ sārūpyavairūpyato vā pratyakṣato vānumānato vāptāgamato vā hito yuktivādaḥ.* "[Logical reason (*hetu*) is] a statement of reason (*yuktivāda*), which is based on example and offered on the ground of similarity and dissimilarity, perception, inference, or reliable authority, for the purpose of the establishment of the meaning itself that is propounded."

[19] The HV introduces each discussion on a new subject by putting forward a simple question with *katama* and a subject like this. Hence I interpret this interrogative pronoun *katama* as a strengthened substitute for *kim*.

[20] I have added the phrase *kenacid eva* in accordance with the parallel lines on *vairūpya*. Yaita has added only *kenacit* (HV 5*,9).

[21] It may be safe to treat the words *sārūpya* and *sādṛśya* as synonymous.

[22] HV 5*,9-12 (3.24, trans. Yaita 1992: 552): *sārūpyaṃ katamat. yat kasyacid dharmasya kenacit* [*eva*] *sādṛśyena kasyacid eva sādṛśyam. tat pañcavidhaṃ draṣṭavyam, liṅgasādṛśyaṃ svabhāvasādṛśyaṃ karmasādṛśyaṃ dharmasādṛśyaṃ hetuphalasādṛśyaṃ ca*; HV 6*,5ff. (3.25, trans. Yaita 1992: 553): *vairūpyaṃ katamat. yat kasyacid kenacid eva vaisādṛśyena kasyacid eva vaisādṛśyam. tad apy etadviparyayāt pañcavidham eva draṣṭavyam.* As indicated in the notes of Yaita's edition, there are some textual problems. The Tibetan version omits all *eva* (D189b1f., 6f.). The manuscript lacks the first *kenacit* and *dharmasādṛśyam*.

One should note that the five divisions by sign etc., have an entire correspondence in the SNSū's explanation of the fourth characteristic (**d**), i.e., *sarvavairūpyopalabdhi*. Because the HV also classifies inference (*anumāna*) into the same five kinds,[23] it is evident that the concepts of similarity and dissimilarity are closely connected with the formulation of an inference, as Yaita (2003a) has pointed out. In an inference, one of these five divisions, viz., sign, nature, action, quality, or cause and effect, takes a place as a proof (*sādhana*), whereas, in the above definition of *sārūpya* and *vairūpya*, they offer themselves as the features, from the respect of which similarity or dissimilarity is cognized. The possessor of similarity expressed by the genitive *kasyacid* is modified by *dharmasya*.[24] Supposing that the text be correct despite the disappearance of *dharmasya* in the definition of *vairūpya*, this *dharma* can be identified with *dharma* in the sense of the object of mind (*manas*). I assume that the word *dharma* is used in this sense by both the SNSū and the HV in the context of logical investigation. The SNSū has explicitly stated the idea that all things (*sarvadharma*) are known by mental consciousness (*manovijñāna*), explaining the aforementioned third impure characteristic (**c**) of *sarvasārūpyopalabdhi*. By saying "all" (*sarva*), the *Sūtra* signifies all kinds of thing to be known by mind. A *dharma* is not to be reduced to an individual existent. It may rather refer to a material or non-material entity, an idea, an action, an event, or a quality, which is designated by a generic singular such as the impermanent (*anitya*), the produced (*kṛtaka*), tree (*vṛkṣa*), and so on. The quali-

---

[23] HV 11*,5f. (3.27, trans. Yaita 1992: 558): *tat punaḥ pañcavidhaṃ draṣṭavyam. liṅgataḥ svabhāvataḥ karmato dharmato hetuphalataś ca.* Here I do not touch upon the definition of inference given by the HV (see HV 11*,4f.), according to which the inference is identified as some object (*viṣaya*). There is most likely something wrong in the text.

[24] Yaita has interpreted *kasyacid dharmasya* differently. In his reading, *kasyacit* is a thing in the sense of *dharmin* and *dharmasya* is its property. I do not think that this separation of *kasyacit* from *dharmasya* is necessary. Neither in the explanation of *sārūpya* nor in that of *anumāna*, the HV ascribes an independent role to property-possessor (*dharmin*).

ties such as impermanence (*anityatā*) and painfulness (*duḥkhatā*) are called *dharma* too, as in the expression *dharmasādṛśya*, which is replaced by *dharmatā* in the HV (see HV 5*,17f. cited below in footnote 29). The manifestation of a quality and the quality itself are not really separated, as the SNSū adopts the phenomena such as death and birth to illustrate the quality of directly cognizable coarse impermanence.

Granting this assumption of the meaning of *dharma*, one may proceed to interpret the HV's definition *kasyacid dharmasya kenacid eva sādṛśyena kasyacid eva sādṛśyam*. The most controversial point is the reading of the phrase *kenacid eva sādṛśyena*. My proposal is to read it as a particular similarity by any of the five features. It might be possible to interpret *kenacit* as referring to another *dharma*, to which the first *dharma* (i.e., *dharmasya*) has a similarity,[25] but it is unlikely to be the intention of the HV, because the HV never specifies two different entities, between which a similarity is to be cognized. The text speaks solely of a mutual similarity (*anyonyasādṛśya*), explaining each of the five kinds of similarity:

> What is the similarity by sign? It is a mutual similarity (*anyonyam sādṛśyam*) based on the connection of mark and [its] base, which is present or has been seen before.[26]

---

[25] Yaita (1992: 552) has adopted this interpretation. In his edition, he supplies *kenacit* only, not *kenacid eva*.

[26] HV 5*,13f. (3.241, trans. Yaita 1992: 552): *liṅgasādṛśyaṃ katamat. yad vartamānena vā pūrvadṛṣṭena vā cihnanimittasambandhenānyonyaṃ* * *sādṛśyam*.

*Emended by Yaita : *-sambandhena nānyonya* Ms.

Cf. further HV 11*,7–12*,5 (3.271, trans. Yaita 1992: 558f.) on *liṅgato 'numānam*, where numerous examples of inference such as the inference of a (war-) chariot (*ratha*) from a banner (*dhvaja*), that of fire (*agni*) from smoke (*dhūma*), that of a kingdom (*rāṣṭra*) from a king (*rājan*), and that of a wife (*strī*) from a husband (*pati*) are adduced. Yaita's explanation (2003a: 135, 138; 2003b: 35f.) that the similarity by sign consists between smoke and fire and between banner and chariot is hardly acceptable. The inference of a war-chariot from a banner is possible under the condition that one has cognized a similarity among war-chariots from the respect of their having a banner as sign. Nor do I agree with his reading of *cihnanimittasambandha* as "the connection of the object [to be in-

What is the similarity by nature? It is a mutual similarity by characteristic (*anyonyaṃ lakṣaṇasādṛśyam*).[27]

What is the similarity by action? It is a mutual similarity by act (*anyonyaṃ kāritrasādṛśyam*).[28]

What is the similarity by quality? It is a mutual similarity by quality (*anyonyaṃ dharmatayā sādṛśyam*). For instance, there is [a mutual similarity] in the impermanent [i.e., among impermanent phenomena] by the quality of being painful (*anitye duḥkhadharmatayā* [*anyonyaṃ sādṛśyam*]), there is [a mutual similarity] in the painful [i.e., among painful phenomena] by the quality of selflessness, there is [a mutual similarity] among those which lack the self by the quality of birth, there is [a mutual similarity] among those which has the quality of birth by the quality of becoming old, ...[29]

---

ferred such as chariot] with mark and characteristic", nor his interpretation of *sambandha* as the connection between proof (*sādhana*, i.e., *liṅga*) and that which is to be proven (*sādhya*, i.e., *liṅgin*).

The idea of sign and these examples seems to have been known to Buddhists since the earliest time, because it appears in *Saṃyutta Nikāya* 1.8.2: *kiṃsu rathassa paññāṇaṃ* ll *kiṃsu paññāṇam aggino* ll *kiṃsu raṭṭhassa paññāṇaṃ* ll *kiṃsu paññāṇam itthiyā ti* ll ll *dhajo rathassa paññāṇaṃ* ll *dhūmo paññāṇam aggino* ll *rājā raṭṭhassa paññāṇam* ll *bhattā paññāṇam itthiyāti* ll "What is the sign of chariot? What is the sign of fire? What is the sign of kingdom? What is the sign of wife? A banner is the sign of chariot. Smoke is the sign of fire. A king is the sign of kingdom. A husband is the sign of wife." The Chinese version of this *Nikāya* (雑阿含, Taishō no. 99, vol. 2, 266b) interprets these verses to mean a sort of inference that one knows the existence of a chariot by seeing a banner and so on.

[27] HV 5*,15 (3.242, trans. Yaita 1992: 552): <u>*svabhāvasādṛśyam*</u>* *katamat. yad anyonyaṃ lakṣaṇasādṛśyam.*

*According to Yaita, it was written down in the margin seemingly by another hand than that of the scribe.

Cf. further HV 12*,6-14 (3.272, trans. Yaita 1992: 559) on *svabhāvato 'numānam*, according to which one can infer, for instance, something past from something present if they are identical by nature. In this case, similarity seems to be close to identity.

[28] HV 5*,16 (3.243, trans. Yaita 1992: 552): *karmasādṛśyaṃ katamat. yad anyonyaṃ kāritrasādṛśyam.* Cf. further HV 12*,15–13*,3 (3.273, trans. Yaita 1992: 559f.) on *karmato 'numānam*, according to which it is the inference of agent or the subject of action (i.e., *karmāśraya*) from its act (*kāritra*) such as the inference of a horse (*aśva*) from its neighing (*haiṣita*). In this case, a similarity consists among horses by their act of neighing, not between horse and neighing as Yaita has interpreted (2003a: 138; 2003b: 37).

[29] HV 5*,17–13*,1 (3.244, trans. Yaita 1992: 552): *dharmasādṛśyaṃ katamat. yad anyonyaṃ dharmatayā* sādṛśyam. tad yathā,** anitye duḥkhadharmatayā*

> What is the similarity by cause and effect? It is a mutual similarity by cause among those which are produced and by effect among those which produce (*anyonyaṃ hetutaḥ phalataś ca niṣpādananiṣpattisādṛśyam*).[30]

"Mutual similarity" is presumably intended for a mutual resemblance among individual entities or phenomena subsumed under one and the same *dharma*. Insofar as they are cognized to be similar by one feature, this *dharma* is said to have a similarity. The compounds *liṅgasādṛśya* etc. are accordingly to be analyzed into

---

*duḥkhe*** nairātmyadharmatayā**** nirātmakānāṃ jātidharmatayā**** jātidharmakāṇāṃ jarādharmatayā ...*

* Yaita has emended the manuscript and given *dharmatāyāḥ*, which does not seem necessary.

** Added by Yaita in accordance with the Tibetan and Pandey 1986.

*** Emended by Yaita : *dharmatā yad duḥke* Ms.

**** Emended by Yaita : *-tāyā* Ms.

Cf. further HV 13*,4-14 (3.274, trans. Yaita 1992: 560): *dharmato 'numānaṃ katamat. yad anuśliṣṭena*(?) *dharmasambandhena tatsambaddhāyā dharmatāyā* abhyūhanam. tadyathā, anityasambandhena duḥkhatām anuminoti, duḥkhasambandhena śūnyatātmatām, ...*

* According to Yaita, it seems to have been noted by another hand than that of the scribe.

"What is the inference from essential quality? It is the conjecture based on the clinging (?) connection with a *dharma* with regard to the quality that is connected with this [*dharma*]. For instance, one infers the painfulness based on the connection with the impermanent, the essence of being empty based on the connection with the painful, ..."

[30] HV 6*,2f. (3.245, trans. Yaita 1992: 553): *hetuphalasādṛśyaṃ* katamat. yad anyonyaṃ hetutaḥ phalataś ca niṣpādananiṣpattisādṛśyam.*

*Emended by Yaita : *-sākṣāddṛśyam* Ms.

Yaita's rendering of the compound *niṣpādananiṣpattisādṛśyam* by "the similarity between the cause to accomplish and that which is accomplished" (Yaita 1992: 553; 2003a: 137) well reflects his interpretation that there is a similarity between cause and effect, which I do not think correct. Cf. further HV 13*,15–14*,5 (3.275, trans. Yaita 1992: 561): *hetuphalato 'numānaṃ katamat. yad dhetunā phalasya phalena vā hetor abhyūhanam. tad yathā ... prāktanena sucaritaduścaritena sampattivipattii, sampattivipattibhyāṃ prākkṛtaṃ* sucaritaduścaritam,....*

* Emended by Yaita : *prākṛtaṃ* Ms.

"What is the inference from cause and effect? It is the conjecture of effect from cause or cause from effect. For instance, [one infers] ... [present] fortune and misfortune from previous good and bad deeds, and previous good and bad deeds from [present] fortune and misfortune ..."

liṅgena sādṛśyam, "similarity by sign", etc., as suggested the appearance of the instrumental case *dharmatayā*[31] in the illustration of the similarity by quality (*dharmasādṛśya*). The first example of the similarity by quality, *anitye duḥkhadharmatayā*, for instance, means that a *dharma* qualified as the impermanent has a similarity by the quality of being painful. That is to say, impermanent phenomena are mutually similar in the respect of being painful. Although they are not said to be similar to each other from other respects, as impermanent human beings are not similar to impermanent jars with regard to their shape, it is safe to posit that they have a similarity if they have one particular feature in common. Therefore, the HV says at the beginning, "Insofar as any *dharma* has any particular similarity, this *dharma* is said to have a similarity."

The way in which the cognition of similarity serves as the proof of inference is as follows: If *dharma* X is known to have

[31] *Dharmatā* is a substitute for *dharma* of *dharmasādṛśya*, as indicated above in the body of this paper. In the explanation of the inference from quality (*dharmato 'numānam*), however, the HV adopts *dharma*, not *dharmatā*, as a proof, and *dharmatā* as the object to be proven, by saying that the essential quality of being painful (*duḥkhadharmatā*) is inferred based on its connection with the impermanent (*anityasambandha*), which is a *dharma*. This replacement could be explained as follows: First, any similarity cannot be attributed to one *dharmatā* or essential quality; secondly, the connection of one *dharmatā* with a *dharma* is nothing other than the connection between two qualities such as the impermanence and the painfulness in the sense that that which is impermanent is painful. In this case, it might be possible to apply the idea of *dharmin* to "that which is impermanent", although the HV never specifies a property-possessor like sound (*śabda*); thirdly, all the qualities enumerated by the HV are commonly attributed to conditioning factors (*saṃskāra*). That means, that which is impermanent is painful as well as that which is painful is impermanent. Accordingly, one can say that the impermanent (i.e., *dharma*) is similar by the quality of being painful (i.e., *dharmatā*) and *vice versa*, and infer the painfulness (i.e., *dharmatā*) based on its connection with the impermanent (i.e., *dharma*) and *vice versa*.

In this regard, I do not agree with Yaita's interpretation (2003a: 138; 2003b: 39f.) that the similarity by quality (*dharmasādṛśya*) consists between the impermanence and the painfulness and that this similarity signifies the connection (*sambandha*) between these two qualities. Since the similarity by quality consists among impermanent phenomena with regard to their being painful, it is not identical with the connection between the two qualities.

similarity through feature Y (i.e., individual X-s commonly have feature Y), one can infer *dharma* X from the perception of feature Y. For instance, war-chariots are known from experience to be similar to each other by their having a banner as sign. On this ground, one can infer the existence of a war-chariot from the perception of a banner alone. The credibility of the proof as well as the inevitable connection between the proof and the object to be proven is thus established based on the similarity of war-chariots subsumed under the *dharma* called "war-chariot", which consists in their having a banner. This is, I think, the method of the HV to confirm the concomitance (*anvaya*) of the proof and the object to be proven on the basis of similarity (*sārūpya*). Dissimilarity (*vairūpya*), in turn, seems merely to dissolve such a positive concomitance, although the HV never speaks thereof in detail. If there are many war-chariots that have no banner, war-chariots are dissimilar to each other in the respect of having a banner. In this case, the cognition of a banner does not help one to infer a war-chariot.[32]

Since the concomitance is indeed ascertained based on experience, it does not cover all cases. With regard to the similarity by sign, one can never avoid exceptions. There must exist a chariot without banner and fire without smoke. In this regard, one should also recognize the possibility that there might arise a case in which the HV's inference based on similarity does not function. For example, one cognizes a similarity among Śiṃśapā trees by the nature of being trees. The inference of Śiṃśapā from the treeness is, however, impossible. Nor can one say, if seeing many Śiṃśapā trees, that there is a similarity among trees in the respect of their being Śiṃśapā. This may well support the assumption that the theory of pervasion (*vyāpti*) is not yet introduced into this early logical system of Yogācāra literature.[33]

---

[32] In my view, dissimilarity (*vairūpya*) actually has nothing to do with the negative concomitance (*vyatireka*) of the proof with the object to be proven. Negative concomitance should also be confirmed by the cognition of similarity in the way that the non-fire has a similarity in the respect of having no smoke.

3.2.2. tadanyasārūpyopalabdhi and tadanyavairūpyopalabdhi in the SNSū

In the consequence of the preceding analysis of the HV's description of *sārūpya* and *vairūpya*, one can hypothetically reconstruct the inferential reasonings of the SNSū, in which the concomitance of the proof with the object to be proven is established on the basis of *sārūpya* and *vairūpya*. I should here like to advert to the SNSū's first two inferences, viz., the inference of the momentariness (*kṣaṇikatva*) and that of another world (*paraloka*), for they are respectively understood to correspond to the inference from quality (*dharmato 'numānam*) and that of cause from effect (*phalato* [*hetuno*] *'numānam*) taught in the HV[34]:

1) There is a mutual similarity in the momentary (i.e., among momentary phenomena) by (the quality of) being impermanent. There is also a mutual similarity in the impermanent (i.e., among impermanent phenomena) by (the quality of being) momentary. Hence it is ascertained that the impermanence is concomitant with the momentary and that the momentariness is concomitant with the impermanent.[35] Consequently, the momentariness of all conditioning factors is inferred based on its connection with the impermanent.[36]

---

[33] Regarding the various qualities of conditioning factors, a complete pervasion in the sense that whatever is impermanent is painful might well be accepted, as suggested above in n. 31. This is, however, defined as such in accordance with the fundamental Buddhist doctrine that all conditioning factors are impermanent, painful and non-self, rather than a logical consequence.

[34] The SNSū's third inference of the imperishability of the influence of past deeds can also be subsumed under the inference of cause from effect in terms of the HV.

[35] As for the relation between *dharma* and *dharmatā*, see footnote 31 above.

[36] This reasoning can be reformulated in the Sanskrit by applying the HV's expression: *kṣaṇike anityatayā anyonyaṃ sārūpyam. anitye kṣaṇikatvena anyonyaṃ sārūpyam. anityasambandhena sarvasaṃskārāṇāṃ kṣaṇikatvam anuminoti.* Although the SNSū has "all conditioning factors" in this inferential reasoning, I do not think that it is intended for the subject (*pakṣa*) or property-possessor (*dharmin*). For the *Sūtra*, the thesis, "all conditioning factors are momentary", is given by the Buddha. In its logical system, the property-possessor

2) There is a mutual similarity among various deeds performed in the previous world by the feature of causing the variety of living beings such as human beings, animals, and insects in the present world. Hence it is ascertained that the variety of present living beings is concomitant with the variety of past deeds. On this ground, one infers various past deeds as well as the existence of the previous world from various living beings in the present world.[37]

In this manner, the cognition of similarity and dissimilarity links up with inference and contributes to ascertain the concomitance (*anvaya*) of the proof (*sādhana*) and the object to be proven (*sādhya*). Accordingly, from an inappropriate cognition of similarity and dissimilarity would follow only an inconclusive (*anaikāntika*) and therefore faulty reason. Such is the very case in the first four "impure" characteristics.

Let us first examine the third characteristic of **(c)** *sarvasārūpyopalabdhi*. If one cognizes a similarity in all things by a single feature, one cannot infer anything specific from this feature, since the concomitance of this feature is established with everything. The fourth characteristic of **(d)** *sarvavairūpyopalabdhi*, on the contrary, refers to the absurd cognition that all things have no similarity on any account if they are dissimilar in one respect. In this case, inference is impossible either because no concomitance is established.

The first two characteristics, viz., *tadanyasārūpyopalabdhi* and *tadanyavairūpyopalabdhi*, may be analyzed from the same perspective, although it is indeed difficult to offer a complete parallel interpretation for both characteristics. I take the pronoun *tad* to indicate

---

is, if separately posited from the property, "that which is impermanent", as discussed above in footnote 31.

[37] Although this reasoning is too complicated to reduce into a simple form of inference and to reformulate in the Sanskrit, it is possible to apply to it the general form that HV 13*,15ff. presents (cited above in footnote 30). In fact, one sees therein a similar type of the inference of past deeds from present states.

the object to be proven in accordance with the *Sūtra*'s usage thereof with regard to the five "pure" characteristics. On this initial assumption, I tentatively propose to interpret *tadanyasārūpyopalabdhi* as the cognition that what is other than the object to be proven have a similarity. Supposing that the momentariness (*kṣaṇikatva*) be the object to be proven, the non-momentary (*akṣaṇika*), that is the thing other than the object to be proven (*tadanya*), is cognized to have a similarity by the feature of being non-produced (*akṛtakatva*). This cognition itself is not wrong and even implies a negative concomitance. Nevertheless, this alone cannot lead to any knowledge of momentariness, since no similarity is cognized among momentary phenomena. One can find neither proper proof (*sādhana*) for nor concomitance with the object to be proven (*sādhya*). In this cognition, the SNSū says, there exists the cognition of *sarvavairūpya*. Thereby the *Sūtra* presumably suggests that the cognition of dissimilarity of all things would follow from this single observation of being non-produced, unless any other cognition of similarity is introduced, since things are dissimilar at all in this sole respect.

The cognition of *tadanyavairūpya* is accordingly to be interpreted as the cognition of dissimilarity in the things other than the object to be proven. This cognition does not help either to know the object. Supposing that some non-momentary (*akṣaṇika*) or permanent (*nitya*) phenomena be imperceptible, the permanent is said to have a dissimilarity by the feature of being perceptible. Another possible cognition of this kind is that the permanent has a dissimilarity by the feature of being produced (*kṛtakatva*), since there exists nothing permanent that is produced. From these cognitions, which are essentially irrelevant to the momentary, does not arise any knowledge of concomitance with regard to the momentariness. Moreover, if similarity is cognized by any feature neither in the domain of the object to be proven nor in that of the other things, there might remain the cognition of similarity alone that all things are known by mental consciousness. This is the cognition of similarity in all things (*sarvasārūpyopalabdhi*). The SNSū seems to intend such an absurd possibility by saying that there exists the cognition of *sarvasārūpya* in the cognition of *tadanyavairūpya*.

In this consequence, both characteristics, viz., *tadanyasārūpyopalabdhi* and *tadanyavairūpyopalabdhi*, are regarded to be inconclusive (*anaikāntika*) with regard to the object to be proven and hence incomplete (*aparinişpanna*).

4. CONCLUDING REMARKS

To sum up, similarity (*sārūpya*) and dissimilarity (*vairūpya*) are extremely important ideas underlying the establishment of right reasoning in the SNSū as well as in the HV. The authors of these texts made use of neither *trairūpya* formulae, nor *dharma-dharmin* relation, nor the theory of *vyāpti*, which became popular among logicians soon after their time. Instead, they ascertain the concomitance of the proof (*sādhana*) with the object to be proven (*sādhya*) based on similarity and dissimilarity which consist among individual entities to be proven from the respect of a particular feature as a proof. One could say, on one hand, that their logical method was primitive and still developing. On the other hand, it may also be said that they impressively attempted to give a plausible explanation for various interrelations by using their own terminology, the full comprehension of which we have not yet attained.[38]

[38] I hope that this paper would be a contribution to the study of early Indian logic, despite an accumulation of hypotheses. My sincere thanks are due to Prof. B. Gillon, who stimulated me to confront the logic of the SNSū again and offered an opportunity to present the earlier version of this paper at the panel on logic during the 12th World Sanskrit Conference (Helsinki, July 2003), and helped me to improve this paper by his careful proofreading. I am also indebted to all the participants in the panel who gave me valuable suggestions and comments.

REFERENCES[39]

Texts and abbreviations

AKBh = [*Abhidharmakośabhāṣya*]. *Abhidharmakośabhāṣya of Vasubandhu*. Ed. by Pradhan. Patna 1975.

AS = [*Abhidharmasamuccaya*]. *Abhidharma Samuccaya of Asaṅga*. Ed. by P. Pradhan. Santiniketan 1950; D4049, P5550; Taishō 1605.

BBh = [*Bodhisattvabhūmi*]. *Bodhisattvabhūmi. A Statement of Whole Course of the Bodhisattva (Being Fifteenth Section of Yogācārabhūmi)*. Ed. by Unrai Wogihara. Tokyo 1930-36; D4037, P5538; Taishō 1579.

D = sDe dge edition.

Dhammapada = *Dhammapada*. Ed. by O. von Hinüber & K. R. Norman. Oxford 1995.

mDo btus pa = Khri srong lde btsan, *bKa' yang dag pa'i tshad ma las mdo btus pa*. D4352, P5839.

HV = [*Hetuvidyā*]. In: Yaita 1992 and 2005; manuscript in the ŚrBh (Ms).

MAV = [*Madhyāntavibhāga*]. In: Vasubandhu, *Madhyāntavibhāga-bhāṣya. A Buddhist Philosophical Treatise*. Ed. by Gadjin M. Nagao. Tokyo 1964; D4021, P5522; Taishō 1601.

MSA = [*Mahāyānasūtrālaṃkāra*]. Asaṅga, *Exposé de la doctrine du Grand Véhicule selon le système Yogācāra*. Ed. by Sylvain Lévi. Paris 1907-11; D4020, P5521; Taishō 1604.

Mvy = [*Mahāvyutpatti*]. *Honyaku meigi taishū*. Ed. by Ryōzaburō Sakaki. Tokyo 1982 (reprint).

Mvy [N] = [*Mahāvyutpatti*]. *A New Critical Edition of the Mahāvyutpatti, Sanskrit-Tibetan-Mongolian Dictionary of Buddhist Terminology*. Ed. by Yumiko Ishihama & Yoichi Fukuda. Tokyo 1989.

P = Peking edition.

RGV = [*Ratnagotravibhāga*]. *The Ratnagotravibhāga Mahāyānottaratantra*. Ed. by E. H. Johnston. Patna 1950.

Saṃyutta Nikāya I = *The Saṃyutta-Nikāya of the Sutta-Piṭaka*, I: *Sagāthavagga*. Ed. by L. Feer. Oxford 1991.

Shōmonji = [*Śrāvakabhūmi*]. Bonbun Shōmonji 8 (The *Śrāvakabhūmi*, Part 8, Sanskrit Text and Japanese Translation). *Taishō daigaku sōgō bukkyō kenkyūsho kiyō* (*Annual of the Institute for Comprehensive Studies of Buddhism, Taishō University*) 11 (1989): 81-85.

[39] The English translation of Japanese titles in brackets is given by the present author.

SNSū = [*Saṃdhinirmocanasūtra*]. *L'explication des mystères*. Ed. by Étienne Lamotte. Louvain 1935; D106, P774, Them spangs ma, *mDo, na*, Stein 194 (in Hakamaya 1987); Taishō nos. 675, 676 and 679.

SNSūV = Byang chub rdzu 'phrul, *Saṃdhinirmocanasūtravyākhyāna*, P5845.

ŚrBh = [*Śrāvakabhūmi*]. *Śrāvakabhūmi of Acārya Asaṅga.* Ed. by K. Shukla. Patna 1973; D4036, P5537, Taishō no. 1579.

ŚrBh (Ms) = [*Śrāvakabhūmi*]. *Facsimile Edition of the Śrāvakabhūmi Sanskrit Palm-leaf Manuscript.* Beijing 1994.

Taishō = *Taishō shinshū daizōkyō* (大正新修大蔵経. The new Taishō edition of the Chinese translation of the Tripiṭaka).

Vyākyāyukti = Vasubandhu, *Vyākhyāyukti*; D4061, P5562.

Secondary literature

EIMER, Helmut 1983. *Rab tu 'byuṅ ba'i gźi. Die tibetische Übersetzung des Pravrajyāvastu im Vinaya der Mūlasarvāstivādins, 1. Teil.* Wiesbaden.

—— 1992. *Ein Jahrzehnt Studien zur Überlieferung des tibetischen Kanjur.* Wien.

FRANCO, Eli 2002. Towards a reconstruction of the Spitzer Manuscript – The dialectical portion. *Wiener Zeitschrift für die Kunde Südasiens* 46: 171-224.

HAKAMAYA, Noriaki 1982. Yugagyōha no bunken (The literature of the Yogācāra school). In: *Kōza daijō bukkyō* 8: *Yuishiki shisō* (*Lectures on Mahāyāna Buddhism* 8: *The theory of vijñaprimātratā*): 43-76. Tokyo.

—— 1984. The old and new translations of the *Saṃdhinirmocanasūtra*: Some notes on the history of early Tibetan translation. *Komazawa daigaku bukkyōgakubu kenkyū kiyō* (*Journal of the Faculty of Buddhism, Komazawa University*) 42: 193-176.

—— 1987. A comparative edition of the old and new Tibetan translations of the *Saṃdhinirmocanasūtra* III. *Komazawa daigaku bukkyōgakubu ronshū* (*Journal of Buddhist Studies, Department of Buddhist Studies, Komazawa University*) 18: 572-606.

HARRISON, Paul 1992. Meritorious activity or waste of time? Some remarks on the editing of texts in the Tibetan Kanjur. In: *Tibetan Studies. Proceedings of the 5th Seminar of the International Association for Tibetan Studies, Narita 1989*, I: 77-93. Narita.

KAJIYAMA, Yūichi 1984. Bukkyō chishikiron no keisei (The formulation of Buddhist epistemology). In: *Kōza daijō bukkyō* 9: *Ninshikiron to ronrigaku* (*Lectures on Mahāyāna Buddhism* 9: *Epistemology and Logic*): 1-101. Tokyo.

KATŌ, Kōjirō 2003. Kawaguchi-bon 'Gejinmitsukyō' Chibetto-go yaku tekisuto ni tsuite (Remarks on the text of the *Saṃdhinirmocanasūtra* found in the Tōkyō [Kawaguchi] Manuscript Kanjur). *Indogaku bukkyōgaku kenkyū* (*Journal of Indian and Buddhist Studies*) 51-52: 142-144.

KATSURA, Shōryū 1986a. On *trairūpya* formulae. In: *Bukkyō to Ishūkyō* (*Buddhism and Its Relation to Other Religions. Essays in Honor of Dr. Shōzen Kumoi on His Seventieth Birthday*): 161-172. Kyoto.

—— 1986b. *Indo ronrigaku ni okeru henjūgainen no seisei to hatten, Carakasaṃhitā kara Dharmakīrti made* (*The Origin and Development of the Concept of vyāpti in Indian Logic, from Carakasaṃhitā up to Dharmakīrti*). (Hiroshima daigaku bungakubu kiyō [The Hiroshima University Studies, Literature Department], 45, Tokushūgō [Special Volume] 1.)

PANDEY, Jagadīśvara 1986. Bauddācārya Asaṅgakṛta Yogācāraśāstra meṃ Hetuvidyā. In: *Homage to Bhikkhu Jagdish Kashyap. Commemoration Volume*: 315-349. Nalanda.

POWERS, John 1993. *Hermeneutics and Tradition in the Saṃdhinirmocana-sūtra.* Leiden.

—— 1995. *Wisdom of Buddha, the Saṃdhinirmocana Sūtra*. Berkeley.

SAITŌ, Kōjun 1977. Kawaguchi Ekai shi shōrai Tōyō Bunko shozō shahon chibetto daizōkyō chōsa bibō (A Report of the investigation of the Tibetan Kanjur Manuscript brought by Ekai Kawaguchi and preserved in Tōyō Bunko). *Taishō daigaku kenkyū kiyō* (*Memoirs of Taishō University*) 63: 406-345.

SCHMITHAUSEN, Lambert 1969. Zur Literaturgeschichte der Alteren Yogācāra-Schule. *Zeitschrift der Deutschen Morgenländischen Gesellschaft, Supplementa* 1, XVII. *Deutscher Orientalistentag*, Teil 3: 811-823.

SUGURO, Shinjō 1976. Yugaron no seiritsu ni kanrusu shiken (Remarks on the establishment of the *Yogācārabhūmi*). *Osaki gakuhō* 129: 1-50.

TUCCI, Giuseppe 1929a. Buddhist logic before Dignāga. *Journal of the Royal Asiatic Society* 1929: 451-488.

—— 1929b. *Pre-Dignāga Buddhist Texts on Logic from Chinese Sources.* (Gaekwad's Oriental Series, 49.) Baroda (reprint: Madras 1981).

UI, Hakuju 1929. Jinna izen ni okeru bukkyō no ronrisetsu (Pre-Dignāga Buddhist Logic). *Indo tetsugaku kenkyū* (*Studies in Indian Philosophy*) 5: 387-503.

—— 1933. *Bukkyō ronrigaku* (*Buddhist logic*). Tokyo (reprint 1966).

VERHAGEN, P. 2008. Studies in Indo-Tibetan Buddhist hermeneutics (6): Validity and valid interpretation of scripture according to Vasubandhu's *Vyākhyā-yukti*. In: R. Gombrich & C. Scherrer-Schaub (eds.), *Buddhist Studies* (Papers of the 12th World Sanskrit Conference, 8): 233-258. Delhi.

YAITA, Hideomi 1992. Yugaron no inmyō: bonbun tekisuto to wayaku (The Sanskrit edition and the Japanese translation of the *Hetuvidyā* of the *Yogācārabhūmi*). *Naritasan bukkyō kenkyūshokiyō* (*Journal of Naritasan Institute for Buddhist Studies*) 15: 505-576. (Revised version in Yaita 2005: 22-41, 95-124.)

Cf. also. Hideomi Yaita & Masahiro Takano, Index to the Hetuvidyā text in the Yogācārabhūmi. In: *Bongo buttennno kenkyū* (*Studies on the Buddhist Sanskrit Literature*), Taishō daigaku sōgō bukkyō kenkyū sho (The Institute for Comparative Studies of Buddhism, Taishō University): 217-284. Tokyo, 1995.

—— 2003a. Yugaron inmyō ni okeru *sārūpya* to *vairūpya* ni tsuite (On *sārūpya* and *vairūpya* in the *Hetuvidyā* of the *Yogācārabhūmi*). *Indogaku bukkyōgaku kenkyū* (*Journal of Indian and Buddhist Studies*) 51-52: 134-138. (Revised version in Yaita 2005: 10-18.)

—— 2003b. Hosshō no ni shōin (jishōin/kekkain) to Yugaron inmyō (Dharmakīrti's two Reasons [svabhāva-/kārya-hetu] and the *Hetuvidyā* in the *Yogācārabhūmi*). *Bukkyō-gaku* (*Journal of Buddhist Studies*) 45: 31-46. (Revised version in Yaita 2005: 10-18.)

—— 2005. *Bukkyo chisikiron no genten kenkyū* (*Three Sanskrit Texts from the Buddhist Pramāṇa-Tradition – The Hetuvidyā Section in the Yogācārabhūmi, the Dharmottaraṭippanaka, and the Tarkarahasya*). Narita.

YOSHIMIZU, Chizuko 1996a. *Die Erkenntnislehre des Prāsaṅgika-Madhyamaka nach dem Tshig gsal stoṅ thun gyi tshad ma'i rnam bśad des 'Jam dbyaṅs bźad pa'i rdo rje*. Wien.

—— 1996b. *Saṃdhinirmocanasūtra* X ni okeru shishu no *yukti* ni tsuite (On the four kinds of *yukti* in the tenth chapter of the *Saṃdhinirmocanasūtra*). *Naritasan bukkyō kenkyūsho kiyō* (*Journal of Naritasan Institute for Buddhist Studies*) 19: 123-168.

Obversion and Contraposition in the *Nyāyabhāṣya*

BRENDAN S. GILLON

1. INTRODUCTION

Most texts treating inference (*anumāna*) in early classical India are devoted to inference as argument in debate. Two of the earliest texts, the *Nyāyasūtra* (NS 1.1.32) and the *Carakasaṃhitā* (CS 3.8.31), clearly enumerate the parts of an argument. They are given as the thesis (*pakṣa*), or proposition (*pratijñā*), the ground, or reason (*hetu*), the corroboration (*dṛṣṭānta*), the application (*upanaya*), and the conclusion (*nigamana*). Of the two texts, only the *Carakasaṃhitā* furnishes examples of arguments. Here is one:

pratijñā:	*nityaḥ puruṣaḥ*
proposition:	the soul is eternal
hetu:	*a-kṛtakatvāt*
ground:	because of being un-created
dṛṣṭānta:	*yathā ākāśam*
corroboration:	like space
upanaya:	*yathā ca a-kṛtakam ākāśam tat ca nityam tathā puruṣaḥ*
application:	as the sky is uncreated and it is eternal, so is the soul uncreated
nigamana:	*tasmāt nityaḥ*
conclusion:	therefore, the soul is eternal

This form of the argument clearly reflects the debate situation. First, a proposition is set forth. Second, a reason is given to support the proposition. Third, a corroborating instance is provided. Fourth, the similarity between the corroborating instance and the subject of inference is made explicit. Finally, the proposition propounded is restated. Moreover, the use of the correlatives *yathā* (as) *tathā* (so), which spell out the similarity between the object of inference, namely the soul, and the corroborating instance, namely space, makes clear the essentially analogical basis of the reasoning in the argument.

In contrast, the *Vaiśeṣikasūtra*, attributed to Kaṇāda (ca. 1st century CE) and the *Ṣaṣṭitantra*, attributed by some to Pañcaśikha (ca. 2nd century BCE) and by others to Vārṣagaṇya or Vṛṣagaṇa (ca. after the 2nd century CE) treat inference only as an epistemic process (*anumāna*), whereby awareness of one fact, corresponding to the ground (*hetu*), permits one to infer a second fact, corresponding to the propounded proposition (*pratijñā*), on the basis of knowledge of a connection between the two. Thus, the *Ṣaṣṭitantra* defines inference as the establishment of one thing through another perceived thing because of a relation (between them) (*anumānam sambandhāt ekasmāt pratyakṣāt śeṣa-siddhiḥ*) (Frauwallner 1958: 123). Both texts provide an inventory of material relations. These relations include: contact, inherence, exclusion, causation, etc.

The idea that there should be a single, formal relation first appears in the extant literature with the work of the Buddhist philosopher Vasubandhu (ca. 5th century CE). He maintains that the relation of the property to be established (*sādhya*) to the property which is the ground (*hetu*) be that of indispensability (*a-vinā-bhāva*, literally, not being without). This line of thought ultimately culminates, through Dignāga (ca. beginning of the 6th century CE), in the conception of inference put forth by Dharmakīrti (ca. 7th century CE).

The first elaboration of the notion of inference found in the *Nyāyasūtra* is given in its earliest known commentary, the *Nyāyabhāṣya*, composed by Vātsyāyana (5th CE), who seems to have preceded the Buddhist Vasubandhu (Randle 1930: 18-19). The question arises: what is his conception of inference? Vātsyāyana gives examples of inference, as we shall see below, and they are formulated in the same manner as the example from the *Caraka-saṃhitā* cited above. In particular, there is a statement that two properties, the establishing property (*sādhana-dharma*), corresponding to the ground (*hetu*) above, and the property to be established (*sādhya-dharma*), corresponding to the property of the proposition (*pratijñā*) above, occur in a corroborating instance, and a statement that the first property also occurs in the object of inference. Nonetheless, as I shall show below, Vātsyāyana's conception of inference is not analogical. Rather, as I shall also show, his conception of inference is similar to the one found in the *Ṣaṣṭitantra* and the *Vaiśeṣikasūtra*, even though he provides no list of material relations to underpin inference. More specifically, I shall show that Vātsyāyana clearly rejects mere similarity and mere dissimilarity as a sufficient for the soundness of inference, rather, as we shall see, he thinks that inference is based on some kind of special material relation, established by concomitance (*anvaya*) and exclusion (*vyatireka*)[1], though he does not use these terms. We shall also see that Vātsyāyana does not hold the relation to be the formal relation of indispensability, at least not the formal relation of indispensability as introduced by Vasubandhu and elaborated by Dignāga and Dharmakīrti. As will be shown in addition, the proposition which Vātsyāyana takes to be established by concomitance corresponds to the categorical form *All A's are B's* or the propositional form *if p, then q* and that the proposition which he takes to be established by exclusion has either the categorical form *All non-A's are non-B's* or the propositional form *if not p, then not q*, respectively. These propositions are obverses of one another and they are not, in general, logically equivalent. In fact, Vātsyāyana, as I shall show, takes them to be equivalent. This contrasts with later thinkers, who, like Dharmakīrti, while taking the propositicn

[1]Indeed, this claim has already been made in unpublished work by Sh. Katsura.

established by concomitance (*anvaya*) to have either the categorical form *All A's are B's* or the propositional form *if p, then q*, take the proposition established by exclusion (*vyatireka*) to have the categorical form *All non-B's are non-A's* or the propositional form *if not q, then not p*, respectively. These propositions are contrapositives of one another and hence logically equivalent. This logical equivalence is clearly and explicitly recognized by Dharmakīrti and accepted by all later thinkers.

2. VĀTSYĀYANA'S CANONICAL INFERENCE FORM

In the *Nyāyabhāṣya*, Vātsyāyana points out two ways in which one property, a ground (*hetu*) or an establishing property (*sādhana-dharma*), serves to make known another, the property to be established (*sādhya-dharma*). One way is through similarity (*sādharmya*) (ad NS 1.1.34); the other is through dissimilarity (*vaidharmya*) (ad NS 1.1.35). These two ways of establishing a conclusion are illustrated with two virtually identical arguments.[2]

ARGUMENT FROM SIMILARITY:

pratijñā:	*a-nityaḥ śabdaḥ*
proposition:	sound is non-eternal
hetu:	*utpatti-dharmakatvāt*
ground:	because of having the property of arising
udāharaṇa:	*utpatti-dharmakam sthālī-ādi dravyam a-nityam*
corroboration:	a substance, such as a pot, having the property of arising, is non-eternal
upanaya:	*tathā ca utpatti-dharmakaḥ śabdaḥ*
application:	and likewise, sound has the property of arising
nigamana:	*tasmāt utpatti-dharmakatvāt a-nityaḥ śabdaḥ*
conclusion:	therefore, sound is non-eternal because of having the property of arising

[2]In his commentary to NS 1.1.33-38, Vātsyāyana uses the same example several times, with some very slight variation in formulation. For detailed discussion of the variations, the reader should see Gillon 2003.

ARGUMENT FROM DISSIMILARITY:

pratijñā:	*a-nityaḥ śabdaḥ*
proposition:	sound is non-eternal
hetu:	*utpatti-dharmakatvāt*
ground:	because of having the property of arising
udāharaṇa:	*an-utpatti-dharmakam ātma-ādi dravyam nityam dṛṣṭam*
corroboration:	a substance, such as the self, not having the property of arising, is eternal
upanaya:	*na ca tathā an-utpatti-dharmakaḥ śabdaḥ*
application:	and obversely, sound does not have the property of not arising
nigamana:	*tasmāt utpatti-dharmakatvāt a-nityaḥ śabdaḥ*
conclusion:	therefore, sound is non-eternal because of having the property of arising

It is possible to abstract from these two arguments their respective canonical forms:

MEMBERS	SIMILARITY ARGUMENT FORM	DISSIMILARITY ARGUMENT FORM
pratijñā:	S_1 p_1	S_1 p_1
proposition:	p is S	p is S
hetu:	H-*tvāt*	H-*tvāt*
ground:	because of H-ness	because of H-ness
udāharaṇa:	H_1 d_1 S_1	$-H_1$ d_1 $-S_1$
corroboration:	d being H is S	d being –H is –S
upanaya:	*tathā ca* p_1 H_1	*na tathā ca* p_1 $-H_1$
application:	and likewise, p is H	and obversely, p is not –H
nigamana:	*tasmāt* H-*tvāt* S_1 p_1	*tasmāt* H-*tvāt* S_1 p_1
conclusion:	therefore, because of H-ness p is S	therefore, because of H-ness p is S

(–H and –S are the contradictory properties of H and S respectively.)

As the reader can see from simple inspection of the forms, the two arguments are the same except for the formulation of the corroboration (*udāharaṇa*) and application (*upanaya*) statements. First, where the properties of the first are H and S, the properties of the second are their contradictories, –H and –S; and second, the application statement of the second contains a negation (*na*: *not*), while the first does not.

3. INADEQUACY OF MERE SIMILARITY AND MERE DISSIMILARITY

Though Vātsyāyana uses the terms *similarity* (*sādharmya*) and *dissimilarity* (*vaidharmya*), it is clear that he does not simply mean mere similarity (*sādharmya*) and dissimilarity (*vaidharmya*), for, on several occasions, he explicitly excludes inference based on *mere* (*mātra*, *eva*) similarity (*sādharmya*) or on *mere* (*mātra*) dissimilarity (*vaidharmya*):

> *vyavasthite hi khalu dharmayoḥ sādhya-sādhana-bhāve dṛṣṭānta-sthe gṛhyamāṇe sādhana-bhūtasya dharmasya hetutvena upādānam na sādharmya-**mātrasya** na vaidharmya-**mātrasya** vā iti* (*Bhāṣya* ad NS 1.1.39).
>
> For, as is well known, when two properties are settled to be in the relation of establishee and establisher in an instance being grasped, the property which is the establisher, and neither **mere** similarity, nor **mere** dissimilarity, is presented as the ground.

This is not the only passage in which Vātsyāyana points out that *mere* (*mātra*, *eva*) similarity (*sādharmya*) and of *mere* (*mātra*) dissimilarity (*vaidharmya*) are an inadequate basis for proper inference. He makes the same point in his discussion of the deficiency of various rejoinders (*jāti*).

> *sādharmyeṇa upasamhāre sādhya-dharma-viparyaya-upapatteḥ sādharmyeṇa **eva** pratyavasthānam a-viśeṣyamāṇam sthāpanā-hetutaḥ sādharmya-samaḥ pratiṣedhaḥ* (*Bhāṣya* ad NS 5.1.2).
>
> A rejection known as sādharmya-sama, (that is,) a reply (based on) **mere** similarity (whose ground) is not different from the ground of (the proponent's) argument, arises because an opponent sets forth the property opposite to the one to be established when the proponent draws his conclusion.

The same point is made still again in his discussion of the kind of rejoinder known as *vaidharmya-sama*, (that is,) a reply (based on) mere dissimilarity, as noted by Frauwallner (Soni 1994: 82).

> *sādharmya-**matreṇa** vaidharmya-**mātreṇa** ca sādhya-sādhane pratijñāya-māne syāt a-vyavasthā* (*Bhāṣya* ad NS 5.1.3).
>
> If an argument to establish the sādhya is propounded through **mere** similarity or **mere** dissimilarity, there can be no settlement (of the issue).

4. OBVERSION AND CONTRAPOSITION

But what are similarity and dissimilarity, if they are not mere similarity and mere dissimilarity? The hint of an answer to this question comes from Vātsyāyana's discussion of pseudo-grounds (*hetu-ābhāsa*), or pseudo-inferences. The author of the *sūtra*s states that pseudo-grounds, or pseudo-inferences, are of five kinds (NS 1.2.4). One kind comprises those in which the ground (*hetu*), or the establishing property (*sādhana-dharma*), deviates from the property to be established (*sādhya-dharma*). The author of the *sūtra*s explains deviation (*sa-vyabhicāra*) as non-one-sortedness (*an-aikāntika*). In his commentary to NS 1.2.5, Vātsyāyana explains one-sorted-ness (*aikāntika*) as existence in one sort of thing (*ekasmin ante vartate*), and he explains its opposite, non-one-sorted-ness (*an-aikāntika*), as a case of one property being pervaded by another property and its contradictory.

This gloss of one-sorted-ness (*aikāntika*) suggests, but does not state, that what is at stake in an argument, or in an inference, is a universal claim to the effect that whenever one state of affairs holds another does too. That this is indeed how one-sorted-ness is to be interpreted comes from another passage.

At the beginning of *Nyāyasūtra* 2.2, its author returns to his view that there are only four means of epistemic cognition (*pramāṇa*), namely, perception (*pratyakṣa*), inference (*anumāna*), analogy (*upamāna*) and testimony (*śabda*) (NS 1.1.3). In particular, he maintains that *arthāpatti* (implication) is a form of inference. While the author of the *sūtra*s neither explains what implication is nor does he provide any illustration of it, Vātsyāyana, fortunately, does both.

> *yatra abhidhīyamāne arthe yaḥ anyaḥ arthaḥ prasajyate saḥ arthāpattiḥ. yathā megheṣu a-satsu vṛṣṭiḥ na bhavati iti. kim atra prasajyate? satsu bhavati iti* (*Bhāṣya* ad NS 2.2.1).
>
> An implication is the fact which is concluded when another is being stated. What is concluded with respect to the statement that when there are no clouds, there is no rain? That when there are clouds, there is rain.

In his commentary to the next *sūtra*, Vātsyāyana goes on to make clear that implication is just inference.

> *pratyakṣeṇa a-pratyakṣasya sambaddhasya pratipattiḥ anumānam. ... vākya-artha-sampratyayena an-abhihitasya arthasya pratyanīka-bhāvāt grahaṇam arthāpattiḥ anumānam eva* (*Bhāṣya* ad NS 2.2.2).
>
> Inference is the awareness through something perceptible of something imperceptible connected with it. ... Implication is the grasping of something unexpressed from the understanding of something stated through their opposition. (But this is) just inference.

In the next *sūtra* (NS 2.2.3), an objection is entertained to the effect that implication (*arthāpatti*) need not be one-sorted (*aikāntika*). This objection has force only under the assumption that being one-sorted is a necessary condition of a inference. Thus, if it can be shown that implication is not one-sorted, it follows that implication is not a form of inference. In the commentary, Vātsyāyana considers a claim by a critic that implication is not one-sorted.

> *a-satsu megheṣu vṛṣṭiḥ na bhavati iti satsu bhavati iti etat arthāt āpadyate. satsu api ca ekadā na bhavati. sā iyam arthāpattiḥ a-pramāṇam iti* (*Bhāṣya* ad NS 2.2.3).
>
> From the meaning (expressed by the sentence) when there are no clouds there is no rain, it follows that when there are (clouds) there is (rain). Yet, sometimes, even when there are (clouds) there is no (rain). Such an implication is not a means of epistemic cognition.

In other words, the critic maintains that the first statement below has the second as an implication, but that the second does not follow from the first.

(1.1) *a-sati kāraṇe kāryam na utpadyate*
when a cause does not exist, its effect does not arise

(1.2) *sati kāraṇe kāryam utpadyate*
when a cause exists, its effect arises

Clearly the issue is whether or not, whenever the state of affairs described in (1.1) holds, the one described in (1.2) does too. One-sorted-ness, then, is a fact corresponding to a universal proposition.

The two statements in (1) are obverses of one another. Obverses, as stated above, do not, in general, entail one another. Yet, Vātsyāyana maintains that what is stated in (1.1) entails what is stated in (1.2). Here is what he says:

> *a-sati kāraṇe kāryam na utpadyate iti vākyāt pratyanīka-bhūtaḥ arthaḥ sati kāraṇe kāryam utpadyate iti arthāt āpadyate. a-bhāvasya hi bhāvaḥ pratyanīkaḥ iti. saḥ ayam kārya-utpādaḥ sati kāraṇe arthāt āpadyamānaḥ na kāraṇasya sattām vyabhicarati. na khalu a-sati kāraṇe kāryam utpadyate. tasmāt na anaikāntikakī* (*Bhāṣya* ad NS 2.2.4).
>
> From the statement that, when a cause does not exist, its effect does not arise, the meaning which is opposite – namely, that when a cause exists, its effect arises – follows from (the statement's) meaning. For existence is the opposite of absence. The arising of an effect, when its cause exists, which is implied by (the statement's) meaning, does not deviate from the existence of its cause. It is well known that an effect does not arise when its cause does not exist. Therefore, (implication) is not non-one-sorted.

What is important here is not that Vātsyāyana has made an error, but why he might have been prone to make it. In particular, let us inquire into why he thinks that the relation between the corroboration statement (*udāharaṇa*) in an argument from similarity conveys what is expressed by the first universal statement above (1.1) and that the corroboration statement (*udāharaṇa*) in an argument from dissimilarity conveys what is expressed by the second universal statement above (1.2).

The previous passage is not the only one in which Vātsyāyana shows that he thinks that the corroboration statement in the argument from dissimilarity and its obverse are logically equivalent. Here is another:

> *ātmā-ādau dṛṣṭānte utpatti-dharmakatvasya a-bhāvāt a-nityatvam na bhavati iti upalabhamānaḥ śabde viparyayam anuminoti utpatti-dharmakatvasya bhāvāt a-nityaḥ śabdaḥ* (*Bhāṣya* ad NS 1.1.37).
>
> One who apprehends that non-eternality does not occur in such instances as the soul because they do not have the property of arising, infers the opposite in sound, namely, that sound is not eternal because it has the property of arising.

In other words, the force of the statements of corroboration is this:

(2.1) *sādhana-dharme sati, sādhya-dharmaḥ asti*
when an establishing property exists, the property to be established exists

(2.2) *sādhana-dharme a-sati, sādhya-dharmaḥ na asti*
when an establishing property does not exist, the property to be established does not exist

Again, these statements are obverses of one another. This is different from those statements associated with the same part of the inference by Dharmakīrti.

(3.1) *sādhana-dharme sati, sādhya-dharmaḥ asti*
when an establishing property exists, the property to be established exists

(3.2) *sādhana-dharme a-sati, sādhana-dharmaḥ na asti*
when the establishing property does not exist, the property to be established does not exist

The statements in (3) are contrapositives of one another, not obverses. As stated earlier, contrapositives are logically equivalent; obverses are not.

Let us return to Vātsyāyana's logical error. To understand why he made it, let us consider the remainder of his reply to the objection he has raised.

> *yat tu sati kāraṇe nimitta-pratibandhāt kāryam na utpadyate iti kāraṇa-dharmaḥ asau. na tu arthāpatteḥ prameyam. kim tarhi asyāḥ prameyam? sati kāraṇe kāryam utpadyate iti. yaḥ asau kārya-utpādaḥ kāraṇasya sattām na vyabhicarati tat asyāḥ prameyam.* (*Bhāṣya* ad NS 2.2.4).
>
> But it is a property of causes that, when a cause exists, its effect does not arise, because of an immediately efficient obstruction. But that is not to be known by implication. What then is to be known by implication? The arising of an effect which does not deviate from the existence of its cause is the fact to be known by implication.

The reply is clearly inadequate. The statement in (1.2) clearly does not follow from the one in (1.1), as Vātsyāyana has himself admitted. Moreover, his reply does not address this fact. All that he has said is that, even if the claim in (1.2) fails, what is expressed by the claim in (1.1) remains.

Why might Vātsyāyana think that he has given an adequate reply? To answer this question, let us return to Vātsyāyana's view of inference.

5. INFERENCE AND RELATION

Vātsyāyana indicates in several passages that the two properties involved in a canonical inference must be linked by a relation. We saw one such passage already above (*Bhāṣya* ad NS 2.2.2). In another passage, Vātsyāyana refers to the relation as one obtaining between the sign and that of which it is a sign (*liṅga-liṅgi-sambandha*).

> *tat-pūrvakam iti anena liṅga-liṅginoḥ sambandha-darśanam liṅga-darśanam ca abhisambadhyate. liṅga-liṅginoḥ sambaddhayoḥ darśanena liṅga-smṛtiḥ abhisambadhyate. smṛtyā liṅga-darśanena ca a-pratyakṣaḥ arthaḥ anumīyate* (*Bhāṣya* ad NS 1.1.5).
>
> The expression *tat-pūrvakam* refers both to the observation of the relation between the sign and the thing of which it is a sign and to the observation of

the sign (itself). A recollection of the sign is connected with the observation of the sign and the thing of which it is a sign, as related. An unobserved thing is inferred by recollection and by the observation of its sign.

In still another passage, he refers to the relation as one obtaining between what is to be established and what does the establishing (*sādhya-sādhana-sambandha*).

saḥ ayam ekasmin dvayoḥ dharmayoḥ sādhya-sādhana-bhāvaḥ sādharmyāt vyavasthite upalabhyate. tam dṛṣṭānte upalabhamānaḥ śabde api anuminoti. śadbaḥ api utpatti-dharmakatvāt a-nityaḥ sthāli-ādi-vat iti. udāhriyate anena dharmayoḥ sādhya-sādhana-bhāvaḥ iti udāharaṇam (*Bhāṣya* ad NS 1.1.37).

This relation of establishee and establisher between two properties in one place is apprehended in that which has been settled on as similar. The one apprehending it there infers it (to be) in sound too, (thinking) sound too is non-eternal because it has the property of arising, like a pot. Something which exemplifies the relation of establishee and establisher between two properties is an example.

What might that relation be? Unfortunately Vātsyāyana offers no further details about the relation. He certainly provides no list of material relations, as do, say, the authors of the *Ṣaṣṭitantra* and the *Vaiśeṣikasūtra*. However, we note that in his discussion of implication that causation is one relation which could underpin inference, and causation is one relation which figures on the list of material relations found both in the *Ṣaṣṭitantra* and the *Vaiśeṣikasūtra*. Moreover, we know that the causation relation has been the object of interest in Indian philosophical thought dating back to early Buddhism and there, as elsewhere, the causation relation is formulated in terms of a pair of universal claims one of which is the obverse of the other. Thus, as Jayatilleke (1963: 449) reports, causally related items are so expressed by formulae such as

(4.1) *asmin sati, idam asti*
when A is present, B is present

(4.2) *asmin a-sati, idam na asti*
when A is absent, B is absent

found in *Udāna* 2 and *Majjhima Nikāya* 1.264.

The state of affairs underlying claims of the form in (4), as Cardona (1967; 1981; 1983: 37-43) has shown, came to be known in grammar as (*anvaya*) and (*vyatireka*), respectively

Strikingly, we find Vātsyāyana to refer to precisely these correlations as *sādharmya* and *vaidharmya*, a fact already noted by Katsura (1992: 33).

> *nidarśanam: nityaḥ śabdaḥ a-sparśatvāt, sparśavān kumbhaḥ a-nityaḥ dṛṣṭaḥ. na ca tathā sparśa-vān śabdaḥ. tasmāt a-sparśa-tvāt nityaḥ śabdaḥ iti. dṛṣṭānte sparśavattvam a-nityatvam ca dharmau na sādhya-sādhana-bhūtau gṛhyete sparśavān ca aṇuḥ nityaḥ ca iti. ātmā-ādau ca dṛṣṭānte "udāharaṇa-sādharmyāt sādhya-sādhanam hetuḥ" (NS 1.1.34) iti a-sparśa-tvāt iti hetuḥ nityatvam vyabhicarati, a-sparśā buddhiḥ a-nityā ca iti. evam dvi-vidhe api dṛṣṭānte vyabhicārāt sādhya-sādhana-bhāvaḥ na asti iti lakṣaṇa-abhāvāt a-hetuḥ iti* (*Bhāṣya* ad NS 1.2.5).

> Here is an illustration: sound is eternal because it is intangible. A pot, being tangible, is observed as non-eternal. And obversely, sound is not tangible. Therefore, sound is eternal because it is intangible. The two properties in the illustration should not be taken to be related as establishee and establisher, (even though) an atom is both tangible and eternal. Yet, according to NS 1.1.34, the ground, namely intangibility, (though found) in instances such as the soul, (nonetheless) deviates from eternality, (for) thought is both intangible and non-eternal. So, because deviation obtains in both kinds of examples, there is no relation of establishee and establisher. So, since it lacks the requisite conditions, it is not a proper ground.

Though the pseudo-inference is formulated as an argument from dissimilarity, for the sake of clarity, both forms of the argument are given below.

ARGUMENT FROM SIMILARITY:

pratijñā:	*nityaḥ śabdaḥ*
proposition:	sound is eternal
hetu:	*a-sparśatvāt*
ground:	because of intangibility
udāharaṇa:	*a-sparśavān ātmā nityaḥ dṛṣṭaḥ*
corroboration:	a soul, being intangible, is observed to be non-eternal
upanaya:	*tathā ca a-sparśavān śabdaḥ*
application:	likewise, sound is intangible
nigamạna:	*tasmāt a-sparśatvāt nityaḥ śabdaḥ*
conclusion:	therefore, sound is eternal because of intangibility

ARGUMENT FROM DISSIMILARITY:

pratijñā:	*nityaḥ śabdaḥ*
proposition:	sound is eternal
hetu:	*a-sparśatvāt*
ground:	because of intangibility
udāharaṇa:	*sparśavān kumbhaḥ a-nityaḥ dṛṣṭaḥ*
corroboration:	a pot, being tangible, is observed to be eternal
upanaya:	*na ca tathā sparśavān śabdaḥ*
application:	and obversely, sound is not intangible
nigamana:	*tasmāt a-sparśatvāt nityaḥ śabdaḥ*
conclusion:	therefore, sound is eternal because of intangibility

As Vātsyāyana makes clear, counter instances can be found to both forms of the argument: thought (*buddhi*) provides a counter instance to the version of the argument based on similarity, as thought is intangible yet it is not eternal. In other words, thought is a counter instance of the universal claim: whatever is intangible is eternal. At the same time, atoms (*aṇu*) provide a counter instance to the version of the argument based on dissimilarity, as atoms are tangible yet they are eternal. That is to say, an atom is a counter instance of the universal claim: whatever is tangible is non-eternal. But this latter claim is simply the obverse of the former claim.

	ARGUMENT FROM SIMILARITY		ARGUMENT FROM DISSIMILARITY	
	soul (*ātman*)	thought (*buddhi*)	pot (*kumbha*)	atom (*aṇu*)
intangibility: (*a-sparśatva*):	+	+	–	–
eternality: (*nityatva*)	+	–	–	+

In spite of the fact that Vātsyāyana's formulation of the corroboration (*udāharaṇa*) and the application (*upanaya*) retain the vestiges of analogical reasoning, he clearly associates with these parts of the inference a causal relation, which, as we have seen from his treatment of implication (*arthāpatti*), can be equivalently formulated as either a universal proposition or its obverse.

6. CONCLUSION

This paper examined how Vātsyāyana, the author of the *Nyāyabhāṣya*, views similarity (*sādharmya*) and dissimilarity (*vaidharmya*) in inference (*anumāna*). What we have seen is that, while the form of inference he uses retains the vestiges of its analogical antecedents, Vātsyāyana rejects the mere similarity and the mere dissimilarity, which underlie analogical reasoning, as underlying inference. Instead, he believes that inference is underpinned by the relation of causation, an idea which is consistent with at least two other important texts of the period, namely, the *Ṣaṣṭitantra* and the *Vaiśeṣikasūtra*. This conception of inference is a material one, distinct from the formal one first found in the work of his contemporary, the Buddhist Vasubandhu, and developed by Vasubandhu's Buddhist successors, Dignāga and Dharmakīrti.

REFERENCES

CARDONA, George 1967. Anvaya and vyatireka in Indian grammar. *Adyar Library Bulletin* 31-32: 313-352.

—— 1981. On reasoning from anvaya and vyatireka in early Advaita. In: *Studies in Indian Philosophy: A Memorial Volume in Honour of Pandit Sukhalji Sanghavi*: 79-104. Ahmedabad: L. D. Institute of Indology.

—— 1983. *Linguistic Analysis and Some Indian Traditions*. (Post-graduate and Research Department Series, 20.; Pundit Shripad Shastri Deodhar Memorial Lectures.) Poona: Bhandarkar Oriental Research Institute.

FRAUWALLNER, Erich 1958. Die Erkenntnislehre des klassischen Sāṃkhya-Systems. *Wiener Zeitschrift für die Kunde Süd- und Ostasiens und Archiv für Indische Philosophie* 2: 84-139.

GILLON, Brendan S. 2003. Nyāya-sūtra 5.1.2: Anomalies in the Bhāṣya. *Journal of Indian Philosophy* 31: 47-60.

JAYATILLIKE, K. N. 1963. *Early Buddhist Theory of Knowledge*. London: George Allen and Unwin Ltd.

KATSURA, Shoryu 1992.The origin and development of the concept of vyāpti in Indian logic: From the *Caraka-saṃhitā* up to Dharmakīrti. Unpublished manuscript. (Transcription of lectures given between March and June 1992 in Vienna.)

RANDLE, H. N. 1930 *Indian Logic in the Early Schools. A Study of the Nyāya-darśana in its Relation to the Early Logic of Other Schools*. Oxford: Oxford University Press.

SONI, Jayandra (trans.) 1994. *Erich Frauwallner's Posthumous Essays*. New Delhi: Aditya Prakashan.

Anumāna in Bhartṛhari's *Vākyapadīya*

AKIHIKO AKAMATSU

The aim of this paper[1] is to elucidate the view of *anumāna* expressed in the *Vṛtti* of the first *kāṇḍa* of Bhartṛhari's *Vākyapadīya*. Careful consideration of Bhartṛhari's historical context shows that his view has been misunderstood, a misunderstanding which also makes it difficult to grasp properly criticisms of his view by the Buddhist philosopher Śāntarakṣita and by the Nyāya thinker Jayantabhaṭṭa. The paper divides into two parts: a reconsideration of the relevant passage from Bhartṛhari's *Vṛtti* and then a review o[f] the criticisms by Śāntarakṣita and by Jayantabhaṭṭa.

We begin with the passage from the *Vṛtti* to VP 1.32 and [its] translation:

> *ihāvyabhicaritābhimatasāhacaryasya dṛṣṭasya saṃbandhinaḥ tatsad[…] vā darśanād adṛṣṭe saṃbandhini yaj jñānam utpadyate tenāpra[…] syārthasya prasiddhir duravasānā.*[2]

> In this world, it is very difficult to establish (the existence of) an obj[…] is not being perceived through a cognition which arises from the o[…] of an observed object, either related to the unobserved object or s[…] by someone who has accepted the concomitance (of the former […] the latter object) as non-deviating.

---

[1] I would like to thank Prof. Dr. Brendan Gillon, editor of thi[s …] critical comments at the 12th WSC and the valuable suggestions [… an] earlier version of this paper.

[2] *Vṛtti* ad VP 1.32, p. 88,5-6.

This statement has three parts which deserve mo scrutiny. The first part is that the person who performs an i e accepts the concomitance as non-deviating (*avyabhicaritābhimata-sāhacarya*); the second is that what is established by inference is an unperceived object (*tenāpratyakṣasyārthasya prasiddhiḥ*); the third is that such an establishment is very difficult to come by (*duravasānā*). Let us consider each of these parts in turn.

According to *Paddhati*, the sub-commentary of the first *kāṇḍa* of the *Vākyapadīya*, the compound *avyabhicaritābhimatasāhacarya* is taken to express a property of the object, or hetu, whose observation plays a crucial role in an inference.[3] This interpretation seems to be the one followed by Iyer in his translation.[4] However, this is not the only interpretation, as shown by my translation bove, nor is it the one favored by the historical context. To see , let us consider some of the definitions of *anumāna* accepted me contemporaries of Bhartṛhari (ca. second half of the 5th AD), such as that of the Vṛttikāra, cited in *Śābarabhāṣya* 6th century), that of Dignāga (ca. 480-540), that of Pra- ca. early 6th century) and that of Candrānanda (9th or

a says:

mbandhasya ekadeśadarśanād ekadeśāntare 'saṃnikṛṣṭe

dge of an object unconnected (with the senses) from by <u>someone who knows their relation</u>.

und *jñātasambandhasya* can only be , of *buddhi*. As such, it must refer to

abhimataṃ sāhacaryam avyabhicāro *hacaryam.*

nvariably concomitant".

slated in Frauwallner 1968: 31: , der die Verknüpfung (beider) s den andern Teil, der ein nicht in nnt."

someone who knows the relation, and not to something whose relation is known.

A similar statement is found in Dignāga's *Vṛtti* to verse 2.20 of his *Pramāṇasamuccaya*.

> *nāntarīyakārthadarśanaṃ tadvido* ***'numānam***.[6]
>
> Experience of a thing as inseparably connected is the instrument of inference, for a person who knows this inseparable connection (Randle 1930: 155).

Praśastapāda also mentions the role of the inferrer in the process of inferential cognition.

> *vidhis tu yatra dhūmas tatrāgnir agnyabhāve dhūmo 'pi na bhavatīty evaṃprasiddhasamayasyāsandigdhadhūmadarśanāt sāhacaryānusmaraṇāt tadanantaram agnyadhyavasāyo bhavatīti.*[7]
>
> The formula (*vidhi*) is 'Where there is smoke, there there is fire: and in the absence of fire smoke also does not occur'. In the case of a person who knows the connection in this way (*prasiddhasamayasya*), the conviction of fire arises, as the result of an undoubted experience of smoke and as the result of remembering the accompaniment of smoke by fire (*sāhacaryānusmaraṇāt*). (Randle 1930: 154.)

Finally, Candrānanda makes a similar statement.

> *evaṃvidhaprasiddhasambandhasyārthaikadeśam asaṃdigdhaṃ paśyataḥ śeṣānuvyavasāyo yaḥ sa liṅgadarśanāt saṃjāyamāno laiṅgikam iti vṛttikāraḥ.*[8]
>
> For a person, says Vṛttikāra, who establishes the relation in this way and who is undoubtedly observing an object, an inference of another arises, and because it is produced from the observation of a mark, it is the knowledge based upon a mark.

All the definitions cited above contain reference to a person who knows the relation between an observed object and an unobserved object. As Randle remarks:

---

[6] Cf. NV, p. 300,1.

[7] PBh, p. 205,10-13.

[8] Candrānanda's commentary on VS 9.18 (p. 69,16-18).

> It seems to have been common to the logic of the time to insert into the definition of the instrument of inference a proviso that the person drawing the inference should be aware of the relation between the terms which makes the inference possible (Randle 1930: 155).

Therefore, construing *avyabhicaritābhimatasāhacarya* as referring to the person who knows the concomitance is fully warranted by the historical context.

An important point to emphasize, however, is that Bhartṛhari does not use the epistemically strong words *jñāta* (known) or *prasiddha* (established), but the epistemically weaker word *abhimata* (accepted). This suggests that he is sensitive to the fact that people's beliefs are fallible: what one believes to be true may turn out to be false; in particular, beliefs in non-deviation may turn out to be wrong. We shall return to this point later.

We now turn to the second part of Bhartṛhari's view, namely, to establish (the existence of) an object which is not being perceived (*tenāpratyakṣasyārthasya prasiddhir.)* It was common to the thinkers of the time to refer to the object of inference as unperceived (*adṛṣṭa, asaṃnikṛṣṭa, apratyakṣa*). This is shown in the sentence from the Vṛttikāra mentioned by *Śābarabhāṣya*, cited above. It is also shown by the following remarks made by Nyāya philosopher Vātsyāyana.[9] He says:

> *smṛtyā liṅgadarśanena cāpratyakṣo 'rtho 'numīyate.*[10]
>
> Through recollection and through seeing the mark, the unperceived object (= possessor of the mark) is inferred (Schuster 1972: 392, note 56).

He also says:

> *pratyakṣenāpratyakṣasya sambaddhasya pratipattir anumānam.*[11]

---

[9] NBh, p. 16,10; p. 17,3; p. 17,4; p. 18,3; p. 18,4; p. 127,5.
[10] NBh, p. 16,9-10 (to NS 1.1.5).
[11] NBh, p. 127,5 (to NS 2.2.2).

Inference is certain knowledge of the unperceived connected (entity, which is attained) through the perception (of what is connected with it) (Schuster 1972: 392, note 56).

Once again we see that Bhartṛhari's view of inference is in keeping with similar formulations of the day, referring to the object of inference as unperceived (*apratyakṣa*).

Finally, we come to the last part of Bhartṛhari's view. Bhartṛhari says that it is difficult to establish (the existence) of such an unperceived object. Why might this be so? Here the following statement from Vātsyāyana is of help. He says:

kenacid arthena liṅgasya sāmānyād apratyakṣo liṅgī gamyate.[12]

Because of the similarity of the mark with some other thing, the unperceived possessor of the mark is known (Schuster 1972: 393, note 59).

Whereas for Vātsyāyana, dependence on the similarity must be the ground for the validity of knowledge, for Bhartṛhari, the same dependence on the similarity is the reason why *anumāna* is unreliable. Notice what Bhartṛhari says about similarity:

tatra rūpasāmānyād apahṛtabuddhiḥ parokṣaviśeṣo durjñānaṃ bhedam arvāgdarśano darśanamātreṇāgamyam āgamenaiva prapadyate | kālabhedād api | grīṣmahemantādiṣu kūpajalādīnām atyantabhinnāḥ sparśādayaḥ dṛśyante | tatra sūkṣmam avasthānaviśeṣaṃ prākṛtam aprākṛtagamyam āgamacakṣur antareṇāpratyakṣam ***anumānamātreṇā****niścitaṃ kaḥ sādhayitum asaṃmūḍhaḥ prayatate ||*[13]

The ordinary man (*arvāgdarśana*), misled by external resemblance, is unable to see the difference and can see it only with the help of tradition. Similarly, properties of things change with time. The temperature of the waters of a well and the like is very different in summer and winter. Which intelligent man would try to demonstrate, by mere reasoning, this subtle difference in nature, imperceptible to the ordinary man, unascertainable by inference and incomprehensible except through knowledge derived from tradition? (Iyer 1965: 44.)

---

[12] NBh, p. 18,3-4.

[13] *Vṛtti* ad VP 1.32, p. 89,2-6.

This passage confirms what we hinted at above when we noted that Bhartṛhari does not use the epistemically strong words *jñāta* (known) or *prasiddha* (established) to characterize a person's grasp of the relation underlying inference, but the epistemically weaker word *abhimata* (accepted). The problem is that the process of inference depends on one's beliefs, in particular, one's belief about the relation between an observed object and the unperceived object of inference.

It is precisely this point to which later thinkers such as the Buddhist philosopher Śāntarakṣita and the Nyāya-thinker Jayantabhaṭṭa took exception,[14] as noted by Abhyankar and Limaye.[15] We are now in a position to appreciate Jayantabhaṭṭa's criticism. According to Jayantabhaṭṭa, unreliability of *anumāna*, insisted by Bhartṛhari, does not result from the faults of *anumāna* itself, but from the faults of knower (*pramātṛ*),[16] because *anumāna* is based on pervasion (*vyāpti*), a formally and ontologically fixed relation, and it is independent of subjective human knowledge. In fact, at the later time when the question how to ontologically determine the logical relation between two terms will be the most important problem, the insertion of such word must be regarded as inappropriate to the definition of *anumāna*.

In the foregoing, we examined the view of *anumāna* put forth by Bhartṛhari in the *Vṛtti* to the first *kāṇḍa* to his *Vākyapadīya*. By

---

[14] VP 1.32: *avasthādeśakālānāṃ bhedād bhinnāsu śaktiṣu* | *bhāvānām* ***anumānena*** *prasiddhir atidurlabhā* || (Iyer 1965: 44: "It is extremely difficult to establish by reasoning the nature of objects, because their properties differ according to difference in circumstances, place and time"). The verse is cited in TS 1459 and NM, p. 314,3-4, and is criticized in TS 1475: *avasthādeśakālānāṃ bhedād bhinnāsu śaktisu* | *bhāvānām* ***anumānena*** *nātaḥ siddhiḥ sudurlabhā* || and NM, p. 325,4-6. VP 1.34: *yatnen**ānumito** 'py arthaḥ kuśalair* ***anumātṛbhiḥ*** | *abhiyuktatarair anyair anyathaivopapādyate* || is cited in TS 1461 and NM, p. 316,14-15, and is criticized in TS 1476: *yatnen**ānumito** 'py arthaḥ kuśalair* ***anumātṛbhiḥ*** | *nānyathā sādhyate so 'nyair abhiyuktatarair api* ||, and NM, p. 326,5-6: *yatnen**ānumito** yo 'rthaḥ kuśalair* ***anumātṛbhiḥ*** | *abhiyogaśatenāpi so 'nyathā nopapādyate* ||

[15] Abhyankar & Limaye 1965: 200-204, 305-308.

[16] NM, p. 325,6: *pramātur eva tatra tatrāparādhaḥ, nānumānasyeti.*

paying careful attention to the historical context, we arrived at a construal of one of the key phrases different from the one found in the *Paddhati* and followed by Iyer in his translation. The construal arrived at here not only fits better with the historical context, it also helps to make clearer objections raised to Bhartṛhari's view of *anumāna* by Śāntarakṣita and by Jayantabhaṭṭa.

REFERENCES

Texts and Abbreviations

NBh = [*Nyāyabhāṣya*]. *Nyāyasūtram of Gautama, with Vātsyāyana's Nyāyabhāṣyam, etc.* Ed. by Gaṅgānātha Jhā. (Poona Oriental Series, 58.) Poona: Oriental Book Agency, 1939.

NM = [*Nyāyamañjarī*]. *Nyāyamañjarī of Jayantabhaṭṭa. With Ṭippaṇī – Nyāyasaurabha by the Editor,* I. Ed. by K. S. Varadacharya. (Oriental Research Institute Series, 116.) Mysore: The Oriental Research Institute, University of Mysore, 1969.

NV = [*Nyāyavārttika*]. *Nyāyadarśana of Gautama. With the Bhāṣya of Vātsyāyana, the Vārttika of Uddyotakara, the Tātparyaṭīkā of Vācaspati, and the Pariśuddhi of Udayana,* Volume 1, Chapter 1. Ed. by Anantalal Thakur. (Mithila Institute Series, 20.) Darbhanga: Mithila Institute of Post-Graduate Studies and Research in Sanskrit Learning, 1967.

PBh = [*Praśastapāda Bhāṣya*]. *The Bhāṣya of Praśastapāda. Together with the Nyāyakandalī of Śrīdhara.* Ed. by V. P. Dvivedin. (Vizianagram Sanskrit Series, 6.) Benares: E. J. Lazarus, 1895 (Reprint: Delhi.)

Vṛtti = [*Vṛtti* of *Vākyapadīya, kāṇḍa* I]. Cf. VP I.

VP = [*Vākyapadīya*]. References to the *kārikā*s follow W. Rau's critical edition of the *kārikā*s (Rau 1977).

VP I = [*Vākyapadīya, kāṇḍa* I]. *Vākyapadīya of Bhartṛhari, with the Commentaries Vṛtti and Paddhati of Vṛṣabhadeva, kāṇḍa* I. Ed. by K. A. Subramania Iyer. (Deccan College Monograph Series.) Poona: Deccan College, Postgraduate and Research Institute, 1966.

VS = [*Vaiśeṣikasūtra*]. *Vaiśeṣikasūtra of Kaṇāda with the commentary of Candrānanda.* Ed. by Muni Sri Jambuvijayaji. Baroda: Oriental Institute, 1961.

Secondary literature

ABHYANKAR, K. V. & V. P. LIMAYE 1965. *Vākyapadīya of Śrī Bhartṛhari.* (University of Poona Sanskrit and Prakrit Series, 2.) Poona: University of Poona.

AKAMATSU, Akihiko 1999. The two kinds of *anumāna* in Bhartṛhari's *Vākyapadīya*. *Journal of Indian Philosophy* 27: 17-22.

FRAUWALLNER, E. 1968. *Materialien zur ältesten Erkenntnisslehre der Karmamīmāṃsā.* (Österreichische Akademie der Wissenschaften, Philosophisch-historische Klasse. Sitzungsberichte, 259. Band, 2. Abhandlung; Veröffentlichungen der Komission für Sprachen und Kulturen Süd- und Ostasiens, Heft 6.) Wien: Hermann Bohlaus Nachf.

IYER, K. A. Subramania (trans.) 1965, *The Vākyapadīya of Bhartṛhari with the Vṛtti. Chapter I.* Poona: Deccan College.

RANDLE, H. N. 1930 *Indian Logic in the Early Schools. A Study of the Nyāyadarśana in its Relation to the Early Logic of Other Schools.* Oxford: Oxford University Press.

RAU, W. 1977. *Bhartṛhari's Vākyapadīya. Die Mūlakārikās nach den Handschriften herausgegeben und mit einem Pada-Index versehen.* (Abhandlungen für die Kunde des Morgenlandes, 42.4.) Wiesbaden: Franz Steiner.

SCHUSTER, Nancy 1972. Inference in the Vaiśeṣikasūtras. *Journal of Indian Philosophy* 1: 341-395.

INDEX

(Italicized page numbers refer to the footnote section)